NICK
SABAN

★ ★ ★ ★ ★ ★ **VS.** ★ ★ ★ ★ ★ ★

COLLEGE
FOOTBALL

CHRISTOPHER WALSH

TRIUMPH
BOOKS

To my spouse and to those of coaches everywhere,
for everything they have to put up with

Library of Congress Cataloging-in-Publication Data

Walsh, Christopher J., 1968–
Nick Saban vs. college football / Christopher Walsh.
    pages cm
    ISBN 978-1-60078-912-0
    1. Saban, Nick. 2. Football coaches—United States—Rating of. 3. University of Alabama—Football—History. I. Title. II. Title: Nick Saban versus college football.
    GV939.S35.W35 2014
    796.332092—dc23
    [B]
                            2014005377

This book is available in quantity at special discounts for your group or organization. For further information, contact:
    Triumph Books LLC
    814 North Franklin Street
    Chicago, Illinois 60610
    (312) 337-0747
    www.triumphbooks.com

Printed in U.S.A.
ISBN: 978-1-60078-912-0
Design by Patricia Frey
Photos courtesy of T.G Paschal unless otherwise indicated

★ ★ ★

Contents

Part IV

★ ★ ★

Foreword

On January 1, 2007, I was in Jacksonville, Florida, working the Gator Bowl for CBS Sports with my colleagues Tim Brando and Spencer Tillman. During our pregame show, the subject turned to Nick Saban who, it appeared, was ready to leave the Miami Dolphins and become the next head coach at the University of Alabama.

Various media reports said that Alabama was willing to give Saban an unprecedented college football contract of eight years at $4 million per year. So the natural topic for us to discuss was whether or not *any* college football coach was worth that kind of money.

At some point in the broadcast I said that if it happened, if Nick Saban did go to Tuscaloosa, "someday Alabama would look back and realize they had gotten a bargain."

Two days later Saban told Dolphins owner Wayne Huizenga that he was going to Alabama. Today, after winning three national championships and coming painfully close to two others, Nick Saban is making more than $7 million per season. Alabama fans, alumni, and administration all know that they are *still* getting a bargain.

With keen insight that comes from years of being inside the Alabama program, Christopher Walsh tells us why Saban is such a bargain in this book.

Alabama's need for a "rock star" as head coach and Saban's need for a different kind of challenge was nothing less than a harmonic convergence. But the complete story of Saban's hire in 2007 goes back more than three decades.

Since the death of the iconic Paul W. "Bear" Bryant in January 1983, Alabama fans had been waiting for the next savior of the program, the next authoritative figure and singularly powerful voice who would return Alabama to its rightful place as one of the superpowers of the college football universe.

During the 25 years under Bryant (1958–82) Alabama didn't just win 232 games, 13 SEC championships, and six national championships. Bryant, by the sheer force of his personality, controlled a lot of what happened in college football during his era. He had the power to pick his own bowl game and, more important, to pick the opponent that would put his team in the best position to win the national championship. The other coaches and the other bowl representatives knew they could not lock in their matchups until Coach Bryant had made his decision.

Having that kind of power for 25 years was heady stuff to the Alabama faithful, and when Bryant was gone, they wanted it back as quickly as possible. There were moments when Alabama came close:

- Bill Curry, a Georgia Tech man, got the Crimson Tide to No. 2 in 1989 but lost 30–20 at Auburn in Alabama's first-ever trip to Jordan-Hare Stadium. Curry went 10–2 that year but was forced out.
- Gene Stallings won 70 games in seven years as Alabama's head coach (1990–96). In that run was the 1992 national championship. But he left after a 10–3 record in 1996.
- Alabama won an SEC championship in 1999, but then–head coach Mike DuBose was embroiled in a scandal (extramarital affair) and was out after a 3–8 season in 2000.
- Dennis Franchione stayed two years and then left due to NCAA sanctions for rules violations committed by the previous staff. Former Crimson Tide quarterback Mike Shula stayed four years with only one winning season (10–2 in 2005).

So understand that Alabama didn't just *want* Nick Saban after the 2006 season (6–7), it *had* to have him. By that point the football program had pretty much been in the wilderness for almost a quarter century.

Saban had been on the job about two months when I went to Tuscaloosa to see him in March 2007. He knew there was much work to do because, for a long time—too long, in fact—Alabama's people had been *talking* about winning national championships but not really putting in the work necessary to do it.

I came away from that meeting with two points that Saban wanted to make:

First, it was in this meeting that he made me aware of "the Process," something you'll read a lot about in Chris' book. The Process, simply put, is a series of steps taken every day in order to improve and work toward a goal. The focus is not on the goal itself. The focus is on the tiny building blocks of work that ultimately move an individual in a positive direction toward the goal. In order for the program to be successful, everybody has to buy into the Process.

Second—and this was even more important—Saban had made it his No. 1 goal that from that point forward Alabama football would speak with only one voice. And that would be his.

Bear Bryant's death in 1983 created a power vacuum in the football program at the University of Alabama. And, like any great football power, Alabama had a lot of people who wanted to rush in and fill that void. There were a lot of voices speaking for the program. Many of them were well intentioned, but in the 24 years since Bryant's passing, it didn't appear like one person was in control. That all changed when Saban arrived in Tuscaloosa like the conquering hero he eventually turned out to be.

Less than a month later, on April 21, 2007, I had all the proof I needed that Saban would fulfill his vision and the hopes and dreams of the Alabama faithful. It was Saban's first spring game, and school officials decided to throw open the gates to Bryant-Denny Stadium and not charge admission.

I was there to write a column for the *Atlanta Journal-Constitution* on the reaction and feelings of the fans. The excitement level was off the charts. And this was only April!

After I took my seat in the press box, I watched while the fans kept coming, and coming, and coming into the stadium. Soon school officials announced that Bryant-Denny, which held 92,138, was full and that the fire marshals had ordered the gates closed for safety reasons.

It was only the beginning.

So enjoy this story that my friend Chris Walsh has prepared for you. If you're an Alabama fan, it is a piece of history to be savored with the realization that, as all great dynasties do, the Saban era will someday come to an end. Enjoy the ride while it is happening, and just be grateful that you were here to experience it.

—Tony Barnhart
CBS Sports

★ ★ ★

Introduction

Although there's really no such thing as a college football off-season anymore, it's become one of Nick Saban's annual rituals, between National Signing Day and the start of spring practices.

That's when he holds court, so to speak, on a semiregular basis with what he calls the NBA—which in this case stands for the Noontime Basketball Association.

It's an intense pickup game that the football staffers participate in on the University of Alabama campus, and Saban goes from being coach to commissioner. He picks the players, the teams, and even the person who will guard him in the game (and sometimes how well). They don't keep stats, and no one films a thing. "There are only two guys in the organization who are shorter," Saban once explained with a smile. "Every now and again I call a foul on myself."

Yes, to borrow a line from Mel Brooks, "It's good to be the king," and in college football there's absolutely no doubt about who reigns.

Saban won his fourth national championship at the end of the 2012 season, each coming within one 10-year span during which Saban also spent two seasons in the National Football League. By the end of the 2013 regular season, oddsmakers had made the Crimson Tide the favorite in 53 consecutive games, dating all the way back to the 2009 Southeastern Conference Championship Game against Florida. To put a little perspective on that, Saban won a total of 48 games the entire time he was at LSU, when the Tigers tallied their first national championship since 1958, two SEC titles, two SEC Western Division crowns, and three bowl wins (two in the Sugar Bowl).

Even though he never won 10 games in back-to-back seasons on the bayou, there was still a general feeling throughout college football that Saban was transforming LSU into a perennial powerhouse that would regularly be in the national championship chase for years to come. He left, of course, for the Miami Dolphins, but it still turned out to be true, so much so that a few years later Alabama's biggest nemesis turned out to be his former team. Meanwhile, the future appeared to be even brighter in Tuscaloosa, where there wouldn't be as many distractions as in Baton Rouge or New Orleans. There were no professional franchises to share the sports landscape, and—no disrespect to LSU—Alabama just had a much better brand label when it came to college football.

Alabama and Saban turned out to be the perfect fit for both sides, and the perfect example of what can happen when the right person is in the right place at the right time. Saban had total control of the football program at the Capstone. (In a 1913 speech, university president George Hutcheson Denny extolled the university as the "Capstone" of the public school system in the state, thus the nickname.) The administration was not only eager to have him coach, but also to use football and other sports as a vehicle to dramatically upgrade the entire university. Fans were hungry for the program's next great run.

What occurred, though, exceeded everyone's expectations, leading to some amazing statistics, such as the following: from the fall of 2008 through 2013, the Crimson Tide were on the cover of *Sports Illustrated* 17 times, not including the three commemorative national championship editions. T.J. Yeldon was the fifth straight starting running back to be on the front of the magazine at least once, following Glenn Coffee, Mark Ingram Jr., Trent Richardson, and Eddie Lacy.

In the 60 seasons from 1948 to 2007, no program led the Southeastern Conference in total defense (yards allowed per game) for more than two consecutive seasons. Between 2008, when it tied Tennessee for first, and 2013, Alabama topped the league six straight times.

When Saban and Alabama had at least a month to rest up and prepare for an opponent, the Crimson Tide was 12–2, with the only losses in the Sugar Bowl at the end of the 2008 and 2013 seasons when the team really wasn't playing for anything.

Saban by the Numbers

Seasons: 18
Consensus national championships: 4
Record in BCS title games: 4–0
Record in conference title games: 4–1
Top five finishes: 4
Top 25 finishes: 11
Overall record: 165–57–1*
Winning percentage: 74.2*
Losing seasons: 0*
Bowl record: 8–7#
Bowl winning percentage: 53.3#
Conference titles: 5
Conference record: 101–39–1
Consensus All-Americans: 23
First-round draft picks (through 2013): 19 (X)
Record against ranked teams: 51–35 (59.30 percent)
Record against top-10 teams: 27–17 (61.36 percent)

Ratios

National title seasons: One every 4.5 seasons
Consensus All-Americans: 1.28 every season
First-round draft picks (through 2013): 1.12 every season
Average number of wins vs. ranked teams: 2.83 each season
Wins over top 10 teams per year: 1.50 every season

* Saban went 7–6 in 2007, but five wins were later vacated.
\# Saban left Michigan State in 1999 before it defeated Florida in the Citrus Bowl.
X-Another seven of his former players were selected in the first round within three years after he left Michigan State and LSU.

Moreover, Saban didn't inherit strong programs at LSU or Alabama. The 11 years at LSU prior to his arrival, 1989–99, had one 10-win season but eight with losing records. Alabama, meanwhile, was coming off years of scandals, NCAA sanctions, and numerous coaching changes when Saban arrived. After his first season with the Crimson Tide, the team didn't have a single player selected in the NFL Draft for the first time since 1970.

But three national championships over a four-year period is the kind of success that's not supposed to happen anymore. This is the age of parity in sports. Programs such as Ohio State, Penn State, and Southern California demonstrated that the bigger you are, the harder you can fall. Dynasties were thought to have gone the way of the dinosaurs, and like the pros, college football was discouraging one-team domination.

Instead, this has become college football's age of Saban, who is the epitome of the slogan heard at every game in Bryant-Denny Stadium: "At some places they play football. At Alabama, we live it."

Or as President Obama put it when Alabama visited him yet again at the White House after winning the 2012 title, "In Miami on the night the Tide won the championship, one Notre Dame fan apparently asked if 'Roll Tide' is a noun or a verb—to which another fan dressed head-to-toe in crimson replied, 'It's a way of life.'"

That's why when a player's parent accidentally tripped over a rug, causing the 2011 crystal football to fall off its pedestal and shatter, the joke heard around Tuscaloosa was, "That's okay, we'll just get another one."

Alabama did, the very next year.

After covering Saban through his first seven seasons at the Capstone, I can confirm that the man is about opportunity. That's all he promises recruits, and the one thing above everything else he tries to provide his players. He's very aware that there are exceptionally few guarantees in life, and almost none in football.

Saban runs a team like it's a business and he's the CEO. His employees are expected to work hard and be faithful, and he in return is extremely loyal as well. He's also a master at squeezing everything he can out of a day. It reminds me a little of the television show *The West Wing* with every detail scheduled out, and as soon as one major hurdle is cleared, someone asks "What's next?" (Fans may remember the episode in which the president brings out a former Duke player, played by Juwan Howard, to be his partner on the basketball court. Likewise, Saban loses in basketball about as often as he does in football.)

But we'll get to all that in the pages to follow. First, a few notes about the book and how it came together:

In no way is anything in it meant to diminish the careers of other coaches or try to make anyone look bad. The intent is to do quite the opposite because anyone who is listed in these pages has to be one heck of a good coach.

Saban himself had no part in this book whatsoever, which was done by design. We never discussed the book or sat down and did formal interviews for it, and no one associated with him attempted to steer me in any direction. Actually, Saban probably hates the idea of his career numbers being listed side by side with many of the game's greats, people he looks up to and admires.

Also, for the record, I didn't attend Alabama. I grew up in Minnesota and graduated from the hockey-crazed University of New Hampshire. My father attended Minnesota, my mother graduated from Northwestern, and my sister got her degree from Tufts University. I had no ties to the area before moving to Alabama for a job to cover the team for a media outlet. My favorite football teams are the Minnesota Vikings (which as of this writing is one of just a handful of NFL teams that does not have any former Crimson Tide players) and those representing the schools I attended.

With that in mind, the idea here was simply to present the facts and try to do the impossible: put perspective on Saban's career (so far) while relating what coaches are doing now to what they did yesterday and what they'll try to do tomorrow. It's a broad attempt at measuring and celebrating accomplishments.

In addition to making the case that Saban is already one of the best coaches in college football history, the book includes what would be college football's version of Mount Rushmore if one existed. However, selecting the four most worthy coaches proved to be a monumental task, and I didn't enter into it with the names predetermined.

First, I had to decide if some of the game's early innovators should be included, even though they were coaching football when it was nothing like it is now. Considering the few number of schools that even had teams around 1900, the sport's evolutionary process, and the lack of any measuring sticks like polls, etc., the answer had to be no. While that will disappoint some, there's just no way to draw any sort of parallels or to know just how good a given coach was, except against his few peers.

Having said that, my Mount Rushmore of the game's pioneers would feature Fielding Yost, Walter Camp, Pop Warner, and Howard Jones (although Amos Alonzo Stagg is certainly deserving as well).

As the numbers started to unfold, I started to get a feeling that the four would be Paul W. "Bear" Bryant, Knute Rockne, Bobby Bowden, and Saban, but hardly

Saban by the Team Numbers

Year	Overall	Conf	Place	Bowl	Coaches Poll	AP Poll
Toledo Rockets (Mid-American Conference)						
1990	9–2	7–1	T1st			
Toledo totals: 9–2 (7–1), .818						
Michigan State Spartans (Big Ten Conference)						
1995	6–5–1	4–3–1	5th	L Independence		
1996	6–6	5–3	5th	L Sun		
1997	7–5	4–4	6th	L Aloha		
1998	6–6	4–4	6th			
1999	9–2#	6–2	2nd	Invited to Citrus	9	9
Michigan State totals: 34–24–1 (23–16–1), .585						
LSU Tigers (Southeastern Conference)						
2000	8–4	5–3	3rd (West)	W Peach	22	
2001	10–3	5–3	1st (West)	W Sugar	8	7
2002	8–5	5–3	T2nd (West)	L Cotton		
2003	13–1	7–1	1st (West)	W Sugar	1	2
2004	9–3	6–2	2nd (West)	L Capital One	16	16
LSU total: 48–16 (28–12), .750						

anything was set in stone (pun intended). The second-guessing was nonstop, especially about Frank Leahy. Under his direction the Fighting Irish had six undefeated seasons and one with a single loss (although in four of those seven seasons Notre Dame had a tie).

The decision came down to a couple of small factors, including that Leahy only coached Notre Dame for 11 years. His run was comparable to Bowden's incredible 14-year stretch at Florida State (1987–2000), but while Leahy had two other years as a head coach at Boston College, Bowden had roughly 30.

Leahy also inherited a team that was already loaded with talent, as Elmer Layden's teams had reached top rankings of No. 2, No. 2, and No. 1, respectively,

Year	Overall	Conf	Place	Bowl	Coaches Poll	AP Poll
Miami Dolphins (NFL)						
2005	9–7		2nd AFC East			
2006	6–10		4th AFC East			
Miami total: 15–17, .469						
Alabama Crimson Tide (Southeastern Conference)						
2007	2–6*	1–4	T3rd (West)	W Independence		
2008	12–2	8–0	1st (West)	L Sugar	6	6
2009	14–0	8–0	1st (West)	W BCS NCG	1	1
2010	10–3	5–3	4th (West)	W Capital One	11	10
2011	12–1	7–1	2nd (West)	W BCS NCG	1	1
2012	13–1	7–1	1st (West)	W BCS NCG	1	1
2013	11–2	7–1	T1st (West)	L Sugar	8	7
Alabama total: *74–15 (43–10), .811						

College total: *165–57–1, .742

#Saban resigned his position before the bowl game to take the LSU job. Michigan State defeated Florida 37–34 to finish No. 7 in both polls.

*Alabama's official record in 2007 was 2–6 after the NCAA ruled that Alabama must vacate 21 victories due to sanctions stemming from textbook-related infractions, 16 of which were under previous coach Mike Shula, discovered during Saban's first season with the Crimson Tide in 2007.

during the previous three seasons (although the 1940 team finished unranked, while 1939 came in 13th and 1938 fifth), while Bowden, Bryant, and Saban transformed their programs into powerhouses. Rockne also inherited a full cupboard from Jesse Harper (34–5–1 over five years), but he's the one who really made Notre Dame the equivalent of college football royalty with five undefeated seasons and six one-loss years during just 13 seasons.

We're splitting hairs here, and at times I found myself asking random people, "Why doesn't Mount Rushmore have five faces?" and getting strange looks. Consequently, it got me thinking about who would be part of a possible second team, or second monument, if more faces were suddenly added in South Dakota.

Actually, the next four were pretty easy to select (in alphabetical order):
Frank Leahy
John McKay
Tom Osborne
Bud Wilkinson

A lot of you are probably wondering, *But what about [insert name here]?* and could make a compelling case for a number of coaches, but then you'd also have to tell me which name to take off the previous list, and that's where it gets much tougher. All four could have been on the original list, and at one time or another I strongly considered each, but in addition to championships, overall program success, and dominance of an era, longevity had to be a consideration.

Which, of course, leads to the obvious question, "What about Joe Paterno?" For purposes of this book, only his official numbers from Penn State were used, minus the vacated wins from 1998 to 2011. Moreover, in the realm of public opinion, the jury is still out about his coaching legacy. Perhaps in the years ahead we'll have a better feel for where it rests, maybe right around the time Saban eventually stops coaching.

Note: for consistency, vacated wins are not included in any coach's record, but a given coach is not credited with having a losing season unless his original record was below .500.

Part I

"Coach Saban tells it to you, you believe him. He looks you in the eyes and says, 'We're going to win championships.' And he lays out a specific plan how he's going to do it. And I think that's what guys buy into."

—Former Alabama offensive lineman Barrett Jones (2009–12)

Reasons Why Saban Is Such a Good Coach

His Parents

Even though Saban had no intention of coaching until after his playing career had ended at Kent State University, football was in his blood from the start.

Nicholas Lou Saban was born on October 31, 1952, and named for his father and his cousin Lou Saban, who coached the Boston Patriots, Buffalo Bills, and Denver Broncos, all at the professional level (and headed a coaching tree that included Marty Schottenheimer, Bill Cowher, and Tony Dungy).

Looking back, though, just about everything in his life helped prepare him for his career choice.

Saban grew up in West Virginia, about a mile from the community of Monongah, where he went to high school. It's just west of Fairmont, not too far from Morgantown, and about 90 miles to the south of Pittsburgh. For football that's strong Steelers territory, but he also liked Roberto Clemente and the Pirates, along with the San Francisco Giants.

With no brothers, there were a number of women who had a significant influence on Saban during his younger years. In addition to his mother, Mary, whom he's always been close to, older sister Dianna was quite an athlete herself. His father had three sisters, and his mother was one of four girls, while young Nick spent a lot of time playing at Grandma Saban's house.

But the person who undoubtedly had the strongest influence on him was his father, who was extremely well-thought-of by the community. "I was very fortunate growing up, and my dad was a coach, but he never went to college, but he coached Pop Warner, American Legion baseball, all those kinds of things. He also had a service station and a little Dairy Queen restaurant, and I started working at that service station when I was 11 years old, pumping gas," Saban said. "Notice I said it was a service station; it wasn't a self-serve. So you cleaned the windows, checked the oil, checked the tires, collected the money, gave the change, treated the customers in a certain way. We also greased cars, washed cars. So the biggest thing that I learned and started to learn at 11 years old was how important it was to do things correctly. There was a standard of excellence, a perfection. If we washed a car…I hated the navy blue and black cars because when you wiped them off the streaks were hard to get out, and if there were any streaks when he came [to check], you had to do it over. So we learned a lot about work ethic. We learned a lot about having compassion for other people and respecting other people and we learned about certainly the importance of doing things correctly.

"When I started to play for him in Pop Warner football, he was the same way as a coach—attention to detail, discipline, do things what you're supposed to do, the way you're supposed to do it, when you're supposed to do it, the way it's supposed to get done, all those things that we've all heard about. Discipline was engrained in just about everything that we did. And I think that sort of perfectionist type of attitude that my parents instilled sort of made you always strive to be all that you could be, and that's probably still the foundation of the program that we have right now.

"We hope that every player in our program has a better opportunity to be more successful in life because he was involved in the program, and that we create an atmosphere and environment for his personal development, his academic development, and his athletic development that actually is going to enhance his future chances of being successful. I think 'Big Nick,' as he was called in those days, had a lot to do with that."

The Pop Warner team was called the Idamay Black Diamonds, and Saban's father also came up with the money to buy a used bus that he drove to the surrounding areas—including Monongah, Idamay, Farmington, Carolina, and Number Nine—to pick up all the kids for football practice. He regularly told the players during games that if they won he'd treat them to Dairy Queen, and then he'd drive everyone home, "so they wouldn't have to hitchhike," Saban said.

Of his father, Saban also reflected, "He was a tough coach…He expected our best all of the time, probably instilled some of the perfectionist-type characteristics in what I try to do. I had a high standard of excellence from what he expected from me. Discipline was a very important part of what you did, being responsible for what you're supposed to do and the way you're supposed to do it, when you're supposed to do it, all that kind of stuff."

The field that Saban's Pop Warner team played on is now known as Nick Saban Field, and it's not because of the guy who won national championships.

There was also a lot of tough love taught in the Saban house. "A lot of us never know growing up why our parents do some of the things that they do, and sometimes we may not like it much. In cases we may resent it some," Saban said in 2012. "There was a bum who used to always come to my dad's service station early in the morning because he would give him free coffee and donuts. We had a tough game the night before, I don't remember if it was a basketball game or a football game or whatever, and the guy was sort of giving me a hard time. I sassed him. I was 17 years old. I got the strap right on the spot. But it was right. I mean it was the right thing. I needed to learn a lesson. I was disrespectful to an older person, regardless of the situation. My parents had tremendous values that I think [have] stuck." Saban added that his mother "reinforced all that stuff" and added, "I had great parents and a great dad."

On the field Saban was a quarterback who became a defensive back at the collegiate level. It wasn't until after he accepted an invitation to stay with the Golden Flashes and be a graduate assistant with Don James' staff that Saban caught the coaching bug. Following the 1973 season opener, a 10–3 upset victory over Louisville, he called his father to tell him that he really liked it and knew what he wanted to do with his life.

A week later, Saban's father died at the age of 46 from a heart attack while jogging. Saban still calls that the toughest part of his life and even offered to come back home and take over the family business, but his mother refused. "Probably when I was a senior in college, that's when I first began to realize [how much I appreciated my upbringing] and then my first year of graduate school when he passed away," Saban said. "I never really ever told him, which I regret."

Saban's Coaching Path

1973–74: Kent State (graduate assistant)
1975–76: Kent State (linebackers)
1977: Syracuse (outside linebackers)
1978–79: West Virginia (defensive backs)
1980–81: Ohio State (defensive backs)
1982: Navy (defensive backs)
1983–87: Michigan State (defensive backs/defensive coordinator)
1988–89: Houston Oilers (defensive backs)
1990: Toledo
1991–94: Cleveland Browns (defensive coordinator)
1995–99: Michigan State
2000–04: LSU
2005–06: Miami Dolphins
2007–Present: Alabama

But Saban has continued to pay tribute to his father in numerous ways, including the Nick's Kids Foundation that helps raise and distribute money to those in need. West Virginia will always be both close to his heart and never far from his mind. That hometown mentality has helped lead to things such as his first offensive line coach at Alabama being none other than Joe Pendry, the college roommate of one of his childhood friends, Joe Manchin, who went on to become West Virginia's governor and a U.S. senator.

"My motivation comes as a coach, to try and help the players on the team be most successful," Saban said. "My motivation as a person would be to serve other people, try and be a good person, which is challenging for all of us, probably, in some circumstance, and hopefully we get better as time goes on, as we have more and more experiences. Try and be a good husband and good father to your children. What else is there?"

His Mentors

Considering the success that one has had at the professional level and what the other has done at the collegiate level, there are a lot of parallels to be drawn between Bill Belichick and Nick Saban.

Not only are they both intensely driven, but they used to be on the same coaching staff together. When Belichick was the head coach of the Cleveland Browns, he made Saban his defensive coordinator. "There's no other coach in this league or any league that I have more respect for than Nick Saban," Belichick said in 2006. "I've said it before, and I'll say it again, I learned a whole lot more from him when he was at Cleveland than I'm sure he learned from me…That guy is a [darn] good football coach."

Head-to-head in the NFL, the coaches split their games in the same AFC East division. However, Belichick appeared to have the better team in New England, going 10–6 and 12–4 while reaching the playoffs. Just imagine what might have happened had Saban decided to stay with the Miami Dolphins.

Nowadays, Belichick visits Tuscaloosa on occasion to see firsthand what kind of talent Saban has developed for the NFL Draft, and when he does, their socializing is usually done while watching game film.

There's no doubt, though, that Belichick has had a profound effect on Saban, and his name usually comes up with reporters a few times a year. For example: "We try to define the expectation for every guy in the organization, and I think any successful business probably does that. So people can be responsible for their own self-determination. They can do their job. When I worked for Bill Belichick, we had one sign in the building; it said 'Do your job.' Now, he defined what he expected from everybody in the organization, but everybody knew what the expectation was for them, whether they were secretary, personnel, or player, what kind of players we wanted to bring to the organization from the personnel department, whatever it was, and then everybody needs to make a commitment to the standard, be a team player, trust and respect the principles and values of the organization as well as each other, be positive about how you go about your work, and know that it's going to take a tremendous amount of commitment and work to be able to accomplish it."

As Saban put it on another occasion, if you don't define every role and expectation, then all you get is chaos, making it impossible to be successful and consistent. That's why, in part, some people have the right makeup to be a head coach, or a leader in general, and others don't.

"It's almost like being a good quarterback," Saban said. "A lot of guys can throw the ball well enough to be a good quarterback, but their ability to process information quickly, make the right decision, deliver the ball at the right time and have the timing to be successful playing the position, I think, separates the men from the boys. It doesn't matter if that guy came up in Division III, Division II, played at the most prestigious school in the country, that's still what's going to separate him as a quarterback. I think that the same is probably true of guys

Though he competed against him in the AFC East for two years, Nick Saban remains close to his mentor, Patriots head coach Bill Belichick. (AP Images)

who are head coaches. They have the right stuff, the right work ethic, the right leadership, the right principles and values in terms of how they develop their organization, provide leadership for their players, hire good people, and have a well-designed system for people to be successful in. I don't think it matters if you come up as a coordinator who becomes a head coach or you're a guy who came up in the ranks."

Any discussion about the people who helped mold Saban into a head coach has to begin with his father, who instilled the sense of discipline that's become his trademark attribute.

Then, of course, there's his college coach, Don James, who had a profound impact on him and got Saban into coaching. When Saban praises peers, the three names that frequently get mentioned are Joe Paterno, Bobby Bowden, and Don James. "Don James did probably more than anyone in this profession to influence me," Saban said. "First of all, I didn't ever want to grow up to be a coach. He kind of recognized that and asked me to be a coach, to be a graduate assistant, and I didn't have any intention…and the only reason why I did it was because my wife had another year of school. I really enjoyed it."

"He was solid, he was good," James said about his former quarterback-turned–defensive back for the Golden Flashes from 1970 to 1972. "You could see he was trying to learn more about the game than just his position."

He added, "Some coaches are just luckier than others, and I was just lucky." James confirmed that a lot of his decision to offer Saban a graduate-assistant spot was right place, right time, saying, "He knew our system, our drills, and our coverages. He could help with the guys right away."

Although James worked longer with future Missouri coach Gary Pinkel, and also had future Pittsburgh Steelers great Jack Lambert on that same Kent State team, he's primarily known for his years at Washington, where during 18 seasons the Huskies went 153–57–2, played in 14 bowls (including six Rose Bowls), and won a share of the 1991 national championship.

His coaching philosophy emphasized defense, teamed with a disciplined offense, and his reputation was that of a stern leader. There was no doubt who was in charge; things had to be done his way, and excuses weren't tolerated. A stickler for details, James was highly organized, and there was little wavering from the set schedule. "A tidy ship is a happy ship" was one of his favorite sayings.

Nick Saban's Coaching Tree

During the 2013 season there were more than 10 former Nick Saban assistant coaches working as head coaches in either the pros or collegiate ranks with nearly another 20 serving as coordinators. Among them, Jimbo Fisher led Florida State to the national championship, Mark Dantonio guided Michigan State to a Rose Bowl win, Jim McElwain took Colorado State to its first bowl game since 2008, Pat Shurmur was the offensive coordinator of the Philadelphia Eagles, and Josh McDaniels was the offensive coordinator of the New England Patriots.

However, none of Saban's former protégés have beaten him as a head coach yet.

Assistants Who Have Gone On to Be Head Coaches after Working for Nick Saban:

Name	Head-Coaching Job (Initial Assistant Coach Under Saban)
Curt Cignetti	Indiana University (Pennsylvania); 2011–Present (Alabama wide receivers 2007–10)
Mark Dantonio	Cincinnati 2004–06; Michigan State 2007–Present (Michigan State defensive backs 1995–2000)
Derek Dooley	Louisiana Tech 2007–09; Tennessee 2010–12 (LSU tight ends 2000–02; LSU running backs/special teams 2003–04; Miami Dolphins tight ends 2005–06)
Jimbo Fisher	Florida State 2010–Present; (LSU offensive coordinator/quarterbacks 2000–06)
Jason Garrett	Dallas Cowboys 2011–Present; (Miami Dolphins quarterbacks 2005–06)
Michael Haywood	Miami (Ohio) 2009–10; (LSU running backs/special teams 1995–2002)
Scott Linehan	St. Louis Rams 2006–08; (Miami Dolphins offensive coordinator 2005)
Jim McElwain	Colorado State 2012–Present; (Alabama offensive coordinator 2008-11)
Mike Mularkey	Jacksonville Jaguars 2012; (Miami Dolphins offensive coordinator 2006)
Will Muschamp	Florida 2011–Present; (LSU defensive coordinator/linebackers 2001–04; Miami Dolphins defensive coordinator 2005)
Pat Shurmur	Cleveland Browns 2011–12; (Michigan State tight ends coach 1990–97)
Bobby Williams	Michigan State 2000–02; (Michigan State running backs 1990–99)

"From an organization standpoint, our program is run a lot the same the way Don James ran his program," Saban said. "They were well organized, efficient, defining things that are the expectations for players, coaches, and everyone in the organization, a systematic approach to almost everything that you're trying to do, and I found that working under that made it easier for me. When I went to other places to coach, I assumed that it was like that everywhere. Not really."

After Kent State, Saban bounced around as an assistant coach, from Syracuse to West Virginia, Ohio State, Navy, and Michigan State, not to mention the Houston Oilers and Cleveland Browns in the NFL. The influences on him were numerous. "George Perles, who was a great coach at Michigan State also at the Pittsburgh Steelers with Chuck Noll, really taught me a lot about developing as a coach," Saban said. "I'm talking about [the] technique of being a good defensive coordinator and a secondary coach, and [he] was great at how he handled people and treated people; [he] was a great recruiter. I learned a lot from him."

Another was Jack Pardee—one of the Junction Boys along with Gene Stallings under Paul W. "Bear" Bryant at Texas A&M—who was Saban's neighbor when he was with the Houston Oilers. "Jack was a really good friend of mine," Saban said after Pardee passed away at the age of 76, on April 1, 2013, following a fight with gall bladder cancer. "You'll never find a better person. He's one of those guys you say you'd like to be like that guy."

Saban's first head coaching job was in the same league as Kent State, the Mid-American Conference, where he turned a 6–5 Toledo team into the 1990 co-league champions at 9–2. It was the only time Saban faced his alma mater—a 28–14 Toledo victory—until Alabama hosted the Golden Flashes in 2011.

So did James know all those years ago that he was starting someone down a Hall of Fame path? Not even close. "You can't predict those things," James said.

Pinkel went on to have a successful coaching career as well, following James to Washington (tight ends 1976, wide receivers 1979–83, and offensive coordinator 1984–1990) before succeeding Saban at Toledo in 1991. The Rockets went 73–37–3 before he was hired away by Missouri in 2001. "[He] had a remarkable influence on me, as he did to Nick Saban," Pinkel said about James, who passed away in October 2013 at the age of 80. "Nick was a head coach at Toledo for one year, then he decided to go with Bill Belichick to the Cleveland Browns, [and he] called me up and asked me if I was interested. I said I was. I'm appreciative to him.

He's a great football coach. I have great respect for him, always have. As a player, great competitor. Very tough, physical player. Very dedicated. Very committed, very team-oriented. I think that reflects the intensity level, very high intensity level. I think that's the same guy you see coach and have the great success he's had in college football. I think historically he'll go down as one of the great coaches in college football, and he should."

The Process

To say that Nick Saban is a creature of habit is like suggesting that the ocean can be a little damp. He wakes up at the same time every day. He has Little Debbie cookies with his coffee. He eats lunch in his office, usually a salad with turkey in it.

You know the car ads boasting about precision engineering? That company has nothing on the Alabama coach. Even when he does his weekly radio show, Saban almost always walks in just after the announcer has just started (skipping the ads preceding the show), and he doesn't eat while there. He's already had meatloaf that an aide picked up from a local diner and on the way makes notes about the points he wants to discuss on the show, regardless of the questions that might be asked.

Saban is the embodiment of routine and consistency, and achieving long-term goals through daily effort and focus is what he refers to as "the Process." It's something that is never-ending, and it is his way of compartmentalizing what's necessary on a regular basis to eventually meet large-scale objectives and accomplishments.

One symbolic thing that Saban does is have a four-row pyramid on a wall that every player has to walk past every day. The only things on each row are large blocks that prominently display the logo of each upcoming opponent that season, with the Week 1 logo in the lower left, followed by the Week 2 team, and so on. The bottom row is the foundation, and with each win the team builds a little more until it finally reaches the top. The players who contribute each week are expected to sign the corresponding block, so with each win, that particular square is full of autographs, but the losses are left completely blank.

Saban doesn't want his players thinking about trying to win a championship, making the SEC Championship Game, or even the score of the game. He wants players to concentrate solely on the things they can influence: the next play, the next rep, the next moment. Here's one of the ways he explains it: "Well, the process is really what you have to do day in and day out to be successful. We try to define the standard that we want everybody to sort of work toward, adhere to, and do it on a consistent basis, and the things that I talked about before, being responsible for your own self-determination, having a positive attitude, having great work ethic, having discipline to be able to execute on a consistent basis, whatever it is you're choosing to do, those are the things that we try to focus on, and we don't try to focus as much on outcomes as we do on being all that you can be and the things that you need to do to be all you can be. Eliminate the clutter and all the things that are going on outside, and focus on the things that you can control with how you sort of go about and take care of your business. That's something that's ongoing, and it can never change. So it's the process of what it takes to be successful, very simply."

The idea is really nothing new. From Vince Lombardi's "Winning is a habit" to Joe Paterno's "You have to perform at a consistently higher level than others," a common characteristic of coaches who have had a lot of success is the ability to get the most out of their players, and obviously Saban has been as good at it as anyone.

He also extends the idea of "good is not good enough" to every aspect of the program. "I came to Alabama, and all the books and all the covers said, 'The process begins,'" Saban said. "The process [is] what it takes to be successful, the hard work, the decision, the discipline, the overcoming adversity, players buying in, being a team, all of the things that you try to build a program with. But then when you have success, everybody starts to think and expect that you're just going to have a continuum of success, which never really ever happens in anything. You know, the process is ongoing. Every year, it's a new process with new players, and 25 percent of your team leaves and you've got new freshmen coming in.

"So you have a new process of what you need to do to make that team sort of be what they need to be. It's the same way in recruiting. It's the same way in academics. It's the same way in personal development. As soon as you lose sight of the process of what it takes to be successful, then I think that it's going to be very difficult to sustain that success. But I also think it's human nature that when things don't go well, people respond to that much better than sometimes they respond to being successful. So on the other side of that spectrum, I think you have to have special people who understand the importance of playing to a standard and know that the importance of what you're doing right now is the most important thing.

"I heard Michael Jordan say this: 'I don't care how many game-winning shots I've ever made and how many games I've ever won with game-winning shots, the one that I'm getting ready to take right now is the only one that matters, because the rest of them don't matter, not in this game.' I think when you're in any kind of competition, any kind of sport, any kind of profession, that's the way it is. Now, that sounds reasonably easy. But from a human-condition standpoint, unless you have special people, special leaders, a special understanding of what it takes to continue to be successful and the standard that you have to play [at] to do it, it is challenging."

Saban has been tweaking his "process" for nearly 40 years, and the key word there is *tweaking*, because he's constantly been evaluating, changing, and updating. Some things that may not have worked well 10 years ago may do so now and vice versa. Over the summer he and his assistant coaches regularly meet with their counterparts from other college and pro organizations to try and discover ways to improve, and to study what worked and didn't work elsewhere and why.

For example in 2013 numerous NFL teams visited Tuscaloosa to study how to defend spread offenses and running quarterbacks because they weren't used to facing them so often. During an ESPN interview, Saban mentioned that the San Francisco 49ers used multiple-formation looks, so more players had to learn how to defend against mobile quarterbacks and be aware of them at all times.

At the time Alabama was coming off a season in which its only loss was to Texas A&M and Heisman Trophy winner Johnny Manziel. Ole Miss had already gone to a quick-snap, no-huddle approach with Auburn and LSU expected to speed things up dramatically as well. It was pretty obvious what the Crimson Tide defense had been working on, with one of the adjustments in recruiting to place a higher emphasis on linebackers who could excel in pass coverage.

So the Process is the vehicle for how Crimson Tide football goes about achieving its objective, which one would think is winning games on a field. It's not—at least it's not the primary aim. To Saban the college game is also part of the collegiate experience, which at its core is about helping and improving students while preparing them for the rest of their lives. It's about fulfilling potential. "Our mission statement has always been to create an atmosphere and environment for players to be successful first of all as people," Saban explained. "Two things, to be successful in life and anything you choose to do: first of all, you have to know what you've got to do. You got to make a commitment to it, be dedicated toward it, have some passion for it, work and invest your time in it, stick with it, have some perseverance relative to all of it, and have the kind of character and attitude, thoughts, habits, and priorities on a day-to-day basis to make good choices about what you do and don't do so you can realize your dreams. That's the first thing we'd like to try to accomplish with our players and provide leadership for.

"The second thing is, we want them to get an education. That's the thing that's going to affect the quality of their life more than anything else, something that we want to provide support for relative to facilities and personnel and people who can affect them and help them reach their full potential academically. We want them to be champions on the football field in terms of developing as players so that they can win a championship someday. And we'd like to use the resource that the institution has at the University of Alabama to help launch their career and get the best opportunities in life."

Although it sounds cliché, and probably just about every coach feels this way, Saban is a great believer that sports are a metaphor for life. At some point everyone is going to face adversity and overcome obstacles. You do that with things like commitment, dedication, hard work, perseverance, character, discipline, and passion. "I don't care what business you're in, I think all those things are probably important to you being successful in that," Saban said. "So really the ingredients that it takes to be successful don't change from one thing to another. Being a competitor, to be able to be consistent in what you do, not get affected by the bad things that happen and get frustrated where it affects your performance, not being able to deal with success when things go well, let that affect your performance, are also lessons that you can learn as an athlete that also are important in life."

As a result, Saban wrote *How Good Do You Want to Be?* in 2005. The book was rereleased in a paperback edition in 2007 after Saban took the job at Alabama, with the color of the coach's shirt on the cover changed to crimson. The book's subtitle is, *A Champion's Tips on How to Lead and Succeed.*

In addition to sports publications like *Sports Illustrated*, numerous business-media outlets have profiled the Process, including *60 Minutes* (and *60 Minutes*

Sports), Fortune, and *The Wall Street Journal.* In August 2008 *Forbes* magazine put Saban on its cover with the headline "Most Powerful Coach in Sports," and later came back with a story titled "What Nick Saban Knows About Success," noting that his coaching Process "applies to business every bit as much as football." *Fortune* had an article "Leadership Lessons of Nick Saban," which stated that "if Saban were running a company instead of a football program, he'd be hailed as an elite manager."

But Saban, like other coaches, has had to come up with different ways to get his message across to young men usually between the ages of 18 and 22, and not just because people don't always react the same way to the same things. Times change, but some of his best deliveries are the same ones he's been using for years.

"You know, there's an old Martin Luther King sermon that talks about, 'There's only one guy who I'd let shine my shoes in Montgomery, Alabama, because of the pride he had in the performance of how he shined my shoes. I didn't want anybody else in the world to shine my shoes, and the enjoyment he got that he did a great job for what you did,'" he said. "You've probably heard this sermon, and I'm just paraphrasing here, but if you're going to be a street sweeper, be the best street sweeper you can be. Sweep the streets like Michelangelo painted the Sistine Chapel, like Shakespeare wrote literature. Let them put a sign up right here that says, 'The best street sweeper in the world lives right here.' And if you can do that, you do the best there is in life, knowing you did your best to be the best you could be, no matter what you choose to do. That's why. Because there's no better feeling than knowing you did the best you could be. I don't care if it's what you do, what I do, what the street sweeper does. It really doesn't matter. It's not all about results."

Going back to the building-block analogy, a similar pattern emerged over Saban's first few years at Alabama. His first couple of recruiting classes led to winning seasons, then division and conference championships, and the 2009 national title. Looking back, players could see the difference and progression. "I remember our recruiting class, we were No. 1, and it was kind of Coach Saban's first entire recruiting class, and we said we were going to win a national championship our second year," former Alabama running back Mark Ingram Jr. said. "It's kind of crazy that we actually did it."

Of course, the following season injury-plagued Alabama had three losses and failed in its effort not only to repeat, but to play in a BCS bowl. It began the next upswing during the practices for the Capital One Bowl, where it absolutely destroyed Michigan State 49–7.

"Having success in a football program can have two [potential] effects. You can demand more success, or you can get a little complacent and be relaxed about what you have accomplished, really think more about what you did rather than what you're going to do," Saban said. "It's human nature to relax, but there's been a lot of examples of very successful people. And I think success should be defined, 'Consistency in performance.' Whether it's the Chicago Bulls in the '90s, the Yankees organization through the years, [or] Roger Federer and Michael Johnson as individual athletes who have had great careers, been successful over a long period of time. We've obviously learned a lot at Alabama over the last [few] years.

"The most important thing we've learned is you got to stay on top of the little things. Things don't happen by accident. You don't win a play by accident. You don't win a game by accident. You don't win a division by accident. You have to make it happen, and you have to make it happen by what you do every day. Your commitment, everything in the organization, to the principles and values of the organization, and the standard that you have set for that organization, become primary in the development of team chemistry. If everybody doesn't buy into those principles and values, everybody doesn't buy into the standard, there's no way you can have the type of team chemistry to be successful, especially at an elite, high level. High achievers don't like mediocre people, mediocre people don't like high achievers. So everybody has to buy into the same principles and values."

Saban used the three-loss 2010 Crimson Tide team as an example for each of the next three seasons. Alabama came back a year later and won the national championship again, avenging an overtime loss to LSU during the regular season with a 21–0 victory in the title game, and in 2012 it returned to the BCS National Championship Game with a team that Saban said exceeded expectations. "We just watched a video of Mariano Rivera, and he talked about [how] he struggled at some time in his career because he was trying to be a perfectionist, and that when he's in the bullpen, he sees the crowd, he hears the crowd, he knows sometimes that he's getting a lot of positive self-gratification for what he does and sometimes getting a lot of negative self-gratification for what he does," Saban said the day before facing Notre Dame. "But when he runs out and they hand him the ball,

17

he's got one focus; he's not worried about the crowd, he's not worried about any of the external factors. One focus: *Three outs. How am I going to get three outs?*

"I think a team's ability to do that, to stay focused on the things that are going to affect the outcome of the game, are critical in games like this, and you know, you could say, 'Well, that's nothing.' Well, believe me, being around young people, being in games like this, that's something, and it's something big. It certainly affects your ability to perform. The way [you perform depends on] your ability to stay focused on the present-moment things that will affect your performance and to stay in the right sort of disposition that way."

Saban's question to his team was: "Can you finish what you started?"

Roughly 24 hours later, the Crimson Tide crushed the Fighting Irish 42–14, and by the end of the week many of the players were back at work, laying the foundation for 2013. "There's no continuum of success," Saban said. "The process begins, but it's ongoing, and if you don't pay attention to that, you're not going to stay up."

In other words, winning is a habit.

Attention to Detail

There isn't a single aspect of Alabama football that doesn't have Nick Saban's fingerprints all over it. From the play calling down to recruiting, everything he does is thought-out, planned, and has a reason behind it.

Every player, when he arrives on the Capstone, is given a binder with everything he needs to know. It is meticulously prepared, from the terminology and how practices are organized to how everyone is expected to conduct himself and what the expectations are not only each day, but over the course of his career.

It's a massive blueprint that Saban has spent years going over, changing, and perfecting, with his assistant coaches and staff held to the same high standards. "He is very detail-oriented. I mean, down to the minute of practice, down to the…I mean, he wants every second of practice organized, every walk-through rep, it doesn't matter if you're in special teams and you're doing walk-through, he wants it organized, he wants to plan for it, he wants it on paper, and he wants you to execute it," longtime assistant coach Kirby Smart said. "In the end it makes your overall program more successful because you don't leave any part of the program uncovered."

The examples are numerous, like the Crimson Tide always arriving at the stadium, home or away, exactly two hours before kickoff. While players start their pregame rituals, Saban alone walks the field to check for any potential distractions and takes note of things like where the 30-second clocks are located. One of the factors in deciding what the priority is for the coin flip is the wind direction, as Saban almost always wants to avoid having the offense and kickers go against it in the fourth quarter when the game could be on the line.

But perhaps the best way to understand Saban's attention to detail is by watching the final couple of minutes of the 2011 title game against LSU, when Alabama was ahead 21–0 and reserve linebacker Alex Watkins jumped offside. Even though the game's outcome was no longer in doubt, and the crystal football was being polished up for the awards celebration, Saban went ballistic along the sideline.

Why? Because it was the kind of mental mistake that he preaches about avoiding every day of the year. Probably the one thing he yells more than any other during practices is, "Do it the right way!" About an hour after the game ended, a reporter actually asked Saban if the competitive fire still burned as hot inside him as when he was a player or graduate assistant.

"What do you think?" Saban responded, drawing a lot of laughter from the room.

The Mental Side of the Game

The 2012 season opener was still weeks away, and yet ESPN dispatched Tom Rinaldi to Tuscaloosa to do a special story associated with the Crimson Tide that would run weeks later on *College GameDay*.

Part of Alabama's training-camp experience is a daily guest speaker, and on that particular night Dewey Bozella was addressing the Crimson Tide. After spending 26 years in prison for a murder he did not commit, Bozella, 52, wanted a chance to fight a sanctioned boxing match and got it, winning a unanimous decision over 30-year-old Larry Hopkins in Los Angeles. Bozella, who had numerous opportunities to be released from Sing Sing Correctional Facility if he would confess to the crime, was honored by ESPN with the 2011 Arthur Ashe Award. "He talked a lot about how important it is to be—who you are is the most important thing about what you do," Saban said. "You can't be mad at the world for your circumstance until you change and you treat people and offer something to a person that's never going to come back to you. It's a great story in determination and perseverance."

"I thought he was very, very inspirational," former offensive lineman Barrett Jones said about Dewey Bozella's "never give up" talk. "For me personally that makes me think when I'm having a tough day, I'm really not having that tough of a day. He had some bad breaks and he still chose to have a positive attitude. A lot about it is, it's your choice, what person you're going to be and what kind of attitude you're going to have about life."

Some of the speakers who Saban brings in are essentially the regular part of camp, like a presentation from the compliance department and a media specialist on how to deal with reporters and conduct interviews. Others, though, would be considered anything from ordinary. He's brought in former NBA player Chris Herren to talk about overcoming his drug-abuse problems, former player and director of football operations for the NFL Gene Washington to discuss life after a career in sports, FBI personnel to discuss gambling, and Michael Franzese, a former New York mobster with the Colombo crime family.

Saban is also huge on motivational speakers and people who can help with the mental part of the game. They include the Pacific Institute, a Seattle-based company that has conducted mental-conditioning classes for the Crimson Tide and taught players to be daily teachers themselves; IMG Performance Institute director Trevor Moawad; and Dr. Kevin Elko, who calls himself a performance consultant. "He was the best speaker I've ever heard," tight end Preston Dial (2007–10) said about Elko. "He spoke on toughness and what it takes to get to the next level."

"He always preaches to us about accepting failure, and if you can accept failure and understand why it happened and what's the reason it happened that way, everything else will be okay," senior linebacker Nico Johnson said of Elko. "Just continue to move forward once the failure happens and keep improving."

Elko and Saban became associated when both were working for NFL teams, and their relationship has gotten tighter over the years. Not only is Elko a regular speaker during camp, but he usually addresses the team at least once more during the season before a big game of some sort and then again in the postseason.

"I've always been interested in it," Saban said about the mental side of the game. "I think I've learned a tremendous amount from them that has really helped me sort of understand the best way to help manage guys psychologically so that they have a better chance of being successful. Not just in football, but in their personal life and academics and anything they choose to do."

A major turning point in that may have occurred at LSU. In 2002 Saban had the team put together a list of goals, and like most others it had "Win the national championship" at the top. The Tigers went on to finish 8–5 and lost four of their last six games.

In 2003 the team's self-proclaimed goals looked much different and were posted on the wall of the corridor leading out of the locker room:

Be a team.
Together everyone achieves more.
Trust.
Dominate your opponent every day.
Discipline, focus and execution.
Finish plays.
Make a positive effect on someone on your team every day.
Be a champion on and off the field.

"My LSU team was the first team I had been associated with in 31 years of coaching that when they made their goals before the season, none of the goals had anything to do with winning a game," Saban said.

Of course, LSU won the national championship. The 2004 team didn't change the goals, because they were considered the principles by which the players already went about things.

"[Saban] goes deep into the mental side," Kirby Smart said in 2013. "He spends as much time on that as he does defensively now, and I think that is where he's grown as a coach, because I can remember being at LSU, I didn't remember the mental side being so great. Now six, seven years later, it's extended so far. He really believes in that, he believes in what you tell the players, he believes in the angle of approach of each game being different and getting their mind-set right for the game.

"To me that's where he has established himself as a coach ahead of the curve because of his ability mentally to create an advantage with his team. Whatever the mind-set is, whether it's physicality, whether it's execution, whatever it is, he does a great job of conveying that to the kids. And he makes us realize as coaches, it's not going to be about what we call, it's not going to be about what we rep, it's going to be about the mind-set in [their] head that's going to make a difference in this game."

Considering Saban has yet to be defeated in a national title game, and has only lost once in the SEC Championship Game, there may not be a better big-game coach in college football. It also didn't happen overnight, as he was on the losing end of his first three bowl games—although Michigan State's best finish in the Big Ten during those seasons was fifth—and he was 3–2 in bowl games with LSU.

"Well, I just think that when you play in games like this, there's always sort of a turning point in the game," Saban said before the 2012 national championship. "First of all, you expect [with] two good teams playing, it's going to be a close game. There's going to be some situations in the game where you need to make a play or they might need to make a play that's going to make the difference in the game, and your ability to rise up in those situations and be able to do that, whether it's a critical third down to maintain possession of the ball on a scoring drive or whether it's a defensive stop, whatever it might be, you know, you have to be ready to execute in those kinds of situations in the game."

It actually hasn't worked out that way, at least in most of the title games. Each successive championship has arguably been more of a blowout: 21–14 over Oklahoma, 37–21 against Texas, a 21–0 shutout of LSU, and the 42–14 rout of Notre Dame.

Before the 2012 title game, Fighting Irish coach Brian Kelly was asked about Saban's approach to the mental aspect of the game and said the following: "Belief is crucial. If you don't believe that you can do it, you probably can't. So I think everything we do is to reinforce all the things that they're capable of doing. Look, they're 18 to 21 years old. The sky's the limit. I don't think there's a football coach out there, I don't think there's a great CEO out there who does not try to employ some form of positive reinforcement and motivation that you can be whatever you want to be. Having said that, there are so many other pieces to it that I think are more important than 'getting them to think that they can do it. They've actually got to go out and do it.' And I think the biggest challenge for me here in the first

The Biggest Line

While some feel that Alabama's 2011 defense may have been the best in college football history, the same could be argued about the 2012 offensive line. With Outland Trophy winner Barrett Jones moving from left tackle to center, the Crimson Tide had the biggest starting five in program history:

Left tackle: Cyrus Kouandjio, 6'6", 311 pounds
Left guard: Chance Warmack, 6'3", 320 pounds
Center: Barrett Jones, 6'5", 302 pounds
Right guard: Anthony Steen, 6'3", 303 pounds
Right tackle: D.J. Fluker, 6'6", 335 pounds

"Besides watching *The Longest Yard*, I'm pretty sure it's the biggest offensive line I've seen," quipped nose guard Jesse Williams, who had to face it every day during practice.

Similarly, when Fluker was asked what it would be like for a defensive end to face he and Kouandjio at the end of an unbalanced line, he responded, "I'd kind of run away."

At the end of the season, guard Chance Warmack was named a unanimous All-American, and Jones was a consensus All-American. According to the organizations the NCAA uses to determine that status, D.J. Fluker was a second-team All-American, but numerous other services had him as a first-team selection.

For a little perspective on that, consider that there hadn't been three consensus All-American linemen from the same team since 1909, when tackle Henry Hobbs, guard Hamlin Andrus, and center Carroll Cooney were all honored at Yale.

couple of years was to get our guys to prepare the right way and to play the game the right way. You've still got to execute and play this game the right way. Belief comes with winning. The best form of confidence is when you make that play."

Maybe that's why part of Elko's deal with Saban is that when the Crimson Tide wins the national championship, he gets a ring too. "The focus that you need to have, the mental toughness you have to have, the ability to lock on to whatever the circumstance is and the perseverance you have to have to be able to overcome little adversities that always crop up, whether you're playing at Missouri and it's pouring down rain, you get 40 minutes in the locker room in the middle of the game. Whatever it is, you have to be able to respond to those things," Saban said.

To anchor the team's massive offensive line, Barrett Jones moved from tackle to center for the 2012 championship campaign.

"A lot of times, we all spend a lot of time figuring out how can we make it perfect for these guys? Well, most of the time it doesn't happen perfectly, so to be able to have an expectation that things may go wrong here, and I have to focus and stay focused even in those circumstances, I think really helps guys when it comes to things like this."

The School

The smile was unforgettable, much like the game that had just been played, and even though athletic director Mal Moore was deep in the recesses of the Rose Bowl, it was easy to tell that no one could have been prouder.

Moore had done it. The rejuvenation, if not resurrection, of the Crimson Tide was already complete, only now with the victory over Texas in the 2009 BCS title game, everyone else knew it as well—and that more championships would follow.

It had all come together, even better than Moore had dared hope, from the renovations of Bryant-Denny Stadium to leaving an open spot along the Walk of Champions where statues of title-winning coaches stood, and would subsequently be filled. "It was put there for this, and I will recommend to the president that we go forth," Moore happily said while waiting to get into the locker room after the 37–21 victory to secure the program's 13th title.

"Immediately?" a reporter asked.

"Yeah. Hell yeah," Moore said. "It is really difficult to express just how proud I am."

It was vintage Moore, who was crimson to the core, or as university president Dr. Judy Bonner once said, "Mal Moore is Crimson Tide sports." No truer words could have been used about the man who was the embodiment of Alabama athletics and who has turned them into the envy of nearly every other school in the nation.

If they kept score with jewelry, Moore would have been considered the Tiffany's of college sports, because no one had a more prestigious ring collection, in addition to bowl watches, pins, and trophies. They dated all the way back to 1958, when Moore was a backup quarterback for the Crimson Tide and three years later helped Bear Bryant win his first national championship.

Moore served as Bryant's graduate assistant in 1964, the defensive backfield coach from 1965 to 1970, the quarterbacks coach from 1971 to 1982, and offensive coordinator from 1975 to 1982. He's the only man connected to the coaching staffs of the 1964, 1965, 1973, 1978, 1979, and 1992 national championship teams.

But when Moore was named the athletic director in 1999, he inherited a program in disarray. The stadium wasn't considered anything special with rundown locker rooms, training facilities that were outdated, and weight-room equipment from the 1970s. Additionally, Alabama had massive issues with the National Collegiate Athletic Association with the Committee of Infractions threatening to issue the death penalty to the football program.

He got through that period and upgraded the facilities, but in order to do so he first had to get people to believe in Alabama again, which was not an easy task. Moore instituted a five-year facilities and endowment initiative, the Crimson Tradition Fund, which initially had a $100 million goal but raised $150 million.

In addition to a major overhaul and expansion of Bryant-Denny Stadium, Coleman Coliseum and nearly every other athletic venue was renovated, while Bryant Hall was converted into an academic center. The project was completed in 2006, setting the stage for greatness. "We all recognize that we're now in position that we can compete with anyone in recruiting," Moore said at the end of the 2006–07 season. "I've said to coaches many times when I'm speaking, and when I'm around and about, we should expect—the coaches should, I should, our alumni, our president, everyone should expect—positive results from this and will [receive them]. I think it's an exciting time for Alabama and for the future down the road at Alabama."

Consequently, in November 2006, the Alabama Board of Trustees renamed the football building the Mal M. Moore Athletic Facility with school president Dr. Robert E. Witt stating, "Mal Moore's leadership in building our athletic programs and facilities has been exemplary."

Then, and only then, came what Moore will always be known for, convincing Nick Saban to leave the Miami Dolphins for the Capstone. The move didn't just change the landscape of Alabama and the Southeastern Conference but all of college football. The Crimson Tide won national titles in 2009, 2011, and 2012, and championships in three other sports. "[Moore's] somebody that I have a tremendous amount of respect for," Saban said.

Feeling that the job wasn't quite done, though, even after adding Saban, Moore orchestrated another expansion of Bryant-Denny Stadium, this time beyond the southern end zone, in time for the 2010 season and at a cost of $65 million. In addition to filling in the last upper deck and adding another two rows of skyboxes along with other amenities, the new seating capacity grew to 101,821, making it one of the largest and desirable home venues in collegiate athletics.

For a program that not too long ago scheduled its biggest home games for Legion Field in Birmingham, it was a remarkable upgrade that served as a monument to a new era for both the program and school while simultaneously adding to an already rich legacy. Nothing like the stadium that originally sat 12,000 when it opened in 1929, Alabama finally had a campus facility that matched its success on the field and to Moore was worthy of the name Crimson Tide. In 2013 *Stadium Journey* magazine tabbed it the best venue to visit in college football.

"Mal wanted to finish the stadium this time," chief financial officer Finus Gaston said upon completion. "He did a great job."

That level of commitment played a huge part in Moore being able to lure Saban, which wouldn't have happened had all the pieces not been in place for the coach to succeed.

The president pro tempore of the Board of Trustees of the University of Alabama System was Paul W. Bryant Jr., son of the legendary former coach Paul W. "Bear" Bryant. Additionally, after 35 years as a faculty member and administrator in the University of Texas System, Witt saw the potential for the university's overall growth to be similar to what Dr. George Hutcheson Denny accomplished in the 1920s and 1930s. Enrollment went from less than 20,000 in 2000 to exceeding 30,000 by 2010 (more than 26,400 high school students applied for a spot in the 2012–13 freshman class, "And the quality of our students, based on ACT scores and high

Athletic director Mal Moore, who forever changed the program by luring Nick Saban to Alabama, speaks during a 2009 national championship celebration.

The Money

When Nick Saban's agent, Jimmy Sexton, initially negotiated an eight-year, $32 million contract with Alabama, it was the highest salary ever paid to a collegiate coach in any sport. Although some claimed that it was helping ruin college athletics and Alabama had become the poster child of excess, others said that it was obvious Saban would only stick around a couple of years, especially since there was no out clause and Saban could leave at any time without a financial penalty.

Apparently they didn't consider that the big contract would A) help keep him at Alabama, B) be necessary to lure him away from the Miami Dolphins, and C) reinforce the school's level of commitment because a lot more would be necessary to return the Crimson Tide to the top of the college football world.

When Saban got a contract extension to pay him $5.32 million in 2012 and $45 million through the 2019 season, in addition to a $5 million life insurance policy, no one argued. "The acceptance of this extension expresses our commitment, my commitment, Terry and [my] commitment, our family's commitment to the University of Alabama for the rest of our career," Saban said. "We made that decision after the season, when other people were interested [in hiring me]."

When asked who was interested, Saban said, "It doesn't really matter. We wanted to stay at Alabama. We're staying at Alabama and weren't interested in going anywhere else. We're really pleased and happy to be here."

Alabama reworked the contract again at the end of the 2013 season to make Saban one of the highest-paid coaches in American sports at about $7 million a season. According to Forbes, of the nine pro coaches who were making more than $6 million a year at the time, eight were in the National Football League: Saints coach Sean Payton ($8 million), Patriots coach Bill Belichick ($7.5 million), Chiefs coach Andy Reid ($7.5 million), Seahawks coach Pete Carroll ($7 million), Rams coach Jeff Fisher ($7 million), Redskins coach Mike Shanahan ($7 million), Giants coach Tom Coughlin ($6.67 million), and Eagles coach Chip Kelly ($6.5 million). The

school GPAs, has never been higher," Bonner said). That, in turn, resulted in a new dorm opening each fall and massive renovations to others, a new home for the College of Nursing, more dining facilities, an elaborate bus system, additional parking lots, and the list goes on and on. "Since Dr. Witt's coming to campus in 2003, there's been an investment of over $1 billion in the physical campus," Tim Leopard, the university's assistant vice president of construction, said at the time. "The approach has been very broad. It has not just been new buildings. It's been new renovations, it's been new infrastructure. It's been roofs, new mechanicals. While new buildings are the most physically apparent change, it's broad across campus other was the National Basketball Association's Doc Rivers, who was making $7 million a season from the Los Angeles Clippers.

Now look at the flip side of it.

In 2006, the year before Saban arrived in Tuscaloosa, the athletic department brought in $67.7 million in revenue, mostly from football, and spent $60.6 million. Five years later, revenue was $124.5 million, and expenditures were $105.1 million for a profit of a $19.4 million. "Nick Saban's the best financial investment this university has ever made," chancellor of the University of Alabama system Dr. Robert Witt, who was the president when Saban was hired in 2007, told the television show *60 Minutes* in 2013. "We have made an investment that's been returned many-fold."

Additionally, according to studies, each Crimson Tide home game was pumping $24.3 million into the state's economy, most directly into Tuscaloosa. Alabama athletics contributed more than $5 million to the rest of the university, and merchandise sales had never been higher. Following the 2009 national championship, the school received an extra $2 million in royalties ($1.4 million after the 2011 title), and year-round sales in merchandise reached $9 million for the first time in school history, second only to Texas.

Meanwhile, with ratings going through the roof, the SEC was arguably enjoying immense success as well, with its TV deals in 2008 worth more than $3 billion over 15 years, and that was before the conference added Missouri and Texas A&M or started its own cable network. All indications were that when new deals were renegotiated, taking into account the new markets and increased demand, they would be the biggest in college sports history.

According to the U.S. Department of Education, the 12 SEC schools combined were making about $620 million. By 2011 that figure was closer to $1.1 billion. That's why when CBS announcer Gary Danielson was asked about the SEC's formula for collecting national championships, he said, "[It] starts with money, I think."

infrastructure. We have 41 buildings that are over 3 million square feet that are new. Currently in design we have almost another million square feet."

One of those changes, specific to football, was the building of a new weight room in the fall of 2012. Costing $9.08 million, it included a cardio/rehab area, strength coaches' offices, graduate-assistant workroom, nutrition bar, juice room, restrooms, medical office suite, elevator, janitor's closet, and storage. "Everything is the best of the best," director of strength and conditioning Scott Cochran said. "Every day I walk in and I'm humbled. It's easy for me. I've never seen anything like it in my life."

The 37,000-square-foot facility (21,000 on the first floor and 16,000 on the second) features numerous large-screen TVs to demonstrate proper technique and a sound system that can drown out even Cochran. Connecting the Mal M. Moore Athletic Facility to the Hank Crisp Indoor Facility, large garage doors separate the first-floor room from the indoor field, making it the envy of even some pro scouts when they come visiting. "Huge!" Cochran said. "It's the biggest, baddest weight room in the country."

Among the motivational signs on the walls is one that reads: "Sweat is just your fat crying."

The work on the new facility was nonstop during the 2012 season, and it opened in January 2013. That was important to Saban because National Signing Day is always the first week of February, and he wanted any wavering recruits to see it before making their final decisions. "I think when people come to Alabama, they expect to see the best, so I think we should always strive to have the best," Saban said. "As long as we have the resources and we can provide the best for our student-athletes, I think that's what we should do in all sports."

Sadly, though, shortly after the new weight room opened, Moore wound up in a Birmingham hospital with pulmonary problems and a few days later was transferred to Duke University Medical Center. He died on March 30, 2013, at the age of 73.

Moore's love affair with Alabama lasted more than 50 years, during which he was a part of 10 football national championship teams as a player, coach, or athletic director (1961, 1964, 1965, 1973, 1978, 1979, 1992, 2009, 2011, and 2012), 16 SEC championships, and 39 bowl trips. Fittingly, his family had all the rings, bowl watches, and other awards he won over the years placed in a glass case shaped like Bryant-Denny Stadium in the lobby of the university building bearing his name.

"I'm just so proud, absolutely, for all of our coaches and the university, our fans and those who pull for the university and everything," Moore said in 2012. "It's a great time in our history right now, what Dr. Witt has done and accomplished. I've said this before, the oneness on the campus is like never before—academics, athletics, and alumni all pulling in the same direction. You see positive results. With the growth of the university, I think it's broken the enrollment record again this year, all of that is kind of interwoven…It's a happy time for all of us."

The People He Surrounds Himself With

Even the biggest leader must have not only his generals, but lieutenants and ser-geants as well, and Nick Saban is no exception when it comes to running an effi-cient football program. But let there be no doubt that even though he's clearly in charge, there are a lot of people making contributions. "I sort of end up driving the bus," Saban said. "But we have good people on the bus and in the right seats. They all buy in and try and do things the right way. That's probably why we're having the success that we've had."

In the front seat at Alabama has been Kirby Smart, who joined Saban at LSU in 2004 as a defensive backs coach, rejoined him in 2006 with the Miami Dolphins, and followed him to Tuscaloosa in 2007, where a year later he became the Crimson Tide's defensive coordinator. In 2009 he won the Broyles Award as the nation's top assistant coach, and three years later he received a similar honor from the American Football Coaches Association.

In both 2011 and 2012, even after losing seven starters, Alabama led the nation in total defense, rushing defense, and scoring defense. About the only thing that didn't change between those seasons was Smart jumping around on the sideline before every play, getting everyone lined up correctly, making adjustments and making quick personnel changes. "If it didn't happen, we probably wouldn't get one play down," former Crimson Tide linebacker C.J. Mosley (2010–13) said.

The defense was set up so that one linebacker communicated with the defen-sive backs and another with the defensive line, prior to every snap, so not only did players relay signals to their position group but also made sure everyone had the same correct call. The tricky part was that more teams were going to no-huddle, quick-snap attacks, and read-option philosophies in an effort to create mismatches and confusion.

"He sees things that we don't see," former Crimson Tide linebacker Nico Johnson (2009–12) said of Smart. "He sees things that happen before they even happen. Every time we come off the field, we're correcting things from the last series or things he thinks are going to happen the next series. It's Coach Smart. He's here for a reason."

Besides, as Saban pointed out, Smart thinks the way he does, which has been a big reason for Alabama's consistent defensive success while other assistant coaches have come and gone. However, as Smart's career progressed, so did the rumors about potential head coaching jobs.

Resisting the urge to jump at his first opportunities just made him more desirable as a candidate. After the 2011 season, Smart interviewed at Southern Miss, only to remove his name for consideration. Instead, the job went to long-term coordinator Ellis Johnson, who had a one-and-done fall. A year later, Smart interviewed at Auburn and made it clear that he wanted similar control to what Saban had at Alabama. Auburn, which had just ended its season with a 49–0 loss to the Crimson Tide, instead brought back former offensive coordinator Gus Malzahn.

Among the team policies that Saban has borrowed from mentor Bill Belichick was to make all assistant coaches off-limits to media, especially during the season. Belichick's thinking (which every reporter everywhere absolutely hates) was that he wanted his team to have one voice, so there would be consistency in its approach, and no one would have to deal with the potential additional distractions. "As an assistant coach, I loved that because I was always nervous that I was going to say the wrong thing, and it wouldn't be the same message that the head coach had," Saban said.

Consequently, Smart regularly talks with reporters only twice a year, during Alabama's Media Day before the start of training camp, when the coordinators are available for about 10 to 15 minutes, and during the postseason if the bowl the Crimson Tide is playing in mandates that coordinators and assistant coaches appear at a press conference.

During these sessions, Smart is almost always asked two things:

1. "When do you think you'll become a head coach?"
2. "What's it like working for Nick Saban?"

Smart once answered, "Well, I'll tell you this: I have become who I've become as a coach from working for Coach Saban. He does an outstanding job of managing our organization. There is nobody I could put him up against…anybody in the country. His ability to facilitate, that's great. He helps game planning on defense, he's a great mind in the room."

To his credit, Smart does vary the responses each year, but the message has remained the same. It also didn't hurt that he was receiving roughly $1 million annually, making him one of the highest-paid assistant coaches in the country, and earning more than a lot of head coaches.

He wasn't alone, though, as Saban has a well-founded reputation for paying his assistant coaches well and working regular raises and bonuses into their contracts. According to *USA TODAY*'s annual report on coaching salaries in college football, Alabama was one of seven schools that paid the assistants more than $3 million in 2012 (and that was before the Crimson Tide beat the Fighting Irish, which kicked in even more bonuses for the staff).

Of course, Saban expects a lot in return and has a reputation for being demanding. "When you say 'demanding,' to me the definition of *demanding* is they require you to do what you're supposed to do, when you're supposed to do it, and how you're supposed to do it," Smart said. "That's what he does. So is he demanding? Yeah, he requires you to do your job, and I appreciate that. That gives me job security knowing that everyone in the organization is held accountable, and he holds everybody accountable. When he's demanding, he's usually right. To me that's probably the greatest feature I've learned or will take with me when I become a head coach, is you have to be demanding. You have to be able to confront people if they're not doing their job or not doing it the way you want it [done]. It's hard sometimes. Just like asking these players to be leaders, to go in front of their peers and challenge a guy, that's tough, and these guys have done it. Coach Saban does it, and it flows down into our organization. He's been a great asset to me, and I'll take a lot of things with me if I ever get the opportunity."

As for what Saban looks for in assistant coaches, three essentials are that they're hardworking, loyal, and can recruit well. While Saban ideally wants his staff to include a mix of coaches with different backgrounds, ages, and geographical familiarity, experience can also be important, especially for the coordinator positions, where he prefers those with both college and NFL backgrounds. If the players come in with the hope and expectation of someday playing in the pros, he wants coaches who know what it takes to best prepare them. "I think that knowledge and experience is really important," Saban said about his hiring process. "I think people look for that, but I also look for people who are going to be a good fit for us in terms of how they are going to fit with the other coaches on the staff, how they get along with people, what kind of relationships [they are] going to be able to build in the organization—players- and coaches-wise—to make people want to achieve at a high level. And I think the right people for us are the people that are willing to do it the Alabama way.

"My sense of it is, what I see happening a lot, sometimes people want to do it the way they do it, the way they've had success with. We want people who will come here and do it the way we do it, the way our players are accustomed to do[ing] it, what they've bought in to and what they['ve] made commitment to. So unless we're looking for input to change something, we're bringing people to do what we do. That's a big part of the fit."

The same holds true for the support staff, which includes the person who probably deals with the players the most during the off-season and is paid more than some of the assistant coaches.

His name is Scott Cochran, and the secret to Alabama's loud and energetic director of strength and conditioning may be lemons. He squeezes them into his water every night to try and help his voice recover from a long day of inspirational yelling and he supplements this regimen with tea in the morning and periodic throat lozenges. "It's kind of funny," he said. "Sometimes I have a little bit left in the tank for my voice, and my kids laugh: 'Daddy has his voice.' Mostly I whisper to them at night when telling them stories."

For those who have never seen Cochran, who's becoming more of a Crimson Tide celebrity with each passing day, he's the one on the Alabama sideline holding up four fingers and jumping up and down through the entire fourth quarter of every game. For most players he's the one waiting for them in the morning when workouts begin at 6:00 AM and the one they occasionally hear in their sleep. "*Yeah, yeah, yeah, yeah!*" has become his trademark call, with the volume only surpassed by its intensity.

"He's always yelling," said tight end O.J. Howard, who quickly found that out during his first few weeks on campus. "He better not catch you walking, that's one thing. But it's fun, and he's always going to push you to be your best."

Cochran makes no apologies. "I'm a strength coach," he said. "I wear shorts and a sweatshirt or a T-shirt to work every single day. I'm changing lives. I don't know, I can't explain it, but to me people get in their car, and they're going to work. I feel like I'm in my car and on my way to the playground, like when I was a kid. I feel like I'm going to swing on the monkey bars. My job requires a lot of energy, but realistically, if I don't have it, how do I expect a player to have it?"

Like numerous others on the staff, Cochran's arrival at the Capstone came through LSU, where he earned a bachelor's degree in kinesiology and a master's degree in sports management while working his way up to assistant strength coach under Saban. He held the same position with the NBA's New Orleans Hornets, working with the likes of Chris Paul, Baron Davis, David West, and Tyson Chandler, when his former coach called and asked if he was ready to get back into football. "I said, 'I am if it's with you.' I came a-running," Cochran said. "It was a Thursday that I came to visit him, and the off-season program began Monday."

The rest of the strength and conditioning staff took a little more time to mold, with Cochran referring to director of player development Willie Carl Martin and assistant head strength coach Terry Jones as his right-hand men. Martin spent 10 years with Edmonton and Winnipeg in the Canadian Football League, where he was named an All-Pro eight times and played in six Grey Cups, while Jones played for Bear Bryant and spent seven years with the Green Bay Packers.

Moreover, Saban promotes the idea of having former players around, whether it's someone who wants to get into coaching or an active player in the National Football League who needs a place to work out during the off-season. They've been through it before and might rub off on their younger counterparts, and to some it's sort of the only home they've ever known. "I think that's kind of what makes this program click is Coach Saban has surrounded these players with former players who are interested in getting these players better," Cochran said, which leads into another secret of his success: having a staff of people paying attention to everyone on the team.

Although someone might notice a technique flaw, and everyone can always use a little extra motivation, Cochran's always checking on the players, and if more than one or two develop the same types of injuries, he'll tweak the team's regimens to avoid it becoming a widespread problem. "I work very close with [director of sports medicine] Jeff Allen," Cochran explained. "Every single day we meet about the issues on the team, the nicks and the little things that you don't see that are bothering the players, that a player would never come and tell me, 'This is hurting.' They don't want to sound or feel like they're soft. We have it set up in the training room where they'll go to certain people and say, 'Hey, this is kind of bothering me; can we put ice on it?' and I find out all that stuff without them knowing, and I can change and adapt the program as long as Coach Saban is okay with it."

For new material, Cochran also notes what music the players listen to in the weight room, and sometimes what they're watching away from football. "I learned a lot from Coach Saban, bringing his work ethic every day, just seeing how hard he works," Cochran said. "What is my job in his army, what is my role, where do I fit in and I can be my best? The thing that I always noticed was energy. They need to be excited about what they're doing. They need to have a sense of urgency when they step on that field. It's not *Oh, it's another day*, I like to bring them some fire, some juice."

Actually, the juice part of it falls more under the direction of Amy Bragg, who was lured away from Texas A&M in 2010, which at the time made Alabama one of roughly 20 Division I athletic departments to have a nutritionist on staff.

Those who saw the ESPN behind-the-scenes special *Training Days: Rolling with the Alabama Crimson Tide* in 2010 got a taste of how nutrition has become a priority when junior running back Mark Ingram showed viewers the bio-pod that measures body fat and subsequently teased teammates about their readings: "What did you get? Oh, you need to eat more."

That's not just being competitive to the end, but looking for any edge that can be found. "She's been a tremendous asset to our team," Ingram said. "Nutrition was emphasized before; now it's a detail."

That's just the tip of the iceberg when it comes to the support system Saban has put in place, which extends from the academic side of things to even trying to make it to the pros. Alabama's NFL liaison is former coach Joe Pendry. In 2007 the well-respected man, who worked for 19 years in the league, signed on to be the Crimson Tide's offensive line coach and liked the place so much he retired in the Tuscaloosa area and joined the support staff. Thus he went from being the one responsible for Alabama nearly never having a holding call to a Capstone fixture and credible promoter of the program.

Many of the other support workers have impressive backgrounds as well but wanted a chance to watch and learn from Saban. "I think that it says a lot about the total program and all the people in it and the great team of people we have here," Saban said. "Whether it's in personal development, academic success, developing the players, being able to recruit quality people to represent the program and develop within the program, I think a lot of people contribute to that."

Terry Saban

Although Nick Saban may have become the pride and joy of Crimson Tide fans everywhere, his wife, Terry, is the one who can be described as beloved. Not only is she the First Lady of Alabama football, she's also the one largely responsible for her husband's success in college football. "I met Miss Terry when she was in seventh grade at science camp and I was in eighth grade, and we were from different schools," Saban said, referring back to his West Virginia upbringing when he was already big into sports. "She did not know what a first down was when we first started dating, and there's no doubt in my mind that she thinks she ought to be the head coach at Alabama right now. No doubt. And she is a hell of an assistant, even though she thinks she's the head coach, which when she's around, I always make her think that. She's quick to tell me when we're running it too much up the middle, when we're not passing enough, when we don't blitz enough on defense. I get lots of feedback on all those things.

Nick Saban may have presided over a championship renaissance at Alabama, but his wife, Terry, the First Lady of Alabama football, rules the Saban roost.

"I would say that she's probably as big a part of the program as anyone in terms of her time, her commitment, and all the things that she does to serve people in a really positive way that is helpful to us being successful, not only in football but in the community and what we can do to serve other people."

Nick Saban and Terry married on December 18, 1971, only she hadn't graduated college yet, so when coach Don James approached Saban about becoming a graduate assistant, football remained in their lives a little longer than expected.

Consequently, like with most developing coaches, they subsequently moved every couple of years for the better part of the next three decades. That's a side of the coaching profession that few outsiders either notice or appreciate—just how difficult it is on any family, especially one that includes two kids. Nick still recalls the day when he was driving around Baton Rouge and a sports talk show was discussing the rumors of his leaving for the National Football League, when his daughter in the backseat said, "Aw, Dad, do we have to move again?"

However, when Alabama's Mal Moore flew to Miami with the intention of trying to convince Saban to leave the Dolphins for the Capstone, the athletic director did something incredibly smart. "The first thing he did was he recruited Terry," Saban said. "I called Terry and said, 'I don't think I'm even going to talk to these guys tonight.' She said, 'Oh, Mal's already here. We've been talking for an hour.' That was his first step in the right direction."

Terry already knew that her husband was happier and better suited for the college game, and before long they were on the plane to Tuscaloosa. Consequently, whenever Saban's name kept getting brought up about possibly going back to the NFL, the coach frequently said that whoever was asking was talking to the wrong person. "We've broken a lot of records while being here," Terry Saban said in 2012. "The one I'm most happy about right now is that we're breaking the record of the longest place we've ever lived. We're very comfortable here."

The Community

The night was reflective of many Alabama football games played during the 2011 season in that the more it progressed, the more it was all about the Crimson Tide.

For half of a two-hour live broadcast celebrating the sport, ESPN announcers had a chance to talk about all the other outstanding players, coaches, and teams during *The Home Depot College Football Awards*, but then the focus moved to Alabama. Running back Trent Richardson was interviewed before winning the Doak Walker Award as the nation's top running back. Barrett Jones, who had already been named the recipient of the Wuerffel Trophy for community service with outstanding achievement, was named the winner of the Outland Trophy for top interior lineman.

Safety Mark Barron and linebacker Dont'a Hightower were up for awards as well and frequently mentioned when the upcoming BCS National Championship Game against LSU was discussed (which was only compounded by the seating chart putting coaches Nick Saban and Les Miles side by side in the audience).

But then as award shows often do, things took a more serious turn during the latter stages when long snapper Carson Tinker took the stage with his teammates for a presentation that brought tears to the eyes of many people watching and silenced everyone in the theater. Tinker, whose girlfriend, Ashley Harrison, had been killed during the April 27 tornado outbreak when she was ripped from his arms as his house was destroyed, accepted the 2011 Disney Spirit Award for most inspirational player or team on behalf of the Crimson Tide. "Some people ask for blessings, but we ask to be blessings," was Tinker's message to millions of viewers on live television. "I'm very proud to say I'm affiliated with the University of Alabama and accept this award."

Although not everything the football program did to lend a helping hand became public knowledge, its contributions were extensive after a tornado carved up a stretch extending 5.9 miles through the Tuscaloosa area with approximately 240 people killed throughout the state and 350 across six states.

Among the well-known efforts were linebacker Courtney Upshaw raising nearly $20,000 in relief funds in his hometown of Eufaula; tight end Preston Dial loading up a semi full of supplies and driving them in from Mobile; and Jones lugging a chain saw for days to remove debris from homes and yards. Numerous players also spent a lot of time in the Holt neighborhood, just east of Tuscaloosa, where the Nick's Kids Foundation played a major part in the rebuilding of 15 homes—one for each championship.

The athletic department also contributed $1 million to the UA Acts of Kindness Fund, which provides relief to faculty, staff, and students experiencing hardship.

Some of the more subtle but just as effective contributions included Nick and Terry Saban going to a shelter to visit with victims and hand out gift cards so they could buy what was really needed, numerous cleanup sessions organized by football officials that were never publicized, and the many donations of blood. Meanwhile, despite the concussion and ankle and wrist injuries he sustained, Tinker put his own loss aside to visit a 10-year-old boy in the same hospital, who had lost his mother, father, and sister in the storm. Tinker later spoke at churches, talked openly about dealing with loss and grief, and tried to take the words "role model" to heart. "Carson Tinker probably lost the most and has given the most," Saban said. "This is a special group."

Alabama, of course, went on to beat LSU, with the Crimson Tide gymnastics, women's golf, and softball teams all following suit before the end of the 2011–12 school year. The football team then successfully defended its title against Notre Dame, and men's golf won its first national championship in the spring of 2013.

But months later when reflecting on everything that had been endured, with the rebuilding process still years away from completion, Saban said that he was prouder of the Disney Spirit Award than of his third crystal football, which had put him in elite company in college football history. "This team reflected the spirit of the people of the state of Alabama in the way that they overcame the adversity that was created by the terrible tragedies of the tornado," he said. "I can't be proud enough of winning the Disney Spirit Award and the way the students represented the spirit of the people of our state, who had so much to overcome, and how you sort of overcome all of that together."

Previous winners of the award had been the United States Service Academy football teams in 2001, Tulane in 2005 following Hurricane Katrina, and in 2009 Boston College linebacker Mark Herzlich, who despite being the reigning ACC Player of the Year was diagnosed with a rare form of bone cancer and overcame Ewing's sarcoma to play again. "This award does not represent me, it represents our team, our university, and the Tuscaloosa community," Tinker said. "Everyone reached out and pulled together as a family in the face of this tragedy. The tornado took so much from us, but with a spirit of hope and a lot of hard work, we have begun the healing process. I am very proud of how this team and this community rallied together after such a devastating storm."

Fast-forward to the summer of 2012: if you only glanced at the neighbor-hood that the Sabans had teamed up with Habitat of Humanity to help rebuild, there didn't appear to be anything out of the ordinary. For the families, it was home.

Garbage bins—which, like the homes, appeared to be new—lined the curbs waiting to be emptied. There were a variety of signs posted on the corner posts, serving notice to everything from missing pets to community events. Fittingly, behind one house was a trampoline that was more than symbolic.

It's only when one stepped back a bit and looked beyond the driveways and toys scattered about the yards that it was apparent that the setting was far from anything that could be considered normal. There was still a massive gap in the horizon, where trees and buildings once proudly stood, along with scores of collapsed structures that had been abandoned and continued to slowly turn into rubble.

"Because of the Sabans and Nick's Kids jumping in, they've been a catalyst for a lot more than just the financial contribution that Nick's Kids made," said Bob Johnson, executive director of Habitat for Humanity of Tuscaloosa, who estimated that the Sabans alone were instrumental in raising approximately $1.4 million for the 14 for 14 Project (another house was added after Alabama won its 15th national championship). The indirect impact of their involvement has been immeasurable. We've raised enough capital to build 25 houses. We've raised about $2.5 million since the storm, which probably means that we've raised more than any local nonprofit in just normal donations and individuals. We haven't gotten any federal assistance. I came through Katrina [in Louisiana], and for a nonprofit to raise as much money as we've raised in 15, 16 months is phenomenal. And I'll tell you, it's not because of me."

Overall, 21 houses were completed by the summer of 2012 with another five under construction. Habitat's plan was to construct between 50 and 75 homes over the following three years in the tornado impact area.

"What we found in Katrina relief is that people would come in and work for a week, and they would give once. They might give twice, they might give once a year. There wasn't that engagement like the Sabans have had, like Nick's Kids has had, and the university has had because of that," Johnson said. "All those folks came after Nick and Terry stepped in and helped us get started. If we hadn't started strong with Nick's Kids, I can tell you all those other folks wouldn't have come along and said, 'Hey, we want to sponsor additional houses.'"

They included Major League Baseball, which sponsored four houses, and Lowe's Home Improvement signed on for five. Meanwhile, after their initial push, the Sabans quietly deflected most attention away from themselves while promising to do more. "They both have really great hearts," Johnson said. "They're incredibly philanthropic. People don't even know all the things that they do. I'm really glad he's a great football coach, but it's so much more than that for me. I can genuinely say that I'd be thankful for him if they weren't great, but I'm incredibly thankful for his heart and all the things he does. I hope people will see that. I think they see him patrolling the sidelines and see all that stuff going on, but I could tell you stories of things they do to help people that no one ever knows about—and it's pretty cool that that's what we've got."

Some of the other ways the Sabans have helped, both large and small, include:

- In June 2008 they announced a $1 million gift, $100,000 each year, to benefit Alabama's first-generation scholarship program. The gift had special meaning, as Nick and Terry were both first-generation graduates. By 2012 they had donated $520,000 to the university.
- When the Gulf Coast oil spill disaster occurred in 2010, Saban made a point to visit and offer support without any TV cameras in tow.
- Although he had to first check and make sure it didn't violate any NCAA rules, Saban sent a letter to the family of a North Carolina high school coach who died September 30, 2012. Mike Crowell, 52, coached the wrestling team at South Davidson High in Denton, North Carolina, for 25 years, the football team for five seasons, and even golf and women's track. He was also a staunch Alabama fan.

"We're always very sorry and compassionate for the family members when they lose a loved one," Saban said. "We wanted to acknowledge his professionalism, his character, and our appreciation for his support."

Meanwhile, the Sabans continue to raise money through the annual Nick's Kids Golf Tournament, speaking engagements, and individual donations. At the 2013 annual Nick's Kids Luncheon, held the day before the football team opened

Four Dead in Ohio

Both a coal-mining explosion that killed 78 people on November 20, 1968, and the Kent State shootings gave Nick Saban early experience in how to deal with life-changing tragedy. However, while the accident known as the Farmington Mine Disaster in West Virginia occurred a few miles away, in 1970 the 18-year-old narrowly missed witnessing the National Guard opening fire on protesters, killing four and injuring nine.

It began with a small demonstration on Friday, May 1, 1970, when roughly 500 people gathered on campus and participated in what turned into a heated protest over Richard Nixon's announcement to invade Cambodia. A copy of the U.S. Constitution was burned, along with a student's draft card. When it finally dispersed, organizers called for another rally Monday, May 4.

Things escalated over the weekend, beginning with downtown rioting late Friday night, and after a state of emergency was declared, an Ohio National Guard unit, made up primarily of those roughly the same ages as the students, arrived Saturday just in time to see the school's ROTC building on fire. Many of those who attempted to stop the blaze were attacked.

Although martial law was declared Sunday, there was a protest, but even the students could feel a confrontation building toward Monday's noon rally. Saban had class at 11:00 AM and afterward decided to eat with a teammate before seeing what was going on. He missed the National Guard advancing, firing tear gas, and eventually discharging their weapons, reportedly 67 rounds over a period of 13 seconds. "I was more interested in having lunch than going there first or I'd have been there," he said.

Among the dead was Allison Krause, a student in Saban's English class who took three bullets to the back, along with two students who just happened to be walking by.

During Saban's senior season, Kent State rallied from a 1–3–1 start to win five of its final six games to move to the top of the 1972 Mid-American standings and earn a spot in the Tangerine Bowl. "All that stuff that happened at Kent State united the students," Saban said during the 40th anniversary. "They were looking for something to identify with. There was probably more interest in the football program at that time than ever before."

fall camp, they distributed $415,644 to more than 100 charities and organizations throughout the state and surrounding areas. It brought the total since the Sabans arrived at the Capstone in 2007 to more than $3 million, not including another million earmarked for tornado relief.

Saban said, "Nick's Kids is not really about me. It's about the legacy of my father, who started an organization to help young people way back when I was nine or 10 years old. My mother and my family always encouraged us to continue that legacy. That is why we do what we do."

Saban always calls it his favorite day of the year. He said, "'No man stands as tall as when he stoops to help a child' is sort of what we all built this on. We appreciate all of the people that dedicate their lives to helping the children in the organizations that we give to. They give their life, their time, and their service to try and help young people, and that is really important. The purpose of this organization is to help people in need in this community. This is the most uplifting, positive day of the year for me because it's what we give, not what we get."

Recruiting

Nick Saban doesn't do anything without a reason, and usually it's because of recruiting (at least in part).

Just like Saban's modus operandi that he's going to outwork the competition on the field and in preparation, it's even more so in recruiting. Whereas most coaches are really good at one or two aspects of the job, Saban is just as driven and probably enjoys recruiting as much as anything else. After all, winning in recruiting is still winning, and it helps lead to success on the field down the road.

One of the first things Saban did when arriving at the Capstone was to upgrade all the areas that recruits frequent, which has only continued. For example, Alabama already had one of the best weight rooms in collegiate athletics before it built a new one in 2013 that instantly became the envy of every school in the nation. Why? Recruiting.

The most off-limits room to outsiders in the football building, maybe the whole campus or even the entire state, is Alabama's recruiting war room, where the staff has the target players listed and ranked on the walls. You've probably seen the NFL equivalent for the draft board on TV, and beside every player's name is a series of grades and codes representing various attributes like height, weight, speed, academics, etc. Saban has minimum requirements for each.

"We certainly have player descriptions, player profiles that we want, and if guys don't fit that certain description, they may be a five-star great player, and there are examples of that this year all over the country, where everybody is like, 'Why aren't y'all recruiting him?' Or he calls us and has great interest, we're just not interested because we recruit to a certain standard. We say we want the guy to be this tall, this big," defensive coordinator Kirby Smart said. "Does that mean there's not exceptions? Sure, there's exceptions to the rule, but we don't want a team full of exceptions."

Specifically, cornerbacks need to be 5'11" or bigger, defensive linemen should be at least 6'2", offensive linemen must have a certain arm length, etc. "Consistency and performance," former defensive end Damion Square said about Saban. "He's a guy who's based on numbers. If we come out and compete, and he believes that if we hit our marks on defense, no matter what opponent is out on the field, and execute the game plan that's put forth, we'll win. He believes that 100 percent, and he never strays from that. He goes after guys who are going to make his team better. If you're one of those guys, you should be honored to be a part of that ['machine'] he's put together. I think those guys understand that when they get recruited."

According to former offensive coordinator Jim McElwain, players can be evaluated almost 10 times before receiving an offer, and Saban's system is so detailed that there are even levels of scholarship offers from immediate offers, preliminary offers, conditional offers, and so on. If a prospect scores high enough in all the evaluations, though, all that's required is for him to just say yes.

Even the Crimson Tide's defensive approach, a base 3-4 defense that has been using more nickel and dime formations with extra defensive backs, is in part due to recruiting. "It gives you ability to recruit more linebackers, more skilled players, so that allows us to do that," Smart said. "We don't always line up in a 3-4, we have to line up in both. In today's day and age, offenses force you to. So our reasoning for doing that is, A) recruiting, B) gives us more skill players, and we can recruit D-linemen that grow or outside linebackers that grow into D-linemen, which has happened to a couple of other guys. It's more about that, and we still think it's the best defense to be in for two-back offenses."

Thus, part of the recruiting pitch to pass-rushers is that more NFL teams are going to the 3-4, and for most players it's easier to go from a 3-4 to a 4-3. "It's a two-way thing," Square summarized. "The program has to benefit the player for him to develop, and then the player has to benefit the program for the program to develop. You've kind of got to meet on both ends."

Even so, there are no guarantees in recruiting, which Saban knows better than anyone, even with his stellar class of 2008 that set the benchmark for the program and helped lead to three national championships. It included the Crimson Tide's first Heisman Trophy winner and 12 players who went on to be selected in the NFL Draft, including five in the first round. At the time running back Mark Ingram Jr., defensive lineman Marcell Dareus (the No. 3 overall selection in the 2011 draft), and junior-college transfer Terrence Cody (a two-time All-American nose guard) were all thought to be closer to the bottom of the recruiting class than the top.

Most recruiting services use a five-star rating system, with five stars meaning the player could contribute immediately, four signifying that he's a year away, and so on. Alabama had three five-star players in 2008 led by Julio Jones, who had a legendary career with the Crimson Tide. The other two were offensive tackle Tyler Love, who never started a game, and B.J. Scott, who had been instrumental in drawing other standout players to join him at Alabama but eventually ended up transferring to South Alabama to get more playing time.

One of Saban's easiest recruiting jobs with that class may have been with prize offensive lineman Barrett Jones, whose father, Rex, had been a Crimson Tide basketball player for Wimp Sanderson (1982–84), and his mother attended North Alabama, where his grandfather Bill Jones had coached the basketball team to a Division II championship in 1979. "One of my favorite things is at [team doctor James] Robinson's office there's a huge picture of Antoine Pettway scoring the winning field goal against Florida to win the SEC championship, and over behind the Alabama bench you see young Barrett Jones jumping up and down, screaming," longtime Crimson Tide broadcaster Tom Roberts said. "His dad had brought him to the ballgame."

Jones went on to win the 2011 Outland Trophy as the nation's best interior lineman, the 2012 Campbell Trophy, commonly referred to as the academic Heisman, and enough other awards to fill a small room. Of course, no one knew that would be the outcome when Jones made his official visit to the Capstone and sat down with Saban in his office, where the coach delivered his pitch. "It's pretty intense," Jones said about the experience, adding that Saban not only told him that he would hoist a crystal football by playing for the Crimson Tide, but how he was going to do it. "When Nick Saban tells you that, for some reason you believe it. You know it's going to happen. He's a hard guy to turn down."

Saban's spiel was touched upon in the movie *The Blind Side*. While most coaches primarily try and sell themselves to recruits and their families (especially moms)—"My mom's always been in love with Nick Saban, so, I mean, that's kind of one of the reasons why I came here," 2010–11 cornerback DeQuan Menzie said—players say that what makes his approach different is that he focuses on his system. It includes the national championship, the number of players who have been drafted, their career spans, and so forth, but it all comes back to the Process.

"It doesn't just happen overnight, and it's not all about football," said former tight end Michael Williams (2009–12). "When he talks about the Process, it's about the classroom, he's talking about your work ethic. You can have all the talent in the world, but if you can't do the right things, [it doesn't matter]. He always talks about being locked in. To this day, I've never seen him yawn once. You can't be more locked in than that. He always has a plan. He just does his job and teaches us to be men."

That plan for the players isn't limited to one season or the team's primary contributors, but everyone—even the last guy on the roster.

Granted, the focus is on the everyday, but there are numerous checkpoints along the way, like Saban meeting with each player after every season concludes and talking over where they are and where they want to be. Another naturally occurs with the start of fall camp, when the difference between high school and college football begins to set in for most new players. It's often a huge reality check. "Yeah, real fast," Williams said. "As soon as camp hits, they hit a wall. You can tell."

But Saban doesn't make guarantees anyway, especially when it comes to starting; he only offers opportunities. Alabama could have no one on the roster at a position, and he would still tell prospects that they'll have to win the job just like everyone else. "Our theory is that we treat every player the same," Jones said. "We don't treat recruits any better or any worse. We don't haze them, we don't shave their heads or anything. We also don't treat them like kings. We tell them that they have as much of a chance to play as our veterans. We earned everything that we did at Alabama. That's why I like it."

It's impossible to argue with the results.

National Team Recruiting Rankings, Top Five (2008–13), from 247Sports
2008: 1. Alabama; 2. Notre Dame; 3. Florida; 4. Ohio State; 5. Miami
2009: 1. Alabama; 2. LSU; 3. Ohio State; 4. Southern California; 5. Texas
2010: 1. Southern California; 2. Florida; 3. Texas; 4. Auburn; 5. Alabama

2011: 1. Alabama; 2. Florida State; 3. Texas; 4. LSU; 5. Southern California
2012: 1. Alabama; 2. Florida State; 3. Texas; 4. Florida; 5. Ohio State
2013: 1. Alabama; 2. Ole Miss; 3. Florida; 4. Ohio State; 5. Notre Dame
2014: 1. Alabama; 2. LSU; 3. Ohio State; 4. Florida State; 5. Texas A&M

Moreover, watching Saban's 2014 class slowly being unveiled was like seeing the cards turned over one by one for a royal flush, giving Saban yet another major infusion of talent. "He recruits like no other," Williams summarized about Saban.

You can see why there's no shortage of people calling him a machine when it comes to acquiring and developing prospects, and not just at Alabama.

When Saban arrived at LSU from Michigan State in 2000, his primary objective was to give the program a complete overhaul, not just with the coaches and personnel, but everything from the attitude down to the facilities. The key, though, was recruiting, and for years many of the top Louisiana prospects had left the state. In the 1990s Baton Rouge athletes Warrick Dunn and Travis Minor took off to become stars at Florida State, and New Orleans high school stars Reggie Wayne and Ed Reed became key components of Miami's 2001 national championship squad.

With stopping the exodus a top priority, Saban was able to keep most of Louisiana's top high school prospects in-state, including running backs Alley Broussard and Justin Vincent and defensive back LaRon Landry. Quarterbacks JaMarcus Russell and Matt Flynn were a part of his stellar 2003 class, as was Miami-area wide receiver Dwayne Bowe.

That year he landed all but two of the top 10 players in the state of Louisiana, all four-star players. Rated No. 1 that year was dual-threat quarterback Robert Lane, whose father played at LSU, but he opted for Ole Miss to be the heir apparent to Eli Manning. Lane never panned out. No. 7 Adam Kraus went to Michigan, where he made 35 starts, mostly at guard. He signed as a free agent with the Baltimore Ravens only to be released a few months later.

A couple of players Saban did hit on with that class, considered by many to be the best in the nation, were Kirston Pittman and Craig Davis. In 2004 Saban landed the state's top seven prospects, including Early Doucet and Glenn Dorsey, and was barely edged out in the recruiting team rankings by Southern California—though the Trojans eventually ended up receiving NCAA sanctions

Talk About a Welcome Party

Each year college football teams are allowed to hold 15 practices in the spring to get a jump on the upcoming season, usually concluding with a public scrimmage of some sort. However, at Alabama the A-Day Game is essentially considered to be a holiday and draws nearly as many people to Tuscaloosa as a game in the fall.

That's not an exaggeration. When Saban first arrived in 2007, so many fans turned out that school officials, who were caught completely off guard, went from having only half the stadium open to the fire marshal needing to turn thousands away after exceeding capacity. Saban called it the defining moment of when he knew he had made the right decision to come to Alabama and was on the verge of experiencing something special.

Alabama's Biggest A-Day Attendances
2011: 92,310
2007: 92,138
2010: 91,312
2009: 84,050
2012: 78,526
2013: 78,315
2008: 78,200

Before Saban, Alabama's A-Day attendance record was 51,117, set in 1988. Only six other times had it attracted 35,000 or more fans. Since Saban, it's become a huge recruiting tool for Alabama.

due to a litany of violations stretching from 2004 to 2008. The year Saban left for the Miami Dolphins, the well-stocked Tigers signed just 13 players and were 22nd in the recruiting rankings.

But while in Baton Rouge, Saban did more than dominate the state. He also snagged recruits from other schools' comfort zones and even developed a knack for finding underrated talent just like he went on to do at Alabama. Les Miles followed suit and for years did a terrific job in keeping the borders closed; however, the one person who regularly snared a prospect or two from his backyard was Saban. With the help of running backs coach Burton Burns, who continued to maintain his strong ties there, Alabama landed numerous star Louisiana prospects like running back Eddie Lacy, safety Landon Collins, and linebacker Denzel Devall.

Meanwhile, Saban also began a pair of important streaks regarding in-state recruiting despite constantly butting heads with rival Auburn. According to BamaOnLine.com and 247Sports, in 2013 Saban swept signing all of the state's top five players for the fourth time in six years, signing all but five of those 30 players offered up in that six-year span. He also had yet to miss on a five-star prospect, having landed all 11 since 2008.

As for his first class at Alabama, in 2007, when Saban was hired a month before National Signing Day, the Crimson Tide added four-star prospects Rolando McClain, Kerry Murphy, and Brandon Gibson, who made up the state's top five with Sidell Corley (LSU) and Michael McNeil (Auburn). Nevertheless, a lot of players in that initial group—like nose tackle Josh Chapman, center William Vlachos, and cornerback Kareem Jackson—made major contributions to one, if not two, national championship teams.

It wasn't until the 2012 season that Saban had a team entirely made up of players he had recruited and signed, with the roster stacked full of three-, four-, and five-star prospects all competing for roles. "[Former coach Don James] used to say if you look at the bottom 40 guys on your roster, and if you have really good quality there, you're going to have a good team," Saban said. "But that means a lot of things. It means that you have a lot of good players, but it also means if the bottom 40 guys are pretty good, the top 40 guys must be pretty good.

"What depth gives you is a better chance to be consistent. You have more players who can have a role, which puts less of a burden on some players, which allows them to be able to sustain their level of performance throughout the year. When you do hit bumps in the road, [such as] losing a player at a critical position for a game or two, somebody else can step up into that role and it's not an issue for your team. Sometimes you have to be a little bit lucky about that."

The Players

Let's face it, playing or working for Nick Saban isn't for everyone. Some people don't mesh with his personality, others can't take the intense dedication, and some are just plain intimidated.

Ask his former players, though, and they usually rave about him and portray a much different image. "Nicky?" former LSU wide receiver Dwayne Bowe

(2003–06) called Saban with a wide smile. "To me he was a great coach. A lot of people think otherwise, but when it comes to football, Nick knows his stuff. He's very disciplined. When he was at LSU, I didn't have a problem with him. I practiced hard, and when it was time to go to work I went to work. It was like a real job, and he was, 'There are going to be some hard times.' I loved him."

Succeeding under Saban isn't that complicated; just work hard and don't stop. He's detail-oriented, driven, and relentless, but he's doing it for his players to try and get the most out of them. "It was tough, but you have to adjust to his style of coaching," former LSU defensive lineman Glenn Dorsey (2004–07) said. "He's one of those guys who will come up and get on you real bad, but you have to understand what he's telling you and don't listen to how he's saying it. He's a very knowledgeable guy. His defense is kind of complicated, but he's [proven]. He's a great coach, but you have to be tough-skinned and adapt to his coaching style."

Well, not all the time.

"Coach Saban keeps us loose," former Alabama running back Trent Richardson (2009–11) said. "Coach Saban is not as much of a taskmaster as people sort of make him out to be."

Wait, what?

"He's really very funny in a kind of sarcastic way. He always has us laughing out there, during flex especially," Crimson Tide offensive lineman Barrett Jones (2009-12) said. "He comes around and pokes fun, especially at the offensive guys. Everyone knows he likes the defense better. We tell him he's spending too much time on the defensive side, not showing us enough love, and he'll fire back with something like he doesn't want to hang out with offensive linemen because they are fat and not athletic."

Regardless, the players are at the heart of college football and the reason why Saban coaches. Over the years some have been nothing short of exceptional, and through the 2013 season, Saban had had at least one All-American at every position except tight end and punter.

Considering the high level of talented players that he's had on his teams, it makes one wonder what an All-Saban Team might look like among all his college players from Toledo (1990), Michigan State (1995–99), LSU (2000–04), and finally Alabama (2007–13).

In terms of pure talent, it's impossible to evaluate—except, of course, for Saban, who only rarely makes comparisons between his various teams and players, and then only to praise someone. However, if going by awards, accomplishments, and status, not only could you put together one impressive All-Star team but have All-Americans on the second-team.

Here are the criteria used for selections:

1. A player had to be named all-conference or All-American (first-team only), be drafted by an NFL team, or have won a major award while Saban was his coach.
2. Any player named all-conference or All-American a year after being coached by Saban or who won a major accolade or was drafted in the NFL within two years of playing for the coach would be considered, though weighed against the time factor.
3. Other players could be considered, especially if recruited/developed by Saban but listed no higher than honorable mention.

For example, LSU quarterback JaMarcus Russell (2004–06) wouldn't be considered for being the first overall pick in the 2007 NFL Draft by the Oakland Raiders, well after Saban left to coach the Miami Dolphins at the end of the 2004 season, but could be for being named the 2006 Manning Award winner and All-SEC (in addition to the 2005 SEC Player of the Year by the Columbus Touchdown Club).

Otherwise, the selections were primarily determined by accolades.

The All-Saban Team

Offense

Quarterback: AJ McCarron (Alabama)—McCarron was the only quarterback in the BCS era to win back-to-back titles. He led the nation in passer efficiency in 2012, and his career school records included passing yards, total yards, completions, touchdown passes, and most consecutive attempts without an interception. He won Alabama's first Maxwell Award for most outstanding player, finished second in the 2013 Heisman Trophy voting, and was Saban's first quarterback to be named an All-American (but was not a consensus selection).

Quarterback AJ McCarron, who shared a special bond with his coach, ranks as the best quarterback Nick Saban has coached.

Second team: Greg McElroy.

Honorable mention: Tony Banks (Michigan State), Josh Booty (LSU), Rohan Davey (LSU), Matt Mauck (LSU), JaMarcus Russell (LSU), and John Parker Wilson (Alabama).

Running backs: Mark Ingram Jr. (Alabama) and Trent Richardson (Alabama)— Ingram won not only Alabama's first Heisman Trophy in 2009, but Saban's as well. He set the Alabama single-season rushing record with 1,658 yards, which Richardson broke with 1,679. Heisman finalist Richardson won Alabama's first Doak Walker Award, and his 24 touchdowns in 2011 tied the SEC single-season record set by Shaun Alexander. He was the third-overall selection in the 2012 NFL Draft, by Cleveland.

Second team: T.J. Duckett (Michigan State) and Eddie Lacy (Alabama).

Honorable mention: Joseph Addai (LSU), Glen Coffee (Alabama), Scott Greene (Michigan State), Sedrick Irvin (Michigan State), LaBrandon Toefield (LSU), Justin Vincent (LSU), Domanick Williams (LSU), and T.J. Yeldon (Alabama).

Wide receivers: Josh Reed (LSU), Julio Jones (Alabama), and Plaxico Burress (Michigan State)—Reed originally signed as a tailback but moved to wide receiver nine weeks into the 1999 season and had a 100-yard performance in just his second game. He caught 94 passes for 1,740 yards his junior season to win the Biletnikoff Award as the nation's top receiver. In 40 games Jones caught 179 passes for 2,653 yards with 15 touchdowns and accumulated 3,084 all-purpose yards. His 179 receptions were second all-time at Alabama, while his 2,653 receiving yards ranked second in school history, and his 15 touchdowns were tied for fourth. Burress only played two seasons with the Spartans but had 131 receptions, 2,155 yards, and 20 touchdowns before being the eighth overall selection in the 2000 draft, by Pittsburgh.

Second team: Michael Clayton (LSU) and Amari Cooper (Alabama).

Honorable mention: Dwayne Bowe (LSU), Bennie Brazell (LSU), Nigea Carter (Michigan State), Craig Davis (LSU), Skyler Green (LSU), D.J. Hall (Alabama), Herb Haygood (Michigan State), Devery Henderson (LSU), Rick Isaiah (Toledo), Derrick Mason (Michigan State), Muhsin Muhammad (Michigan State), and Gari Scott (Michigan State).

Tight ends: Chris Baker (Michigan State) and Michael Williams (Alabama)— Baker made 47 consecutive starts and had a string of 24 consecutive games with at least one reception. He set the school record for tight ends with 133 catches, 1,705 yards, and 13 touchdowns and was selected in the third round of the 2002 draft. The workhorse Williams made 41 career starts and had seven career touchdowns, including one against Notre Dame in the BCS National Championship Game, before being selected in the seventh round of the 2013 NFL Draft.

Second team: Brad Smelley (Alabama) and Robert Royal (LSU).

Honorable mention: Jerry Evans (Toledo), O.J. Howard (Alabama), Josh Keur (Michigan State), Vince Marrow (Toledo), Preston Dial (Alabama), Colin Peek (Alabama), and Nick Walker (Alabama).

Tackles: Andre Smith (Alabama) and Flozell Adams (Michigan State)—Smith won the 2008 Outland Trophy as the best interior lineman and was the subsequent sixth overall pick in the NFL Draft. Nicknamed "the Hotel," Adams was a three-year starter for the Spartans, two at right tackle and one at left, and named both an All-American and Big Ten Offensive Lineman of the Year. Although expected to go higher, he was selected in the second round of the 1998 NFL Draft by Dallas and had an All-Pro career.

Second team: D.J. Fluker (Alabama) and Cyrus Kouandjio (Alabama).

Honorable mention: James Carpenter (Alabama), Craig Kuligowski (Toledo), Greg Randall (Michigan State), Andrew Whitworth (LSU), and Brandon Winey (LSU).

Guards: Mike Johnson (Alabama) and Chance Warmack (Alabama)—Johnson was a two-year All-American who started 41 consecutive games and set an Alabama record by appearing in 54 games. He was also a team captain and lead blocker during Ingram's Heisman Trophy season. Warmack was a unanimous All-American as a senior who made 40 career starts and was selected 10th overall in the 2013 NFL Draft, by the Tennessee Titans.

Second team: Stephen Peterman (LSU) and Anthony Steen (Alabama).

Honorable mention: Herman Johnson (LSU), Tupe Peko (Michigan State), and Scott Shaw (Michigan State).

Center: Barrett Jones (Alabama)—Jones won the 2011 Outland Trophy after making the move from right guard to left tackle and then during his senior season he won both the Campbell Trophy (academic Heisman) and Rimington Trophy (best center).

Second team: Antoine Caldwell (Alabama).

Honorable mention: Rudy Niswanger (LSU), Jason Strayhorn (Michigan State), William Vlachos (Alabama), Ben Wilkerson (LSU), and Louis Williams (LSU).

Defense

Defensive line: Terrence Cody (Alabama), Chad Lavalais (LSU), Glenn Dorsey (LSU), and Marcus Spears (LSU)—All four players were named All-American, although Cody received the honor twice while playing nose guard. Lavalais was the SEC Defensive Player of the Year in 2008, Spears had nine sacks and 17 tackles for a loss as a senior before being the 20th pick in the subsequent draft, and Dorsey won the Outland, Nagurski (defensive), Lombardi, and Lott (defensive impact) awards during his senior season.

Second team: Marcell Dareus (Alabama), Dan Williams (Toledo), Marquise Hill (LSU), and Kyle Williams (LSU).

Honorable mention: Josh Chapman (Alabama), Wallace Gilberry (Alabama), Howard Green (LSU), Jarvis Green (LSU), Melvin Oliver (LSU), Chase Pittman (LSU), Josh Shaw (Michigan State), Robaire Smith (Michigan State), Ed Stinson (Alabama), Dimitrius Underwood (Michigan State), Jesse Williams (Alabama), and Claude Wroten (LSU).

Linebackers: Dont'a Hightower (Alabama), Rolando McClain (Alabama), C.J. Mosley (Alabama), and Julian Peterson (Michigan State)—McClain won both the Butkus and Lambert awards as the nation's best linebacker and was the No. 8 selection in the 2010 draft. During his two years at Michigan State, Peterson recorded 140 tackles and 25 sacks in only 23 games before being a first-round draft pick. Hightower won a starting job as a true freshman and ended up being a two-time team captain and leader of possibly the best defense in college football history. Mosley was a two-time All-American who won the 2013 Butkus Award and finished third in Alabama career tackles despite being a full-time starter for only his senior year, when he was named a team captain.

Second team: Bradie James (LSU), Courtney Upshaw (Alabama), and Ike Reese (Michigan State).

Honorable mention: Matt Eberflus (Toledo), Trev Faulk (LSU), Ali Highsmith (LSU), Adrian Hubbard (Alabama), Josh Thornhill (Michigan State), T.J. Turner (Michigan State), and Lionel Turner (LSU).

Cornerbacks: Corey Webster (LSU) and Dee Milliner (Alabama)—In 2004 Webster became LSU's first two-time All-American since 1987 (Wendell Davis). Originally a wide receiver, he made 33 tackles and two interceptions during his senior season. Milliner was named a unanimous All-American in 2012 after recording 51 tackles, two interceptions, and 18 pass breakups. He subsequently was the ninth overall selection in the 2013 NFL Daft, by the New York Jets.

Second team: Dre Kirkpatrick (Alabama) and Kareem Jackson (Alabama).

Honorable mention: Darren Anderson (Toledo), Javier Arenas (Alabama), Deion Belue (Alabama), Amp Campbell (Michigan State), Simeon Castille (Alabama), Travis Daniels (LSU), Chevis Johnson (LSU), Marquis Johnson (Alabama), Renaldo Hill (Michigan State), and DeQuan Menzie (Alabama).

Safeties: LaRon Landry (LSU) and Mark Barron (Alabama)—The No. 6 overall draft pick in 2007, Landry was a four-year starter with 48 consecutive starts who broke up 40 passes and made 12 interceptions. Barron was a three-year starter, won two national championships, and was twice named a team captain. He finished his career with 237 tackles, including 13 for a loss and five sacks, and 12 interceptions. The hard-hitting safety was the seventh overall pick in the 2012 draft, by Tampa Bay.

Second team: Rashad Johnson (Alabama) and Ha Ha Clinton-Dix (Alabama).

Honorable mention: Norman LeJeune (LSU), Robert Lester (Alabama), Aric Morris (Michigan State), and Craig Steltz (LSU).

Special teams
Return specialist: Javier Arenas (Alabama)—With 1,752 yards, Arenas finished just 10 short of setting the NCAA record for career punt-return yards, while both his total return yards (kicks and punts) of 3,918 and eight touchdowns also ranked second all-time. He received the 2009 Punt Returner Trophy from the College Football Performance Awards.

Second team: Derrick Mason (Michigan State).

Honorable mention: Domanick Davis (LSU), Skyler Green (LSU), Herb Haygood (Michigan State), Christion Jones (Alabama), and Marquis Maze (Alabama).

Kicker: Leigh Tiffin (Alabama)—Although Michigan State's Paul Edinger was also an All-American and a sixth-round draft pick, Tiffin set numerous Alabama career and single-season records and is the Crimson Tide's all-time scoring leader.

Second team: Paul Edinger (Michigan State).

Honorable mention: John Corbello (LSU) and Jeremy Shelley (Alabama).

Punter: Craig Jarrett (Michigan State)—Jarrett landed first-team all-conference honors when he was named All–Big Ten in 1999 after being a second-team selection the year before. The four-year starter was only considered an honorable mention his senior season but was selected in the sixth round of the 2002 NFL Draft.

Second team: Donnie Jones (LSU) and Cody Mandell (Alabama).

Honorable mention: P.J. Fitzgerald (Alabama).

The Saban All-Alabama Team

It's not very often that there are enough quality players seven years into a coach's reign to name an All-Star team, but Nick Saban is obviously not your normal coach, and Alabama is not your normal football program.

Offense

Quarterback: AJ McCarron. Second team: Greg McElroy. Honorable mention: John Parker Wilson.

Running backs: Mark Ingram Jr. and Trent Richardson. Second team: Eddie Lacy and Glen Coffee. Honorable mention: T.J. Yeldon.

Wide receivers: Julio Jones and D.J. Hall. Second team: Amari Cooper and Marquis Maze. Honorable mention: Kenny Bell, Keith Brown, Matt Caddell, Darius Hanks, Kevin Norwood, and DeAndrew White.

Tight end and H-back: Mike Williams and Brad Smelley. Second team: Colin Peek and Nick Walker. Honorable mention: Preston Dial, O.J. Howard, Travis McCall, and Brian Vogler.

Tackles: Andre Smith and D.J. Fluker. Second team: James Carpenter and Cyrus Kouandjio.

Guards: Mike Johnson and Chance Warmack. Second team: Anthony Steen and Marlon Davis.

Center: Barrett Jones. Second team: Antoine Caldwell. Honorable mention: William Vlachos

Defense

Defensive linemen: Terrence Cody, Marcell Dareus, and Wallace Gilberry. Second team: Jesse Williams, Josh Chapman, Brandon Deaderick, and Damion

Square. Honorable mention: Quinton Dial, Jeoffrey Pagan, A'Shawn Robinson, Ed Stinson, and Lorenzo Washington.

Linebackers: Rolando McClain, Dont'a Hightower, Courtney Upshaw, and C.J. Mosley. Second team: Nico Johnson, Adrian Hubbard, and Eryk Anders. Honorable mention: Trey DePriest, Darren Mustin, and Cory Reamer.

Cornerbacks: Dee Milliner and Dre Kirkpatrick. Second team: Javier Arenas and Kareem Jackson. Honorable mention: Deion Belue, Simeon Castille, Marquis Johnson, and DeQuan Menzie.

Safeties: Mark Barron and Ha Ha Clinton-Dix. Second team: Rashad Johnson and Robert Lester. Honorable mention: Landon Collins and Vinnie Sunseri.

Special teams

Return specialist: Javier Arenas. Second team: Christion Jones. Honorable mention: Marquis Maze and Trent Richardson.

Kicker: Leigh Tiffin. Second team: Jeremy Shelley. Honorable mention: Jamie Christensen and Cade Foster.

Punter: Cody Mandell. Second team: P.J. Fitzgerald

Awards

If anyone's searching for the perfect indictment of having too many college football awards, look no further than Nick Saban.

For Coach of the Year awards there's the Paul W. Bryant Award, which has been annually bestowed since 1986, the Associated Press Coach of the Year, Bobby Bowden Coach of the Year, Home Depot Coach of the Year, Walter Camp Coach of the Year, American Football Coaches Association Coach of the Year, the Bobby Dodd Coach of the Year, etc.

There also used to be the George Munger Award, renamed the Joe Paterno Award, discontinued by the Maxwell Football Club, and after a year's absence it was restarted as the Maxwell Football Club's Coach of the Year Award.

There are also the various publications and news outlets that name a coach of the year too, even though there's almost never a set criteria on which to base the decision. Was the best coach the one whose team improved the most, did the most with the least, overcame the most adversity, or simply had the best record?

The Eddie Robinson Award is annually presented to "the nation's most outstanding coach" by the Football Writers Association of America, and dates back to 1957, when Woody Hayes was the inaugural recipient.

Meanwhile, the Liberty Mutual Coach of the Year Award claims to recognize college football coaches who demonstrate "sportsmanship, integrity, responsibility and excellence both on and off the field." It uses a three-pronged selection process with fan voting (counting 20 percent), a selection committee from the College Football Hall of Fame (55 percent), and national media (25 percent).

You get the idea.

So which one of those awards has Saban won during any of the seasons the Crimson Tide captured a national championship? Believe it or not, just the Bowden, which unlike most of the others is selected and presented after the bowl season is completed.

In 2012 most of the Coach of the Year awards went to Notre Dame's Brian Kelly, after the Fighting Irish went undefeated during the regular season. The previous year LSU's Les Miles won after the Tigers ran the regular-season table. The 2009 winner, when Saban had his undefeated season and vanquished Tim Tebow and Florida? Kelly, at Cincinnati.

This isn't to suggest that Kelly or anyone else wasn't worthy of such an honor, especially since each organization can give out whatever hardware it wants, as it deems appropriate. But something seems amiss considering Saban's lack of recognition.

Specific to the 2012 team, the reigning national champions only had nine seniors on scholarship. Essentially seven defensive starters had to be replaced, along with all of the starting offensive weapons surrounding quarterback AJ McCarron, who had to work with a new offensive coordinator. The Crimson Tide was also coming off back-to-back NFL Drafts of having four players selected in the first round, which would have left the cupboard empty with just about any other program.

The strange thing is, Saban had already won nearly all of the previously mentioned coaching awards at some point during his career, and a few of them more than once.

Saban's National Coach of the Year Awards
Associated Press: 2003, 2008
Paul W. "Bear" Bryant: 2003
Eddie Robinson: 2003, 2008
Home Depot: 2008
Walter Camp: 2008
Liberty Mutual: 2008
Sporting News: 2008
Bobby Bowden: 2009, 2011, 2012

Saban actually landed three major national awards when he won his national title at LSU, and more at Alabama when his team didn't win the national championship than when it did.

Meanwhile, Crimson Tide players started becoming regular fixtures at awards banquets and on All-American lists. For example, the 2011 national champions had a whopping seven players picked by various organizations, with Barrett Jones, Trent Richardson, and safety Mark Barron all unanimous selections and linebacker Dont'a Hightower a consensus pick. The other three were cornerbacks Dre Kirkpatrick and DeQuan Menzie and linebacker Courtney Upshaw.

Some of the hardware that the Crimson Tide collected for the first time included the Doak Walker Award for the best running back (Richardson, 2011), the William V. Campbell Trophy for the top scholar-athlete (Jones, 2012), and, of course, Mark Ingram Jr. winning the 2009 Heisman Trophy. "The Heisman was kind of shocking and something I never really expected coming into this year," Ingram said after beating Texas for the national title. "And when I won the trophy, like, it was a great honor to win the trophy, but it was more than just a trophy to me. It was overcoming adversity. All throughout my life, me and my family sticking together overcoming obstacles and people that tried to hold us back. A lot of emotion came from that.

"This national championship was more of everybody. I was so happy to leave my heart out there for the team, and blood, sweat, and tears. We were out there running 110 sprints in 110-degree heat. We were like, 'Why are we doing this?' Some days after practice you're like, 'Why am I doing this?' or you get hurt and you're like, 'Why am I doing this?' Tonight was what it was all for, and just to know all the hard work paid off, it was more of just togetherness and a family and a feeling of all our brothers just being able to accomplish this together was real sweet for all of us. That's what the difference is."

That's why center William Vlachos called Ingram the best player he'd ever been around, and sophomore linebacker Dont'a Hightower was glad not to be on the opposing side. He did what the great ones do: make the tough and nearly impossible appear routine. "I just want to be a better player," Ingram said. "I want to be the best player I can be. I know there's a lot of room for improvement. We can't live off our past success."

Nevertheless, after he "only" had to beat out 2007 winner Tim Tebow, 2008 winner Sam Bradford, Colt McCoy, Toby Gerhart, and Ndamukong Suh, among others, Ingram's victory came following the closest vote in Heisman history. He was also the first running back since Pitt's Tony Dorsett in 1976 to win both the Heisman and the national championship during the same season.

"[Ingram] has a lot of field presence, he has great vision," said former Alabama linebacker Chris Jordan (2008–11), a converted running back himself. "He can see the defense, read the defense, and he knows where the cutbacks are before the cutback is even there, so he's already cutting back before the hole is there, so he's hitting it [at] full speed. He has great vision, footwork, and speed."

It led to his establishing the Alabama single-season rushing record with 1,658 yards, with a whopping 1,075 yards after contact (on 249 carries, 30 receptions), and 20 total touchdowns. Meanwhile, he lost just two career fumbles. "Yards after contact, I think, is a mental thing, not letting the first man bring you down, trying to get as many yards as you can, try[ing to] make a play when your team needs the play," Ingram said. "You just need to make a play for them. It's something mental. I don't think it's something you can work on. You can work on getting your knees up, pad level low. When it comes to game time it's your willingness, your desire to keep getting extra guys, keep fighting, try and make a play for the team."

So that's where the focus remained, beating that first man, then the next one, and so on. Turning small gains into big gains. In the words of Saban, dominating, not just as a player but also as an offense and as a team.

"We definitely want to be the best in school history, the best in the country," Ingram said. "I think that's everyone's goal on our team—the best offense, the

most explosive offense we can be. That's our attitude going into every single practice. It's never gonna be easy."

Yet Ingram, who was just 19 when he won the Heisman, not only became
the face of his team and conference, but of all of college football. Every move he
made was watched more closely than anyone else in Crimson Tide history—yes,
even more than Joe Namath when he was strutting around campus in the 1960s.
"Everywhere I go, people recognize me," Ingram said. "They meet me, want to
take pictures. That's exciting, something you dream of as a kid. Having kids come
up to you, you're a role model for them, they want to grow up like you are, it's
humbling, a blessing. I'm excited I can impact a younger person's life like that.
That's real special to me, real touching to me."

Alabama has been nearly as impressive in the classroom as well. Over a span
of five seasons (2008–12), 58 players competed for the Crimson Tide after having
already graduated, and between 2010 and 2012, the school had a total of 29 SEC
First-Year Academic Honor Roll recipients, topping the conference. Consequently,
Alabama emerged as one of the nation's leaders in keeping its players on track to
earn degrees, and one of the keys to continued success was the university turning
Paul W. Bryant Hall into an academic center before hiring Saban.

Renovated for $10.3 million and rededicated on April 22, 2005, the former
home of Crimson Tide football and men's basketball players was redesigned to
provide support for student-athletes and to provide whatever they could possibly need. From the staff at the Center for Athletic Student Services to the
computer lab and study areas, it could help with everything from long-term
goals to daily needs, such as with the Bryant Sports Grille, which even features
a coffee café. "It's great," described wide receiver Julio Jones. "They have tutors. It
doesn't matter what you're doing, what you major in, they'll get someone for you,
or if you need help. They don't try and punish us, but they make sure that we're
on top of grades. They just try and let us know that academics come first, ahead
of football here."

It's also been reflected in the two ways the National Collegiate Athletic
Association measures academic success among all its institutions, with the
Graduation Success Rate (GSR) and the Academic Progress Rate (APR).

The GSR success rate is just like it sounds, the percentage of student-athletes
earning a degree within six years (although institutions are allowed to subtract

Alabama National Award Winners

Pre-Nick Saban

Butkus Award: Derrick Thomas (1988)
Jim Thorpe Award: Antonio Langham (1993)
Lombardi Award: Cornelius Bennett (1986)
Lott Trophy: DeMeco Ryans (2005)
Outland Trophy: Chris Samuels (1999)
Sammy Baugh Trophy: Steve Sloan (1965)
Paul Warfield Trophy: David Palmer (1993)
Jack Tatum Trophy: Antonio Langham (1993)
Johnny Unitas Golden Arm Award: Jay Barker (1994)
AFCA Coach of the Year: Paul W. "Bear" Bryant (1961, 1971, 1973); Gene Stallings (1992)
Paul W. "Bear" Bryant Award: Gene Stallings (1992)
Eddie Robinson Coach of the Year: Gene Stallings (1992)
Walter Camp Coach of the Year: Gene Stallings (1992)
Bobby Dodd Coach of the Year: Bill Curry (1989)

Under Nick Saban

Heisman Trophy: Mark Ingram Jr. (2009)
Maxwell Award: AJ McCarron (2013)
Doak Walker Award: Trent Richardson (2011)
Butkus Award: Rolando McClain (2009); C.J. Mosley (2013)

student-athletes who leave prior to graduation as long as they would have been academically eligible to compete had they remained).

In October 2013 Alabama's GSR, which was compiled by the NCAA for students from the 2003–06 school years, scored an 86 on a scale of 100. That was the second-best overall score in the Southeastern Conference behind only Vanderbilt.

Of UA's 16 intercollegiate athletics programs that were competing at the time, seven—women's golf, soccer, softball, tennis, and volleyball and men's golf and swimming and diving—achieved perfect scores of 100. Overall, nine programs recorded a GSR score of at least 90, and 12 were above 80.

Football came in at 73, but all indications were that the score would only continue to rise as foreshadowed by the Academic Progress Rate reports. On a scale

Outland Trophy: Andre Smith (2008); Barrett Jones (2011)
Rimington Trophy: Barrett Jones (2012)
Jim Parker Trophy: Andre Smith (2008)
Jack Lambert Trophy: Rolando McClain (2009)
Sporting News Player of the Year: Mark Ingram Jr. (2009)
Johnny Unitas Golden Arm Award: AJ McCarron (2013)
Wuerffel Trophy: Barrett Jones (2011)
William V. Campbell Trophy: Barrett Jones (2012)
Broyles Award: Kirby Smart (2009)
Eddie Robinson Coach of the Year: Nick Saban (2008)
Walter Camp Coach of the Year: Nick Saban (2008)
Bobby Bowden Coach of the Year: Nick Saban (2009, 2011, 2012)
AP Coach of the Year: Nick Saban (2008)
Home Depot Coach of the Year: Nick Saban (2008)

Saban's Consensus All-Americans
Javier Arenas (2009), Mark Barron (2011), Antoine Caldwell (2008), Ha Ha Clinton-Dix (2013), Terrence Cody (2008–09), Dont'a Hightower (2011), Mark Ingram Jr. (2009), Mike Johnson (2009), Barrett Jones (2011–12), Cyrus Kouandjio (2013), Chad Lavalais (2003), Rolando McClain (2009), Dee Milliner (2012), C.J. Mosley (2012–13), Josh Reed (2001), Trent Richardson (2011), Andre Smith (2008), Marcus Spears (2004), Chance Warmack (2012), and Ben Wilkerson (2004)

of 1,000, every Alabama team was well above the 930 cutoff standard that could lead to penalties.

Mika Shula inherited a horrendous 890 score in 2003–04 but led an impressive turnaround with 966 and 971 and then 950 in 2006–07. Under Saban's direction Alabama's one-year score initially dropped to 936 in 2007–08, which can be common during a coaching change, but rose to 972 in 2008–09 and then reached a spectacular 994 in 2009–10. Not only was it the second-best football score in the SEC behind Georgia's 1,000—and tied with Clemson and Duke for the fourth-best single-year score in the nation—it was just three points behind Boise State and TCU.

Among overall scores, which are based on four years of performance (in this case from the 2006–07 academic year to the 2009–10 academic year), football's

963 rose to 970 and was 22 points higher than the national average. For the period extending from the 2008–09 academic year through the 2011–12 academic year, Alabama's 978 topped the conference and was the 11th best in the nation.

It reaffirmed what his players have been saying for years, that not only does Saban graduate his student-athletes, he also prepares them for life in a multitude of ways.

His initial academic All-Star at Alabama was Greg McElroy, whose off-the-field accomplishments would more than fill this page. While earning his undergraduate degree in business marketing, the two-year starting quarterback had a straight-A transcript except for a lone B, ironically from a leadership class. McElroy's pursuit of becoming a Rhodes Scholar was well followed, and *Sports Illustrated* writer Lars Anderson nominated him for the magazine's top honor, the Sportsman of the Year award, because, "More than any other player in the sport, he represents all that is good about college football."

When the College Sports Information Directors of America selected McElroy as the ESPN Academic All-American of the Year, offensive lineman Barrett Jones joined him as a first-team Academic All-American after being a second-team selection the previous year. That made him just the third Crimson Tide player to be twice selected, joining Johnny Musso (1970–71) and Randy Hall (1973–74).

At the time Jones was a sophomore. He went on to be named an Academic All-American after both his junior and senior years as well, and became Alabama's first winner of the William V. Campbell Trophy. It was the second win for Saban, though, as LSU center Rudy Niswanger won it in 2005 after the coach had already left for the Miami Dolphins. Formerly called the Vincent dePaul Draddy Trophy, it's presented to the college football player who demonstrates the best combination of academics, community service, and on-field performance.

"McElroy was a big nerd too," running back Trent Richardson told reporters in 2011. "The team needs a couple nerds, especially the game we're playing. It's a more mental game than anything. I have to say I'm one of them, because I have a high GPA, trying to get the Academic All-American stuff. A lot of people, when they see me in the classroom, I'm sitting up front. A lot of people say I am a nerd because I don't talk in class. I'm just quiet to myself trying to get my work done. But I'm not as near a nerd as Barrett."

Although Jones knew how to play the violin and in eighth grade qualified for the National Scrabble Championship in Boston, he spent the next couple of days making sure Richardson ate his words. "Trent is no nerd," Jones said, smiling. "If you're going to call me a nerd, I'm going to at least make it somewhat of an exclusive club."

The NFL Draft

Although rock musician Tom Petty once said that his song "The Waiting" was generally about not knowing if your dreams will come true, he could have been specifically singing about the National Football League's draft.

Yes, the waiting is the hardest part for the players, but in 2011 wide receiver Julio Jones didn't seem to mind—probably because he quickly found out that he wouldn't be moving too far from home. With the Atlanta Falcons looking to add an impact player, they traded away five draft picks to the Cleveland Browns— their 2011 first-, second-, and fourth-round selections plus their first and fourth in 2012—to move up into the No. 6 slot to take him.

Only one person may have been more thrilled than the person who used to wear No. 8 for the Crimson Tide. "My mom is very excited," Jones said. "You know how moms are, and I'm the baby. When the baby goes off, she gets upset. 'I want to come see you. I want to cook for you.' She's very excited for the whole situation."

But instead of heading out to celebrate in New York after doing his obligatory media interviews, Jones turned around and went back to the area, where the still-undrafted players were waiting to hear their names called, to join former teammate Mark Ingram Jr. With running backs seldom going in the top half of the first round, even if they do have the Heisman Trophy in tow, both got comfortable as the picks went by.

Hours later, things finally began to perk up with New Orleans approaching at No. 24, and many thought the Saints could be just a running back away from returning to the Super Bowl. Yet they ended up addressing a bigger need on the other side of the ball with California defensive end Cameron Jordan.

Moments later, in perhaps the surprise of the first round, Seattle announced Crimson Tide tackle James Carpenter as its selection at No. 25. Although a terrific performance at the Senior Bowl had sent Carpenter rising up many draft boards, the NFL didn't extend an invitation for him to be on hand with the expected first-rounders in New York. "I was in Augusta, Georgia, watching it with my family," Carpenter said.

The wait for Ingram finally came to an end just three picks later when the Saints, as if in direct response to the division-rival Falcons' move with Jones, traded up to snare Ingram at No. 28. Amazingly, that's exactly where the New York Giants had selected his father in the 1987 draft. More specific to the Saints, it's where they ranked in league rushing the previous season: 28th. "It's crazy, but God does everything for a reason," Ingram said. "I have been training down there since January, and now I am going to be playing there. I have rolled by the dome a couple of times the past couple of months, and it's crazy. I'm excited about it."

Thus concluded the first day of the 2011 draft, when Alabama had four selections, beginning with defensive lineman Marcell Dareus at No. 3. While that would gut most teams, the following year the Crimson Tide again had four players selected in the first round—five in the top 35—and the most overall. "Remarkable," ESPN analyst Todd McShay said about the back-to-back four first-round selections. "It's up there with one of the more impressive feats from a school that we've seen in a long time."

From 2009 to 2013, Alabama led all teams with 14 first-round selections after not having any between 2000 (Chris Samuels and Shaun Alexander) and 2009 (Andre Smith), and no draft picks at all in 2008. The 11 first-round picks from 2011, 2012, and 2013 alone equaled the output of the previous six Alabama coaches and 22 years combined.

Overall, through the 2013 NFL Draft, 111 players that Saban either coached or recruited were selected over the years, an average of just less than one per round (.93). Among them were 33 Crimson Tide players picked between 2009 and 2013, whose initial contracts combined added up to more than $280 million.

"He already instilled in us to do it right, stay on time and handle your responsibilities, be accountable for yourself and others," Dareus said about Saban. "I look at that as, like, being on a pro team. So I want to go to the next level and do the same thing. Not someone that's just going to try to be a bulldog and just take over, but lead by example. Learn from the veterans. Learn what you don't know, and it will carry over."

That approach may have especially helped the Alabama players in the 2011 draft. Due to a labor dispute that wasn't resolved until July, when the owners and the players' union both approved a new 10-year collective-bargaining agreement, there were no off-season camps or free-agent signings, with rosters locked in place during the four-and-a-half-month lockout.

The only thing that was business as normal for the league was the draft, and players who were best equipped to make the jump from the collegiate ranks— such as running back Trent Richardson—were highly coveted. During a bag drill (in which scouts and coaches hold big blocking bags and want each player to hit them in rapid succession) on his Pro Day workout, Richardson knocked over the representative from the Cleveland Browns and sent the other two back about five yards, with the last loudly saying how powerful it was, before cursing. "He's a beast," former NFL coach Jon Gruden said. "He broke all of Emmitt Smith's high school rushing records here in Florida. I've seen him run over people, run around people, he protects the ball, he can catch it, he can pick up blitzes. He might be the strongest human being on the planet, and I think his weightlifting proves that."

Sure enough, the Browns gave up their fourth-, fifth-, and seventh-round picks (Nos. 118, 139, and 211) just to go from No. 4 to No. 3 and keep the Minnesota Vikings from trading with anyone else who might want to snag Richardson. "It means a lot," Richardson said. "For them to trade up for me, I've got a lot to prove. Is there any pressure on me? Yes, there's going to be pressure. But do I feel it? No, I don't, because football is football, and no matter what league you play in, no matter who you're playing against, and no matter who straps on their helmet, I'm fixing to play against you, and you have to play for all four quarters. I'm very confident in what I do."

The Heisman Trophy finalist, who set the Alabama single-season rushing record with 1,679 yards to go with 21 rushing touchdowns and won the Doak Walker Award as the nation's top running back, was selected in the exact same slot as Dareus had been the previous year. "I'm happy to be in Cleveland, and I'm proud to be a part of the Cleveland Browns," Richardson said. "It's better than winning the national championship. It's a lot of hard work from my mom, and the feeling that I have right now is incredible. I'm on cloud nine. I'm high on

The Crimson Tide's First-Round Club

Draft Year	Overall Pick	Player	Team	Position
Nick Saban (14) *(through 2013)*				
2013	9	Dee Milliner	Jets	CB
2013	10	Chance Warmack	Titans	G
2013	11	D.J. Fluker	Chargers	T
2012	3	Trent Richardson	Browns	RB
2012	7	Mark Barron	Buccaneers	DB
2012	17	Dre Kirkpatrick	Bengals	DB
2012	25	Dont'a Hightower	Patriots	LB
2011	3	Marcell Dareus	Bills	DT
2011	6	Julio Jones	Falcons	WR
2011	25	James Carpenter	Seahawks	T
2011	28	Mark Ingram Jr.	Saints	RB
2010	8	Rolando McLain	Raiders	LB
2010	20	Kareem Jackson	Texans	DB
2009	6	Andre Smith	Bengals	T
Mike DuBose (3)				
2000	3	Chris Samuels	Redskins	T
2000	19	Shaun Alexander	Seahawks	RB
1999	26	Fernando Bryant	Jaguars	DB
Gene Stallings (5)				
1997	20	Dwayne Rudd	Vikings	LB
1994	9	Antonio Langham	Browns	DB
1993	5	John Copeland	Bengals	DE
1993	6	Eric Curry	Buccaneers	DE
1993	29	George Teague	Packers	DB
Bill Curry (3)				
1990	4	Keith McCants	Buccaneers	LB
1989	S	Bobby Humphrey	Broncos	RB
1989	4	Derrick Thomas	Chiefs	LB

REASONS WHY SABAN IS SUCH A GOOD COACH

Ray Perkins (4)

1987	2	Cornelius Bennett	Colts	LB
1986	4	Jon Hand	Colts	DE
1985	25	Emanuel King	Bengals	DE
1984	U	Joey Jones	Falcons	WR

Paul W. "Bear" Bryant (14)

1983	16	Mike Pitts	Falcons	DE
1981	5	E.J. Junior	Cardinals	LB
1980	21	Don McNeal	Dolphins	DB
1979	6	Barry Krauss	Colts	LB
1979	14	Marty Lyons	Jets	DE
1978	18	Bob Cryder	Patriots	G
1978	23	Ozzie Newsome	Browns	TE
1976	6	Richard Todd	Jets	QB
1974	9	Wilbur Jackson	49ers	RB
1973	4	John Hannah	Patriots	G
1968	20	Dennis Homan	Cowboys	WR
1967	26	Leslie Kelly	Saints	RB
1965	1	Joe Namath	Jets	QB (A)
1965	12	Joe Namath	Cardinals	QB (A)
1963	6	Lee Roy Jordan	Cowboys	LB

Harold Drew (5)

1953	8	Bobby Marlow	Giants	B
1951	9	Clarence "Butch" Avinger	Steelers	B
1948	1	Harry Gilmer	Redskins	QB
1948	4	Lowell Tew	Redskins	B
1948	5	Vaughn Mancha	Yanks	C

Frank Thomas (1)

1936	2	Riley Smith	Redskins	B

S-Supplemental draft; U-Special draft of USFL players; A-Namath was selected in both the NFL and AFL drafts life right now." (Note: Richardson was traded to Indianapolis early in the 2013 season.)

Crimson Tide fans were just getting used to the idea of seeing Richardson's name on the back of another jersey when safety Mark Barron also left the green room at Radio City Music Hall in New York. After coming back for his senior season, the Tampa Bay Buccaneers made it worth his while by making him the highest defensive back selected in franchise history, seventh overall. "I love the way he tackles," Buccaneers general manager Mark Dominik said. "He's a force."

The Cincinnati Bengals took cornerback Dre Kirkpatrick exactly when a lot of people thought he would go, at No. 17. Linebacker Dont'a Hightower lasted until the 25th pick (the same slot in which offensive tackle James Carpenter was chosen by Seattle in 2011), by the New England Patriots. Even though linebacker Courtney Upshaw fell out of the first round, he might have landed with the perfect team, the Baltimore Ravens. Instead of selecting the linebacker with the 29th overall pick, former Alabama legend Ozzie Newsome, the general manager, traded down for an extra late-round selection and still got him with the third pick of the second round, No. 35.

Nose tackle Josh Chapman and defensive back DeQuan Menzie were tapped by Indianapolis and Kansas City, respectively, in the fifth round, and tight end Brad Smelley's late-season surge made him the 40th pick of the seventh round, No. 247 overall, also by the Browns.

Even though Saban had an impressive draft record prior to Alabama, such success was new even to him.

In 2000, mere months after he left, Michigan State had both wide receiver Plaxico Burress and linebacker Julian Peterson selected in the first round. From then through 2013, the Spartans have only had two first-round selections, running back T.J. Duckett in 2002 and wide receiver Charles Rogers the following year.

At LSU, having a first-round player essentially became an annual staple beginning with wide receiver Michael Clayton in 2004 and defensive lineman Marcus Spears in 2005—just after Saban departed. The Tigers peaked with four players in 2007 but have had a regular first-rounder since.

"Obviously it speaks to the coaching staff, how they prepared these guys," McShay said about Alabama's pro-style approach. "Talking with guys in that program and coaches who have been around that program, or with that program, I think that's the thing that may be overlooked. They even have an individual plan for each and every one of these players. We all know where you want to be in three or four years when you leave here, how are we going to get you there, and what do you have to do today, tomorrow, Wednesday, Thursday, and Friday of this week, and then Wednesday, Thursday, and Friday six months from now, in order to get to that point.

"They buy in. They buy in because of the results. If they truly want to be an NFL football player, then they're going to follow this path. And obviously Alabama recruits well, you have to have the talent to get these guys there, but they get the most out of their talent."

"Every Alabama kid has been coached hard," Mike Mayock of the NFL Network said. "They're expected to show up on time, they're program players, you don't have much problem with them. It does help coming out of Alabama today, trust me. It's almost kind of like Miami in the 2000s."

Between 2001 and 2004, the Hurricanes had 19 first-round selections but obviously weren't able to sustain their success. In 2012 Miami still had the most players in the NFL (USC surpassed 15 in 2013) but hadn't won a conference title since 2003, the team's last 10-win season. Miami had also been implicated in another major recruiting scandal, this time centering around a renegade booster.

Even so, coming off back-to-back national championships, the Crimson Tide appeared to be just getting revved up in terms of cranking out NFL prospects. "It's a lot of talent," ESPN analyst Mel Kiper Jr. said. "They're loaded down there. It's going to keep going on and on."

His Schemes

One of the reasons why Nick Saban has so much success recruiting and has so many NFL teams showing up to Alabama's annual Pro Day workout to check out the latest batch of players is that nearly everything the program does is to help prepare players for the next level or whatever they may do after the Capstone.

That includes approach, conditioning, accountability, facilities, etc., as the Crimson Tide went from having no players picked in the 2008 NFL Draft to regularly leading the nation in selections.

The same is true with Saban's schemes on both sides of the ball. Although there are exceptions, Saban's teams are about as pro-like as can be.

Offensively, the Crimson Tide doesn't try to fool the opposition too often but will do enough to keep it off balance. Primarily the offense is going to take care of the ball, play with a lot of toughness, and try and be as imposing as possible and wear down the other team's defense.

The key word is *balanced*. Saban best explained it during the press conference to introduce him at Alabama in 2007: "Offensively, you know, we've always wanted to have balance in the offense. I think it's important to stop the run when you're playing defense, but I also think it's important to be able to run the football effectively, dominate the line of scrimmage…Passing efficiency is really important on third down, really important in making explosive plays. Explosive plays are important in scoring points. Those are all things we want to try to create here in terms of the balance that we have on offense, running and throwing the football.

"I also think it's very important that you utilize the players that you have. I hate to start telling stories up here. You're getting me wound up. When I was in high school in [Monongah,] West Virginia, we were playing at Masontown Valley. You had to walk through the graveyard, the lights were bad, to get to the field to go play. We're third and fifth in the state. Whoever wins the game is getting in the playoffs. In those days only the top two teams got in. We get behind 18–nothing. Walk through the graveyard, come out at halftime through the graveyard. It's 18–12, with 1:27 to go in the game. We get the ball back. Coach [Earl] Keener doesn't call any plays. He made Coach of the Year eight years, and I call every play as a 15-year-old high school [sophomore]. We get down to 4th-and-12 at the 25-yard line, one timeout left. Take it. Everybody in the town where I grew up is at the game, every guy, every person. Last guy turned the lights out to go to the game. I'm saying, 'Thank goodness Coach Keener is going to call this play, then I won't get blamed for calling the wrong play.'

"I said, 'Coach, what do you want to run here?'

"He says, 'What do you think?'

"I said, 'I think you should call this one, last play of the game.'

"He says, 'I tell you what. You have a three-time all-state split end, and the left halfback is the fastest guy in the state. I don't care what play you call, just make sure one of those two guys gets the ball.'

"I call 26 crossfire pass. Threw it to the left halfback, fake to him, post corner off the *X*, 25-yard touchdown, we won the game 19–18.

"After the game, [Coach] told me this: he says, 'It really doesn't make any difference what play you call sometimes; it's what players you have doing it.' I remember that.

"On offense I think sometimes that's important. I think it's important to have playmakers and skill players who can make a difference in making explosive plays."

Despite keeping the same base philosophy, Saban has continually tweaked the offense with his coordinators, with each adding his personal touch. Some call more screens, others have utilized the tight ends better in the passing game, etc.

However, midway through the 2012 season, after Alabama had just crushed Tennessee to improve to 7–0, when asked what was different about having a new offensive coordinator from the previous season, Doug Nussmeier, quarterback AJ McCarron said, "Nothing stands out."

That, in turn, was actually very telling.

"Yeah, definitely," he said. "I think we're putting up good numbers on both sides, the running and the passing game. I think it's been a good transition."

At the time, Alabama's offense had 1,536 rushing yards and 18 touchdowns, compared to 1,541 passing yards and 16 TDs.

From 2009 to 2012, Alabama had accumulated 9,713 rushing yards, compared to 10,364 passing, a difference of just 651 yards. "I think every week, we're trying to put our guys in the best position that we possibly can to create the kind of balance offensively that makes us difficult to defend," Saban said at the time. "I think our offensive staff has done a good job of that for the most part."

As for the defense, it's a 3-4 base, aggressive with a lot of pressure. The 3-4 usually means three defensive linemen with four linebackers, though that's a little misleading, and the cornerbacks don't play too far off the receivers.

"When I went to LSU the first time, they had the Bengal Belles group there, which was the women's quarterback [fan] club," Saban said. "The first time I went to address that group, the first question was from a lady who was about 70 years old, she was about this high, she was all the way in the back of room…reminded me of my grandmother. I'm thinking these ladies are going to ask me questions like, 'Anybody bake cookies for the guys on Thursday night before the game?' This

Nick Saban vs. the Big Ten

It goes without saying that Nick Saban faced some pretty good coaches when he was at Michigan State (1995–99). Those who received the Dave McClain Coach of the Year award, which is now the Hayes–Schembechler award, included Northwestern's Gary Barnett, Purdue's Joe Willer, Wisconsin's Barry Alvarez, and Minnesota's Glen Mason. There was also Ohio State's John Cooper, Michigan's Lloyd Carr, and, of course, Joe Paterno at Penn State.

While Saban went 23–16–1 against conference opponents during those five seasons, the closest he got to the conference title was in 1999, when his final Spartans team finished in a tie for second in the Big Ten and No. 7 in the final Associated Press poll. Michigan State defeated Notre Dame, Michigan, Ohio State, and Penn State in the same year for the first time since 1965 and recorded six wins at home for the first time since 1912. The Spartans led the Big Ten in rushing defense (77 yards per game) and total defense (299 yards per game) while ranking fifth nationally in rushing defense and 11th in total defense. The offense averaged 31 points per game.

Saban was 2–3 against rival Michigan, which won the 1997 national championship the same season Charles Woodson captured the Heisman Trophy.

Michigan State vs. Michigan, 1995–99

Year	Winning Team	Score	Location
1995	Michigan State	28–25	East Lansing
1996	Michigan	45–29	Ann Arbor
1997	Michigan	23–7	East Lansing
1998	Michigan	29–17	Ann Arbor
1999	Michigan State	34–31	East Lansing

little lady gets up and says, 'Are we going to get up and play any close coverage on these people, or are we going to be off and let them catch the ball in front like I've been seeing around here for the last four years?' I said, 'We're in the right spot here now. We're getting coached up on the secondary. That's the style we'd like to play on defense.'"

With Saban there are two important deviations to the standard 3-4 defense. One is the "Jack" linebacker position, which is sort of a hybrid outside linebacker/ defensive end spot, as the player has to be able to both drop into coverage and pass-rush, and usually has his hand down on the line of scrimmage next to the three linemen. When this occurs the line is: defensive end, nose tackle, defensive end, Jack linebacker. On the 2011 national championship team, Courtney Upshaw was the Jack linebacker.

The 1996 game still bothers Saban. "We were ahead like 14–3 and we had the ball," he explained. "I always used the 'When are we going to go two-minute before the half,' based on the field position. We didn't have very good field position. So it was third-and-5, and we threw an incomplete pass. There [were] about 30 seconds to go in the half, and we're going to punt, we were happy to punt and be ahead 14–3. Well, they called roughing the passer. We got a 15-yard penalty, and that put us up right at about the 45-yard line, so we said let's try and steal a field goal out of this. So we go two-minute right out of the box, the quarterback throws a slant, the safety runs it down from a cover-two in a three-deep zone, picks it off, and runs 45 yards for a touchdown. So now there [are] like 25 seconds [left], and it's 14–10. They kick off to us, they pooch-kick, we fumble, they recover it. Woodson was still there because I still remember this: they line up, after the scramble for the ball there's about 15 seconds to go, they run two plays, don't score, there's like seven seconds to go, and they put Woodson in at receiver, he runs a post, and they throw him the ball, he scores a touchdown. So in like 40 seconds, 35 seconds in the game, we go from being ahead 14–3 to behind 17–14 at Michigan. That was the worst story.

"The best story was the last year I was at Michigan State, when [Tom] Brady was playing, and we won. That was probably one of the better wins because they had a really good team. That was a really good team that we had too. I just remember we were 5–0 or 6–0, and we were ranked, and we couldn't live with success, we went and played Drew Brees [and Purdue] the next week, and he drilled us. I remember that too."

The other three linebackers are the typical strongside, middle, and weakside, otherwise known as "Sam," "Mike," and "Will." The Sam is the other outside linebacker, while the two interior spots can be pretty interchangeable. However, when extra defensive backs are necessary, which Saban has used more and more over the years as opposing offenses try and spread defenses out to create more gaps, the Sam and an interior linebacker are usually pulled.

Saban calls his extra defensive backs "money" and "star." He said, "In the old days, I called the fifth defensive back 'nickel back,' and we never really played six defensive backs," he said. "We just left the Mike and Will out there and took the Sam out and put the nickel back in. Well, when I went to Cleveland, everything that Bill Belichick does has some purpose, from what you call 'blitz' to what you call 'fire-zone front.' The star really is the Sam, so he wanted an *S* word for that position. When you put six guys in the game, whether it's a sub linebacker or a sixth defensive back, we had nickel, dime, dollar, different money terms.

"Whoever played star, that was the Sam, and whoever played the money position was the Will. But when you talk to players, you can say, 'Look, these linebackers on the team are all going to play money. These DBs on the team are going to learn how to play money,' because when it comes to the assignments of the defense, the position is the same. It's just they've got four wideouts in there now and the linebacker can't cover, so we put another DB in there. So we just started calling that the money position. It could be nickel, dime, or dollar. That was Bill's sort of system, but it made lots of sense to me. Just like everything else we did, we categorized things for the players. I think it made it better for the players. I think this does too."

The different positions require some different physical characteristics. "You can be a really good star and not have the long speed to be a good corner," continued Saban, "long speed being that if a guy runs a takeoff on you, you have to not get outrun when the ball is in the air.

"If you have really good quickness and cover ability, the slot guy has a hard time beating you in that position because he's closer to the safeties, he's closer to the middle of the field. So a good tackler, a good blitzer, a good cover guy on a slot player, which is different than a good cover guy on an outside player. The money guy has got to have some linebacker characteristics in terms of the run. It helps that the guy's a little bit bigger and physical because sometimes he has to cover a tight end, who is a bigger guy, but he also, unless you change personnel, has to be good enough to do the same things that the star does."

Alabama teaches most of the defensive backs more than one spot, and then it's essentially a mix-and-match process looking for the right combinations. Frequently, though, newcomers who earn immediate playing time concentrate on only one specific position or role during their first season.

"There was a time I thought, *No way I get this*," said former safety Robert Lester (2009–12). He became a three-year starter who finished tied for fifth in Crimson Tide career interceptions (14) and eighth in interception return yardage (183).

Learning From His Mistakes

Nick Saban is not perfect. He's not even close.

Plenty of times he and the rest of the coaching staff have made the wrong decision regarding a recruit. Yes, he makes mistakes in games. There are a number of things he wishes he could have back, like when he didn't call a prospective assistant coach back in 1990 after taking over at Toledo. "He called my house and talked to Terry," Saban said. "Terry really interviewed him. She told me when I came home that night. She said this really interesting guy called and really sounded like a top-notch, bright, articulate…[She said,] 'You really need to talk to this guy.'"

Saban didn't. At the time he was with the Houston Oilers, trying to finish that season while hiring his first staff as a head coach and preparing for the move. It was one of the things that slipped through the cracks.

The guy who had called was Urban Meyer.

Oops.

Instead, when Earle Bruce got the head job at Colorado State, he hired Meyer as his wide receivers coach, and Saban was left with a what-if story that he could joke about when Alabama and Florida played in back-to-back SEC Championship Games in 2008 and 2009. "That was obviously one of the biggest mistakes I ever made," Saban said.

Although the thought of Saban and Meyer working on the same side might be enough to cause some coaches to second-guess their choice of profession, mistakes are simply part of the job, part of the game, part of life. It's what you do after one happens that is the important part, or as writer James Lane Allen once famously wrote, "Adversity does not build character, it reveals it."

"Some of the best lessons you learn are sometimes the mistakes that you make; those are the best opportunities that we all have to learn, and improving is not necessarily [from] the successes but sometimes in the failures," said Saban, who regularly talks to his team about overcoming obstacles and how each season, each game, and each practice is a test.

But that doesn't mean he can stomach losing any more than the fans. "I catch it from everybody," he said after Alabama came up short against Texas A&M in 2012. "My wife's mad. My kids are upset. Everybody. I am too. But how am I going to affect everybody around me so that we respond the right way to the circumstance that we're in?"

A big part of Saban's Process is constantly self-evaluating, and not just plays. He examines everything about himself, on down through the players, during the days, weeks, and months following a loss. "Obviously, when we don't play well, that means, *Did you plan well enough?*" the coach said, starting a list of basic fact-finding. "Did you practice well enough? Did you practice the things that you ended up playing? Were the players prepared? Were they emotionally ready to play the game? All those types of things get analyzed, not only from a big-picture standpoint but also from a group standpoint and individually—with every player in the organization as well as every coach. When you don't play well, obviously you need to do all those things a little bit better at every level—[from] me, right down to the players."

So how well does Saban learn?

Before losing to LSU during the 2011 season, Saban had won 12 straight rematches, with the last coach to beat him in consecutive games being Steve Spurrier when high-flying Florida pounded LSU 41–9 in 2000 and 44–15 in 2001. In those 14 initial defeats, Saban's team lost by an average of 14.4 points. In the rematches, he won by an average of 14.7 points.

Of course, no rematch was bigger than LSU in 2011, when the Crimson Tide lost a grueling regular-season game 9–6 in overtime but came back and not only beat the Tigers in their backyard of New Orleans for the national title, but recorded the only shutout in BCS history, 21–0.

But Saban self-evaluates whether Alabama wins or loses, and not just about games and the big picture, but about specific things. His concerns range from the best way to use timeouts to running a fake punt at the end of the first series in the 2009 BCS National Championship Game against Texas. "To be honest with you, it was probably a mistake because it didn't work," Saban admitted. "But sometimes when you do things like that, the players see you being aggressive, and maybe it's not as bad as you think.

"When I was at LSU and we played Tennessee in the first [SEC] Championship Game, I think it was in 2001…they were [No.] 1 or 2 in the country and going to go play in the national championship game [if they won]. We got behind 14–7 and we were on the 29-yard line with fourth-and-an-inch. I mean an inch. Now, they had [Albert] Haynesworth and some big guys playing in the middle. So I said we're going to go for it on our own 29-yard line on fourth-and-an-inch, and we got stuffed, and we sacked them, and they kicked a field goal and they got ahead 17–7.

"For the next five minutes of the game I was like in la-la land, like, *Why did you do that? That's the dumbest thing you've ever done.* My wife even told me, 'That's the dumbest call I've seen you make since you've been a head coach.' But we were walking off the field after the game, [and] the seniors came up and said, 'You know, Coach, that was the most important thing you did in the game is when you went for it on fourth down.'

"I said, 'Really?'

"They said, 'Yeah, because when you did that, we really thought we could win. You were being aggressive and you were trying to win,' and we were aggressive after that and we ended up winning the game 31–20. So even sometimes the dumbest things you do, you never know how people are going to respond to them, and that was one of the dumb ones."

Yet it goes a lot further than just making corrections and trying to avoid mistakes. In order to stay on top in college football, coaches and their staffs have to continually stay on top of the game's trends and changes, and adapt.

Perhaps the best example in college football history of a coach reinventing (for lack of a better term) his program, was Paul W. "Bear" Bryant, after the Crimson Tide started a clear decline in the late 1960s. Combined with the integration of the Crimson Tide's first black players, Bryant spent part of the summer of 1971 learning the wishbone from Darrell Royal at Texas, who had been part of national titles in 1969 and 1970. With the offense still a secret when the Crimson Tide opened the season at Southern California, a team it had lost to 42–21 the previous season, Alabama unveiled the scheme against a shocked defense, scored two early touchdowns, and stunned the No. 5 Trojans 17–10.

Bryant went on to claim a share of the national championship in 1973, 1978, and 1979, and be in the running for several more.

A little good fortune helps as well.

One game that will always be tied to Saban was the Bluegrass Miracle, when LSU visited Kentucky on November 9, 2002, and the Wildcats weren't given much of a chance to win. The Tigers led by as many as 14 points and were ahead 24–14 after a field goal with 13:58 remaining, only to see the home team rally.

With the game tied and 15 seconds remaining, Kentucky called timeout with first down at the LSU 11-yard line. Coach Guy Morriss decided to go for the win, thinking in part that if anything went wrong there could be a second chance at the field goal. Taylor Begley made the 29-yard FG with just 11 seconds to go and with the subsequent kickoff pinned the Tigers at their own 9.

Game over, right?

LSU went for a short gain, and quarterback Marcus Randall connected with wide receiver Michael Clayton, stopping the clock for a final play. With the Tigers needing 75 yards, Morriss was doused with a Gatorade bath before the final snap, and when Randall reared back and threw the ball as far as he could, victory fireworks went off. Fans even started to storm the field and climb the eastern goalpost.

What they missed was one of the most incredible final plays in college football history. The Hail Mary pass fell about 25 yards short of the end zone, and eight Wildcats had a chance to make a play on the ball. Instead, three defenders deflected it to Devery Henderson near the 15-yard line, with the LSU receiver turning, avoiding the only Wildcat player who had a chance to stop him, and sprinting into the end zone for the stunning game-winning score.

Jefferson Pilot Sports, which was broadcasting the game, accidentally posted the final score of Kentucky 30, LSU 27, even though it was 33–30, and LSU was the actual victor. As the shocked Kentucky fans started to figure out that they had just lost, Saban said during his television interview: "I don't know what to say. I feel bad for Kentucky's players. But this is a big moment for us, and I'm happy as heck for our team. Well, sometimes you gotta be a little lucky, and I think that was our luck right there."

On the 10-year anniversary, Saban said, "I remember it all." He also remembered that Alabama absolutely crushed LSU the following week, 31–0. It was the first time the Tigers were shut out since the Crimson Tide had beaten them 26–0 in 1996, and it was their most lopsided shutout loss since a 35–0 defeat by Oklahoma in the 1950 Sugar Bowl.

The coach himself brought it up to reporters after the Texas A&M loss in 2012, one week after the team had won a dramatic game at LSU. "You all live in the results world, we kind of live in the process world," he said. "It's hard to get people to respond. It's kind of the Bluegrass Miracle phenomenon. You play bad, you win the game, then the next week you get your ass kicked because nobody responded to playing bad, because you won on the Bluegrass Miracle."

However, Saban's biggest professional mistake was probably with the Miami Dolphins, when in 2006 he told reporters, "I'm not going to be the Alabama coach," only to turn around and take the job a few weeks later. To this day he regrets making the statement.

The reason why Saban said what he did during a press conference was that the question kept getting asked, and the Dolphins were still in the middle of their season. It was becoming a distraction, and by just even hinting at considering a move he would have lost the players in the locker room and become a lame-duck coach. "I came to the Miami Dolphins, what, eight years ago, for the best owner, the best person that I've ever had the opportunity to work for," Saban said in 2012, referring to Dolphins owner Wayne Huizenga, who hired him away from LSU. "In the two years that I was here I had a very, very difficult time thinking that I could impact the organization in the way that I wanted to or in the way that I am able to in college, and it was very difficult for me. Because there is a lot of parity in the NFL. There's a lot of rules in the NFL."

It was a tough lesson to learn, because for years reporters continued to ask about his possibly returning to the NFL someday. "I kind of learned from that experience that maybe [college] is where I belong," he said. "I'm really happy and at peace with all of that."

Dolphins fans weren't so forgiving, though, nor was the Miami media, which for years continued to pound away at Saban from afar and never seemed to notice that his going to Alabama involved taking a pay cut. In addition to being rejected in favor of a college program, the Dolphins had sub-.500 finishes in five of the subsequent six seasons with just one playoff appearance.

Meanwhile, at the end of the 2012 season the Orange Bowl Committee got its regular turn to host the BCS National Championship, with Alabama poised to play Notre Dame. Every media outlet was ready to pounce on the "return of Saban" story line, only he defused it by going on a South Florida radio show featuring one of his staunchest critics before the Crimson Tide arrived.

"I think the biggest thing was probably not handling the way I left very well," Saban told 790 AM "The Ticket" in Miami. "That's always been a thing with me that I've never felt good about…The one thing that I don't have any regrets about [is] the relationship that I had with the players and the job that I did for the Dolphins and Mr. Huizenga. We all make mistakes; we all learn about ourselves.

Why Freshmen Are Off-Limits to Reporters

It's known as the Plaxico Burress story, stemming from his time at Michigan State. "I love Plaxico, don't get me wrong," Nick Saban explained. "He was a great player for us and did a good job and all that. We're going to play Michigan, at Michigan, which is the biggest game of the year, and I let freshmen talk to the media. He's a freshman. He says, 'Yeah, going down there will be like taking candy from a baby.' So he just about got killed."

Michigan State lost the game 29–17, but Burress went on to set the Big Ten single-season record by catching 65 passes his first season (a year later he also had 10 catches on 255 yards to help lead a 34–31 victory against the Wolverines).

That helped contribute to another Saban policy, that he uses the best players regardless of age. "The big thing with young players is the maturity to be able to grind through the season," Saban said. "The season is a grind, but you've got to embrace the grind. The younger guys have a more difficult time being able to do that week in and week out, and I think they go through some ups and downs."

As much as I respected the players and the organization, the things we tried to do there, this has been a good thing for my family to be here."

Just like that, the potential firestorm of questions was avoided, and for the second straight year Saban's team was able to win the title game played near where he had previously coached—and where some still held a grudge. "We like to have honesty and integrity in everything that we do. I've obviously been accused of not having that before...maybe rightfully so. I certainly wish that wouldn't have been the case," he said. "[I] just try and set a good example for doing things the right way, whether it's for my children, our players. I don't really treat our players any different than I do my own children in terms of how we make decisions about what we do and what we don't do. No one's perfect, a lot of circumstances come up in your life that are tough decisions. We just try and make them the right way."

The Competition

When Nick Saban returned to the Southeastern Conference in 2007, it had already separated itself as the top league in the nation, and the gap was growing as wide as a canyon. Florida had just won its first national championship under Urban Meyer (beginning the conference's historic run of seven straight titles). For the fourth consecutive year at least five SEC teams finished in the top 25, and many thought that Arkansas running back Darren McFadden would snap the league's drought in Heisman Trophy balloting, in which it had enjoyed just one winner since 1996.

"Great to be back in the SEC," Saban said during his introductory remarks at SEC Media Days. "I've been asked the question on several occasions already today: 'What is the difference in the league now than when you left?' And my response to that is: it seems like it's even tougher now than ever before. The competition from top to bottom, the great coaches in the league, the great programs, more good teams, lots of great players. But I also think that's what makes this an outstanding, competitive venue."

Consider the following:

The NFL Draft: The SEC had 63 selections in the 2013 NFL Draft, 19 more than the previous year, and the most picks of any conference for the seventh straight draft. It was the most any league had produced since the Pac-10's 55 in 1983, and represented one-quarter of all players selected. It also tied another record with 12 first-round selections.

NFL rosters: From 2006 to 2012, the conference averaged 266.1 former SEC players on opening weekend rosters, with the ACC second at 241.6, followed by the Big Ten (228.9), Pac-12 (192.6), and the Big 12 (168.9). In 2013 there were 340 former SEC players on the opening weekend rosters.

Final rankings: In 2012 the SEC finished with a record seven teams in the final top 25 (which it tied in 2013). Ten SEC schools were ranked at some point during the season. From 2006 to 2012, the SEC had the most teams ranked in the final polls, including a combined 36 in the coaches poll, six more than the Big 12 and 10 more than the Big Ten.

Head-to-head: From 2006 to 2012 the SEC had the best nonconference winning percentage (regular season and bowls) of .818 (333–74), with the Big 12 second at .738 (262–93), ahead of the Big East at .700 (222–95), the Big Ten at .687 (252–115), the Pac-12 at .631 (169–99), and the ACC at .611 (239–152).

Bowl games: Although from 2006 to 2013 the SEC didn't have the best winning percentage in bowl games, it did have the most bowl appearances (73) and wins (42) by a wide margin. Second was the Big 12 with 56 and 29, respectively. In January bowl games during that span, the SEC was 27–12 (.692) against nonconference competition and 21–8 (.724) since 2008.

The Bowl Championship Series: The SEC won nine of the 16 national titles during the BCS era, while no other conference won more than two. SEC teams also hadn't just won the title games but had dominated. During its 2006–12 championship streak, the SEC's average margin of victory was 17 points with only one game decided by single digits: Auburn's three-point win

The Hit List

Saban at Alabama vs. SEC

SEC West	*SEC East*
Arkansas 6–0*	Tennessee 7–0
Ole Miss 6–0*	Kentucky 3–0
Mississippi State 6–1	Vanderbilt 1–0*
Auburn 4–3	Florida 3–1
LSU 5–3	Georgia 2–1
Texas A&M 1–1	South Carolina 1–1
	Missouri 1–0

Other schools
Winning or .500 records: North Texas 2–0; Penn State 2–0; Arkansas State 1–0; Chattanooga 2–0; Clemson 1–0; Colorado 1–0; Colorado State 1–0; Duke 1–0; Florida Atlantic 1–0; Florida International 1–0; Georgia Southern 1–0; Georgia State 2–0; Kent State 1–0; Michigan 1–0; Michigan State 1–0; Notre Dame 1–0; San Jose State 1–0; Texas 1–0; Tulane 1–0; Virginia Tech 2–0; Western Carolina 1–0*; Houston 0–0*; Western Kentucky 2–0.
Losing records: Florida State 0–1; Louisiana Monroe 0–1; Oklahoma 0–1; Utah 0–1

*win vacated

Saban Career vs. SEC

SEC West	*SEC East*
Arkansas 9–2*	Tennessee 9–1
Ole Miss 10–1*	Kentucky 6–0
Mississippi State 11–1	Vanderbilt 2–0*
Auburn 6–6	Florida 5–4
LSU 5–4	Georgia 4–2
Alabama 4–1	South Carolina 3–1
Texas A&M 1–1	Missouri 1–0

over Oregon in 2010. Under Saban, Alabama's average margin of victory was 21.7 points.

Also the SEC went 17–10 in BCS bowls and was 80–53 in all bowls, while none of the other major conferences finished above .500 (Pac-12: 47–48; Big 12: 60–66; ACC: 54–61; and Big Ten: 49–64).

Big Ten teams: Illinois 6–0; Indiana 4–0; Michigan State 1–0; Minnesota 3–1; Northwestern 2–1; Ohio State 2–1; Penn State 4–3; Iowa 2–2; Michigan 3–3; Wisconsin 1–2; Purdue 1–3–1

Other Schools
Winning or .500 records: Arkansas State 2–0; Arizona 1–0; Arizona State 1–0; Ball State 1–0; Boston College 1–0; Bowling Green 1–0; Central Michigan 1–1; Chattanooga 2–0; Citadel 1–0; Clemson 1–0; Colorado 1–0; Colorado State 1–1; Duke 1–0; Eastern Michigan 3–0; Florida Atlantic 1–0; Florida International 1–0; Georgia Southern 1–0; Georgia State 2–0; Georgia Tech 1–0; Houston 1–0*; Kent State 2–0; Lafayette 1–0; Louisiana Monroe 1–1; Louisiana Tech 1–0; Louisville 1–1; Memphis 1–0; Miami (Ohio) 2–0; Middle Tennessee 1–0; North Texas 2–0; Northern Illinois 1–0; Notre Dame 4–0; Ohio 1–0; Oklahoma 1–1; Oregon 1–1; Oregon State 1–0; San Jose State 1–0; Texas 1–1; Troy State 1–0; Tulane 2–0; Utah State 1–0; Virginia Tech 2–1; Western Carolina 2–0*; Western Illinois 1–0; Western Kentucky 2–0; Western Michigan 2–0
Losing records: Florida State 0–1; Navy 0–1; Nebraska 0–2; Stanford 0–1; UAB 0–1; Utah 0–1; Washington 0–1

*win vacated

Active Division I Teams with Winning Records Against Alabama (All-Time)
Texas 7–1–1
Notre Dame 5–2
Rice 3–0
Boston College 3–1
TCU 3–2
Oklahoma 3–1–1
UCLA 2–1
Teams 1–0 against Alabama: Central Florida, Louisiana-Monroe, Minnesota, Northern Illinois, Oklahoma State, Utah, Wisconsin

From 2006 to 2013, an SEC team was ranked first in the weekly BCS standings 37 of 64 weeks, with Alabama and LSU combined having led for more weeks than the second- and third-place conferences, the Big Ten and Big 12, combined.

With all that in mind, and all the coaches in the conference who had won a national championship, consider Saban's record in SEC play of 28–12 during his five years at LSU and 43–10 during his first seven years at Alabama (not including three vacated wins) with four of the defeats coming during his first season at the Capstone. Combined, he was 71–22 against the "best."

Hindsight is 20/20, of course, but there's a reason why South Carolina coach Steve Spurrier once quipped, "It's easier to win the national championship than the SEC. Ask Nick Saban."

Nevertheless, there's an underlying, simple truth that applies here, which just about any coach at any level of competition will confirm, that to be the best one has to play the best. "I don't think there's any question about it," Saban said when asked about whether playing in the SEC gives a team an edge in the national championship. "So if you're playing those teams…those kinds of games, that kind of competition, playing against sort of the best, obviously helps you play another good team when you play in a game like [the BCS championship].

"And I don't even think it's just those teams, I think it's the fact that there's a lot of teams in our division that we had very difficult games with. So it's almost every game that you play in the SEC is a game that you could lose, and you have to be very well prepared for and you have to sort of play with a consistency. You can't play up and down, or you're going to have problems. And I think all those things really help the consistency and the players to understand and appreciate what it takes to be successful."

Beating Saban had become such a difficult task for any opposing coach that only six managed to pull it off between 2008 and 2012. With the exception of Texas A&M's Kevin Sumlin pulling off a 29–24 win in 2012, when Alabama was facing its third ranked team in as many weeks, no SEC opponent had a winning record against the Crimson Tide with Saban.

Michigan was one of the few programs with an overall winning record against Saban until Alabama opened the 2012 season with an impressive 41–14 neutral-site win in Dallas. When he was at Michigan State (1995–99), the rivals played every year, with the Wolverines coming out on top three times.

As for which program has had the most success against him, would you believe that it's Purdue? The Boilermakers are 3–1–1 against Saban, and former quarterback Drew Brees is largely responsible for that record.

In 1997 Brees replaced starter Billy Dicken with 4:24 to play and was intercepted by safety Aric Morris at the Purdue 26-yard line with 3:47 left, seemingly sealing the Purdue loss. Ahead 21–10, Michigan State subsequently lined up to attempt a 39-yard field goal, only Purdue defensive tackle Leo Perez broke through the line to block the kick, and defensive end Rosevelt Colvin scooped up the loose ball and scored on a 62-yard return.

The ensuing onside kick was recovered by Boilermakers wide receiver Chris Daniels with 1:58 remaining; Dicken returned and led a touchdown drive to give Purdue its first lead, 22–21. Michigan State got the ball back at its own 33-yard line with 35 seconds remaining and quickly drove, only Chris Gardner missed a 43-yard field goal with three seconds left.

"Divine intervention may have been on our side today," Purdue coach Joe Tiller said in his postgame remarks, while Saban was quoted as saying, "This is about as disappointed as I've ever been."

His anguish against the Boilermakers was only beginning. In 1998 Brees threw two touchdown passes less than four minutes apart in the fourth quarter as Purdue rallied from an 11-point deficit for its fourth straight victory, a 25–24 win.

Finally, in 1999 Brees passed for 509 yards while leading a 52–28 win. He eventually left Purdue in 2001, having set Big Ten records for passing yards (11,792), touchdown passes (90), total offensive yards (12,693), completions (1,026), and attempts (1,678), and he's the last starting quarterback Saban lost to two straight times.

Similarly, winning two straight against Saban as a coach has proven to be nearly as difficult. Heading into the 2014 season the only coach to pull it off with Saban at Alabama was Les Miles with a 24–21 home victory in 2010 followed by the 9–6 overtime win in the 2011 No. 1–vs.–No. 2 showdown at Bryant-Denny Stadium. Of course, Saban more than got even against LSU by winning the game that really mattered, the subsequent BCS championship, 21–0, and a year later the clutch 21–17 victory at Tiger Stadium en route to winning the 2012 title too.

But not even he can win them all. Despite having won four national championships, Saban has had only one undefeated team: 2009. "I think it's very difficult in this day and age," Saban said.

The Drive to Be the Best

You'd probably be surprised at the number of times Nick Saban gets asked if he's enjoying himself as the Crimson Tide keeps notching championships, awards, and accomplishments with each subsequent season. "It depends on how you sort of categorize enjoyment," he said. "I enjoy the competition. I enjoy the fact that our team has an opportunity to play in such a great competitive venue. I enjoy the work of trying to get the team ready to play the way they're going to need to play to have an opportunity to be successful. It's very challenging. So that's my enjoyment."

Saban made that comment in New Orleans, where Alabama was about to face LSU for the 2011 national championship. "Now, maybe your perception of enjoyment is you go out and have a party," he said. "Well, that's not my enjoyment of this experience. We have been to the Sugar Bowl four times, and I really enjoy the relationships that we have with the people here at the Sugar Bowl. So in my own way, as the coach, I enjoy this. Putting the team together, putting the plan together, to have an opportunity to play against a great team and see if you can be successful, that's my enjoyment. So that's my fun. It may not be other people's fun. So I enjoy it. In my own way, I enjoy it. This is what you work for, to have these kinds of opportunities."

Actually, a lot of that is an understatement, as Saban is extremely competitive in everything that he does. It doesn't matter if there's a crystal football at stake or the loser has to do the dishes, he wants to win.

Except for his wife and family, perhaps no one has seen it more firsthand than Kirby Smart, who initially joined Saban's coaching staff at LSU in 2004 and, minus one season at his alma mater, Georgia, has since remained a fixture on Saban's sideline. "I have become who I've become as a coach from working for Coach Saban," said Smart. He added, "There is no question he is driven to be the greatest coach in the game."

Similar to when he plays basketball during lunch in the off-season, or golf in the spring, Saban also likes to stack the deck whenever possible. In college football, you do that by having the best players, in addition to the best assistants, facilities, etc.

You know the saying, "He with the most toys wins"? Well, for Saban it's having human walls like Terrance Cody at nose guard or D.J. Fluker on the offensive line. Opponents look over, and the competition may be already half-over no matter how fired up they may be. However, as every coach in America will tell you, every game is four quarters long. "Well, I don't think that if you're in a boxing match that having great emotion in the first round necessarily will win you the fight," Saban said. "I think you've got to be punching in the 15th round too, and you carry emotion through to that. I think it comes a little bit more to competitive character and determination, a lot of other things that help you overcome adversity as a competitor, the challenges that you have of competing against other people who are exceptional in and of themselves.

"So even though emotion is important, I think more it's competitive character and attitude, intensity that can be sustained for 60 minutes in a game, [that] is probably more important so that you can continue to do the things you need to do to be successful. I mean, I think that regardless of the competitive event, I don't care, everybody wants to win when the game starts, and everybody is emotional about winning. It's who can sustain for the entire game; to play well in a game, I think, is really critical to being successful."

Not to mention having All-American players such as Mark Ingram Jr., Chance Warmack, and Dee Milliner, with more guys just like that behind them waiting for a chance to show what they can do.

A perfect example is the way Saban handles the defense. Even though he isn't the coordinator and doesn't call the plays, he still works with the cornerbacks every day in practice. He's their position coach, which can be pretty rare in college football.

What can you say? He's a defensive coach and plays to his strengths, while having the objective of never having a drop off—ever. That included the 2012 defense, which had to follow the unit that might been the best ever but had to replace practically all of the statistical leaders and seven starters who combined to make 188 starts.

That time, in particular, it appeared to be an extremely daunting task, especially considering all the big names no longer on the roster, such as Mark Barron, Josh Chapman, Dont'a Hightower, Dre Kirkpatrick, DeQuan Menzie, and

Courtney Upshaw. Yet the previous year there was no Marcell Dareus, and the season before that no Rolando McClain, etc. "Once the defense gets together and has that communication like last year's team had, we can be as good or greater," linebacker C.J. Mosley said in 2012.

When Mosley said that, a disbelieving reporter looked at him and asked, "Really?"

"You never know," Mosley responded with a grin. "Anything can happen."

Alabama got pretty close, but one of the consequences of winning a national championship is that the next team is always compared to its predecessor, perhaps unfairly, just like the 2010 Crimson Tide was to the 2009 team.

With the 2011 title, Alabama's 14th overall, the defense led the nation in nearly every statistical category and by a wide margin. Legendary coach Bobby Bowden called it probably the most physical defense he'd ever seen at the collegiate level. "I was at the first LSU-Alabama game, and [as] soon as that game was over, I said, 'They're going to play again,'" Bowden said. "There was no doubt in my mind they were the two best football teams in the country."

Prior to the rematch in the BCS title game, LSU was 13–0 thanks to its 9–6 overtime victory at Bryant-Denny Stadium and had handily won the SEC championship. There was talk that the Tigers might be the best team in college football history, only for it to end with a shutout and Crimson Tide fans celebrating in and around the Mercedes-Benz Superdome on January 9.

Although LSU had averaged 40.9 points against every other opponent, it scored 4.5 points in two games (nine quarters) against Alabama.

"Let me put it this way: in 13 games last year, they gave up nine touchdowns, against the best opponents in the country," Hall of Fame coach Lou Holtz said about Alabama. "In one bowl game, Clemson gave up 10 touchdowns to West Virginia. It was unbelievable. I was at the national championship game, and I felt that Alabama would win because I think teams are 7-for-7 in return games, the team that lost the opener, but in no way did I expect them to dominate the game the way they did defensively. It was a complete mismatch."

That's the standard.

So while Alabama has gotten used to replacing high-profile players, it's still been ranked in the top five in total defense six straight years through 2013. The only two times it was out of the top three was 2010 and 2013 (both fifth).

"We kind of have a standard here at Alabama," Smart said in 2013. "A lot of people think our standard is to be first in the SEC, be first in the country, first in our red zone and run defense. We really don't go by that motto. We go by, 'Be the best Alabama defense there's been.' We compare ourselves to the last five years of Alabama defenses. When you do that, last year's defense was not exactly up to par, not exactly spectacular. We put in a lot of work to improve on defense."

Best Defense Ever?

By pulling off the first BCS National Championship Game shutout, the University of Alabama's 2011 title team forced its way into the debate about what's the best defense in college football history. Obviously it's a question that's impossible to answer, but there's no doubt that the Crimson Tide is in elite company.

Alabama finished the season by leading the nation in pass-efficiency defense (83.69 rating), pass defense (111.46 yards per game), rushing defense (72.15), scoring defense (8.15 points), and total defense (183.62 yards per game)—in addition to third-down defense, red-zone defense, and three-and-outs.

Alabama also topped each category convincingly.

Defensive Category	Second-Best Team	Statistic	Difference
Pass-efficiency defense	South Carolina	94.23 rating	+10.54
Pass defense	South Carolina	131.69 yards	+20.23
Rushing defense	Florida State	82.69 yards	+10.54
Scoring defense	LSU	11.29 points	+3.14
Total defense	LSU	261.5 yards	+77.88

Additionally, while Alabama gave up just 10.08 first downs on average, the next-best team was Georgia at 14.36.

Only one other time since the NCAA started keeping track in 1937 has a team finished No. 1 in all four key defensive categories: Oklahoma in 1986. The Sooners yielded 169.6 total yards, 60.7 rushing yards, 102.4 passing yards, and 6.6 points per game.

Moreover, of the 47 running backs in the NCAA who had 1,000-yard rushing seasons, Alabama faced five: Michael Dyer of Auburn, Silas Redd of Penn State, Zac Stacy of Vanderbilt, Vick Ballard of Mississippi State, and Lance Dunbar of North Texas. Combined, they had 65 carries for 154 yards against the Crimson Tide, for an average of 30.8 yards, and one touchdown. Against everyone else they accumulated 1,084 carries for 5,826 yards, or a 100.4 average, and 50 touchdowns.

Even more remarkable was that Alabama was consistently doing it while playing in the best conference in the country, against the best players, against the best coaches…and so on…who were spending months during the off-season trying to figure out ways to top the Crimson Tide.

Think about that for a moment. Then start to consider what it takes to stay ahead of them.

Going back to the original question, that's why, in part, Saban is enjoying what he's doing, while making history, even if he doesn't often show that much emotion. Winning is fun, but he also likes the day-to-day aspects of the job. "I kind of take this year-to-year, day-to-day," Saban said during one of his more poignant moments. "God willing, I'd like to coach for a long time, but…you know, as long as I'm happy…

"Sometimes I see coaches on TV, and I say to myself, 'I wonder if that guy is happy in his life.' I think sometimes when you get into this business…everything's about the game. If it gets all about the game and it's not about trying to be a good person, trying to be a good father, trying to be a good role model for the young men that you're trying to affect in a positive way…Trying to serve other people, whether it's through our Nick's Kids or whatever it is, to help other people who have needs. When it leaves and it just becomes all about the game, then I'm not sure you can be happy as a person, because I don't think…you know, you try and give to the game as much…but when you're concerned about the game giving your ego everything it needs for you to sort of survive, I don't think that's a good thing. If that ever happens, maybe I'll start doing something else. I don't know what it would be. I don't think I'm qualified for much."

★ ★ ★

How They Stack Up, Part I: National Championships

The biggest way college football coaches keep score, for lack of a better term, is with titles, and the list of active coaches who have won at least one is short:

Active Coaches Who Have Won Consensus Titles
Nick Saban 4 (3 at Alabama, 1 at LSU)
Urban Meyer 2 (at Florida)
Larry Coker 1 (at Miami)
Jimbo Fisher 1
Les Miles 1 (at LSU)
Steve Spurrier 1 (at Florida)
Bob Stoops 1

Former Auburn coach Gene Chizik was out of football after the 2012 season, while Coker was back in at Texas–San Antonio, which went 8–4 and 7–5 during its first two seasons. Also, Mack Brown stepped down from Texas at the end of the 2013 season.

But even if you added Pete Carroll and Jim Tressel, whose former schools were still feeling the impact of their off-the-field issues, Nick Saban was alone in how often he'd won titles during his 18-year coaching career (one every 4.5 years) and at Alabama (three in seven seasons).

In the broader sense, in terms of all-time "consensus" national championships, the key word being *consensus* (critics will claim that's unfair for a variety of reasons, but there really is no other way of having an equal standard that applies across the board), Saban was already near the top with four.

By that standard, Bear Bryant has five consensus titles, and while some of the Bear's were indeed controversial, he also had a number of teams that ended up on the short end as well. Granted, the school claims six for him, but among them is 1973 for finishing first in the coaches' poll while Notre Dame, which beat Alabama 24–23 in the Sugar Bowl, is considered that year's consensus champion for our purposes.

This is not a complete list and for the most part includes only coaches since the poll era began in 1936:

Multiple National Championships, All-Time
Bernie Bierman 5
Paul W. "Bear" Bryant 5
Nick Saban 4
Howard Jones 3
Frank Leahy 3
John McKay 3
Knute Rockne 3
Barry Switzer 3
Wallace Wade 3
Bud Wilkinson 3
Earl Blaik 2
Bobby Bowden 2
Bob Devaney 2
Woody Hayes 2
Urban Meyer 2
Tom Osborne 2

Ara Parseghian 2
Joe Paterno 2
Darrell Royal 2

While some of the game's great innovators like Fielding Yost, Glenn "Pop" Warner, and Walter Camp aren't included, it should be noted that 78 years before Saban became the first coach during the modern age to win consensus championships at two different schools, Howard Jones did it during the pre-poll era (Yale 1909, Southern California 1931–32).

Here's how the numbers average out over the length of their head coaching careers. The number represents, on average, the season-to-championship ratio for each coach (i.e., if it says 4.3, that means that coach had one championship per every 4.3 seasons of coaching):

Frank Leahy 4.3
Knute Rockne 4.3
Nick Saban 4.5
John McKay 5.3
Barry Switzer 5.3
Bud Wilkinson 5.7
Urban Meyer 6.0
Paul W. "Bear" Bryant 7.6
Wallace Wade 8.0
Howard Jones 9.3
Ara Parseghian 9.5
Darrell Royal 11.5
Earl Blaik 12.5
Bob Devaney 12.5
Tom Osborne 12.5
Woody Hayes 15
Bobby Bowden 20
Joe Paterno 23

★ ★ ★

The Mount Rushmore of College Football: Paul W. "Bear" Bryant

★ ★ ★ ★ ★ ★ ★

"They're much better than we were. I've never seen a coach be able to assemble the kind of talent that Saban has. Coach Bryant... he might have had one or two good players a year. That was about it, and everyone else was an okay college player. He didn't put a whole lot of guys into the pros. But Saban sure has some talent."

—Pro Football Hall of Fame guard John Hannah, who played under Bryant from 1970 to 1972, in 2012

Here's how good of a football coach Paul W. "Bear" Bryant was: from 1946 to 1953 his teams enjoyed eight straight winning seasons to go with appearances in the Orange, Sugar, and Cotton Bowls, and captured the program's first Southeastern Conference title in 1950. That season was capped off with an invitation to face Oklahoma in the Sugar Bowl, which may have seemed like a looming execution considering Bud Wilkinson's Sooners were riding a 31-game winning streak.

Only Bryant came out on top, 13–7…with Kentucky. Yes, the Wildcats, who have since won just one other SEC title, in 1976, and that was shared with Georgia.

Bryant also made his mark at Texas A&M, beginning with his first training camp in 1954, when he took players 250 miles west to a barren army base in Junction, Texas, and put them through the mental and physical equivalent of a meat grinder. More than two-thirds of the players quit, with those who endured dubbed the "Junction Boys," but it also defined the coach's legacy as a hard-nosed disciplinarian. "I don't want ordinary people," Bryant said. "I want people who are willing to sacrifice and do without a lot of those things ordinary students get to do. That's what it takes to win."

Bryant's Aggies were closing in on the 1957 national championship when he was lured away by Alabama and made his famous statement: "Mama called, and when Mama calls, then you just have to come running."

Although originally from Arkansas, where he was born, it was in Tuscaloosa where Bryant changed more lives that he ever knew, and made his biggest impact. It's also where the man who is still regularly quoted for saying "I ain't never been nothing but a winner" did just that: win…a lot.

During his amazing 25 years with the Crimson Tide, Bryant lost just 46 games, compared to 232 wins. No program in the nation won more than Alabama in both the 1960s and 1970s, and Bryant is considered the only college football coach since the Associated Press poll was created in 1936 to successfully lead not one, but two dynasties. "He wasn't just a coach," former Southern California coach John McKay once said. "He was *the* coach."

During his 38-year career, only nine of Bryant's teams finished unranked—including each of his first four years (1945 at Maryland, 1946–48 at Kentucky)—compared to 22 winding up in the top 10. He took 29 teams to bowl games and led 15 to conference championships.

Bryant set a similar standard in the Southeastern Conference with 159 regular-season league wins, which not only remains the record, but just three others have managed to top the century mark. He was named the SEC's Coach of the Year an incredible 12 times.

No coach had his presence, either, as Bryant, the epitome of toughness, became a symbol for a troubled state and region and an iconic presence that transcended

Nick Saban vs. Paul W. "Bear" Bryant

Category	Saban	Bryant
Seasons	18	38
Consensus national titles	4	5 (Z)
Top five finishes	4	13
Top 25 finishes	11	29
Overall record (%)	165–57–1 (74.2%)	323–85–17 (78.0%)
Losing seasons	0	1
Bowl record (%)	8–7 (53.3%)	15–12–2 (55.2%)
Conference titles	5	15
Conference record	101–39–1	177–57–10
Consensus All-Americans	23	23
First-round draft picks (through 2013)	19	19
Record against ranked teams (%)	51–35 (59.30%)	65–43–5 (59.73%)
Record against top 10 teams (%)	25–16 (61.0%)	33–23–1 (58.77%)
Ratios/percentages		
National title seasons	One every 4.5 seasons	7.6
Consensus All-Americans	1.28 every season	.61
First-round draft picks (through 2013)	1.12 every season	.50
Average wins vs. ranked teams	2.83 each season	1.71
Wins over top 10 teams per year	1.50 every season	.87

Z-Alabama claims 1973 for finishing first in the coaches' poll, but Notre Dame is considered the consensus champion.

college football. Even his nickname, which stuck after he actually wrestled a bear at a carnival as a teen, reflected his fierceness as a player with the Crimson Tide in the 1930s, and his stature as a coach.

"Bear Bryant is probably the greatest coach in college football in terms of what he accomplished, what his legacy is," Nick Saban said. "I think the biggest thing that impacts me is how many peoples' lives he affected in a positive way, players who played for him, because they all come back and say how he affected their life. They don't come back and say, 'We won a championship in '78, '79, '61,' whenever it was. They come back and say how he affected their lives. There's a lot of Bear Bryant stories that I've learned a lot from, that have made me a better

Paul W. "Bear" Bryant, who Nick Saban refers to in reverential terms, won five consensus national titles, one more than Saban. (AP Images)

person. I certainly appreciate that, have a tremendous amount of respect for what he accomplished. There's no way that we have done anything close to what he's done in terms of his consistency over time, how he changed what he did to impact the times."

When Bryant retired he was Division I's all-time winningest coach with 323 wins. He guided his teams to 29 bowl appearances, 15 conference championships, won an SEC-record 146 games, 13 league titles, and six national championships, five consensus. No program won more games than Alabama (193–32–5) in both the 1960s and 1970s. "He was simply the best there ever was," former Nebraska coach Bob Devaney said of his peer.

Even though Bryant died on January 26, 1983, at the age of 69, hardly a day goes by that most Crimson Tide fans still don't mention his name at least once, while books and documentaries are still being made about him and his legacy. Fans still proudly wear the pattern of his trademark houndstooth hat around campus, and a good part of Tuscaloosa has been named in his honor.

That's remarkable, especially considering how much things have changed since Bryant was born in 1913, the year when Woodrow Wilson took office as president, Ford Motor Company introduced the first moving assembly line, and Harvard was considered the team to beat in college football.

While some of Bryant's records have been eclipsed, and other coaches have since won championships with the Crimson Tide—including his former player and assistant coach Gene Stallings—Bryant is still considered the one to set the standard, and who many try and emulate in some way. "Coach Bryant, in his tenure here, to have the kind of success that he had over time, consistency in performance over all that time and winning all those championships, the intangibles that his teams always seemed to play with, are the things that you really try to get your team to do," Saban said. "Whether it's the physical toughness, the effort, the finishing, the discipline to execute.

"I know that when I first started coaching, I read Coach Bryant's book, and it had a tremendous impact on me, in terms of some of the important things that would help you be successful as a coach, and I believe strongly in a lot of the same intangible-type things in terms of character, attitude, discipline, hard work. That's the kind of program that we have here. I think that was the foundation, really, of his program."

As a result, his shadow still looms large on the Capstone, similar to how the tower from which he watched practices stands like a monument. "I don't think there's any question that there's probably only a few people in college athletics history who have had as great an impact, maybe John Wooden at UCLA," Saban said about Bryant on what would have been his 100th birthday, September 11, 2013. "I don't think you can really kind of put words into what it really has meant and how it has affected the University of Alabama."

Part II

"A lot of players have a chip on their shoulder, even though we won the national championship. We all want to strive to be the best players at our positions. That's just the mentality that we have at that school and that program that Coach Saban instilled in us."

—Former Alabama guard Chance Warmack (2009–12)

★ ★ ★

Saban's National Championship Teams

2003

Most of the things that Nick Saban does at Alabama stem from his years as an assistant coach, not to mention being the head coach at Toledo, Michigan State, and LSU.

A good example is movie night for the team the evening before games, and when the Crimson Tide was preparing to face Notre Dame for the 2012 championship, Saban was asked if he could remember what the Tigers watched prior to winning his first title in 2003. "Wow, I was hoping you'd say last year, and I might be able to remember," he said with a laugh. "I know last year it was *Red Tails*, but I don't want to say the wrong movie. But I think the movie, regardless of whether it was *The Last Samurai* or whatever movie it was, the message was the honor of being all that you can be, that maybe that might be more important than winning or losing, and that your focus should be on that instead of the outcome. I do remember that was the message that we were trying to get our players to focus on in that particular game."

(Incidentally, the movie was *The Last Samurai*).

Although LSU won the SEC Championship Game in 2001, things really clicked for the Tigers during Saban's fourth season in Baton Rouge. By winning its first five games, including a 17–10 home victory over Georgia, LSU steadily climbed the rankings and found itself in a three-team race for the national title— all of which would have a setback.

Southern California's loss came first, on September 27, 34–31 in overtime at California; two weeks later, LSU lost to Florida, 19–7. Meanwhile, Oklahoma, the top team in the preseason polls, ran the table during the regular season, going 12–0, and was the unanimous No. 1 team across the board.

With USC second, LSU appeared to be on the outside looking in heading into the final weekend of play, but the Tigers had a tougher opponent, a rematch with No. 5 Georgia in the SEC championship. That game wasn't anywhere near as close as the regular-season meeting, with the Tigers dominating the Bulldogs 34–13 at the Georgia Dome. "There's not much to say," Georgia coach Mark Richt said. "We just got whipped."

LSU had an edge in total yards of 444–249, Lionel Turner scored a defensive touchdown on an 18-yard interception return, and running back Justin Vincent— who had started the season fifth on the depth chart—set a championship game record with 201 rushing yards to be named the game's most valuable player. "I'd like to see us have the opportunity to play for a national championship," Saban said at the time. "I think our team deserves that. We've taken care of the business we could take care of."

He got his wish.

The Pac-10 didn't have a championship game at the time, so the Trojans just had to beat unranked Oregon State 52–28 to stay in the hunt. The only top 25 team it faced all season was Washington State, which finished the season at No. 9.

Oklahoma, though, which had been hearing about its eventual place in history, had No. 13 Kansas State in the Big 12 title game in Kansas City, and played horribly. Ell Roberson had four touchdown passes, Darren Sproles ran for 235 yards, and the Wildcats won their first conference title since 1934 (when it was in the Big Six). "I'm not going to sit here and lobby for any bowl," Oklahoma coach Bob Stoops said. "We just got whipped. They outplayed us in every part of the game."

Nevertheless, the results brought chaos to the BCS, as there were three quality one-loss teams and just two spots in the championship game, which was to be played at the Sugar Bowl in New Orleans. On paper, Oklahoma had the only loss against a ranked team, while LSU was 4–0 against top 25 opponents. "If we had not lost that one game, we wouldn't have the problem we have right now," Saban said. "We believe in the system and we will live with the system. It's probably not a perfect system. Until we have a playoff, which I've never been in favor of, we'll probably never know who the best teams are."

One by one the polls came out the next day, with the Associated Press and the coaches both voting Southern California and LSU Nos. 1 and 2. However, the computers, which counted for one-third of the formula, flipped the order, with Oklahoma first, LSU second, and Southern California getting No. 4 Michigan in the Rose Bowl as a consolation prize.

Naturally, the furor was deafening, especially coming from the West Coast, but the matchup was intriguing on paper, as it featured the nation's best offense against the top defense. While the Sooners had Heisman Trophy quarterback Jason White, the Tigers proved once again that defenses win championships, with the game-winning points fittingly scored on a 20-yard interception return by defensive lineman Marcus Spears. "There's no doubt in my mind we're the best defense in the country," prison guard–turned–defensive tackle Chad Lavalais said after the game. "We made the plays when we needed to all year."

White took a pounding and completed just 13 of 37 passes for 102 yards, with no touchdowns and two interceptions, and the Sooners managed just 52 rushing yards on 33 carries (1.6 average). Coming in, they averaged 45.2 points and 461 yards. "We play in the [Southeastern Conference]," defensive end Marquise Hill said. "We're used to playing smash-mouth football, real football. They weren't just going to come in here and blow it out on us. If they thought that, they were sadly mistaken."

But none of that was what Saban highlighted during his postgame press conference: "They believed in themselves, they believed in each other, and this game was no different than a lot of other games we played this year. We get a punt blocked, they score a touchdown, we take the ball, however many yards, 80 yards for a touchdown to answer the bell. It's happened all year long, that we were able to turn around and do whatever we needed to do. We fumbled a snap on second-and-2 on the 2, and intercepted a pass and [got] it back two plays later. And that's happened time and time again because these guys never, ever…when something goes bad in a game, it means nothing. They have tremendous identity, character, and confidence and know how to compete. And that's how you've got to compete. You've got to overcome adversity. And this might sound like a bunch of BS, but I'm telling you that's why we won the national championship, because [of] the character and ability of these guys and the attitude that they played with, and I'm very, very proud of them."

Meanwhile, the Trojans won at the Rose Bowl 28–14, prompting coach Pete Carroll to proudly proclaim: "I think we just won the national championship," and many of his players to say that they wouldn't watch the Sugar Bowl three days later. To the surprise of no one, Associated Press voters still had Southern California at No. 1 in their final poll, as did the Football Writers Association of America, resulting in a controversial split title. "All I know is the powers that be selected us to be here," LSU quarterback Matt Mauck said. "We just received a trophy. We won the SEC championship. I don't know how you could not consider us the national champions."

"Same for me," Spears added. "This game has been set up like this for a long time. We have been using this system and this is the system we deal with, and we are national champions in our minds because we feel like we deserved it and we earned everything we got."

During the 2013 season, LSU celebrated the 10-year anniversary of Saban's first title. He obviously was not able to attend but sent a video greeting for the players. "We had some great players on that team and really had great team chemistry and character, and a lot of guys worked hard," he said. "The thing that made that team special to me is most of the guys that were recruited on that team came to LSU when we weren't all that great, and they came there sort of with a mission to accomplish something special. I love that team. That's the first team that we ever had that had that kind of success. We really had a lot of good players but great team chemistry."

2003 LSU Tigers

Assistant coaches: Kirk Doll, Derek Dooley, Jimbo Fisher, Stan Hixon, Travis Jones, Will Muschamp, Stacy Searels, Lance Thompson, and Tim Walton. Strength and conditioning coach: Tommy Moffitt

Captains: Chad Lavalais, Matt Mauck, Rodney Reed, and Michael Clayton

Date	Opponent	Location	W/L	Score
August 30	Louisiana-Monroe	at Baton Rouge	W	49–7
September 6	Arizona	at Tucson	W	59–13
September 13	Western Illinois	at Baton Rouge	W	35–7
September 20	Georgia	at Baton Rouge	W	17–10
September 27	Mississippi State	at Starkville	W	41–6
October 11	Florida	at Baton Rouge	L	19–7
October 18	South Carolina	at Columbia	W	33–7
October 25	Auburn	at Baton Rouge	W	31–7
November 1	Louisiana Tech	at Baton Rouge	W	49–10
November 15	Alabama	at Tuscaloosa	W	27–3
November 22	Ole Miss	at Oxford	W	17–14
November 28	Arkansas	at Baton Rouge	W	55–24
December 6	Georgia SEC championship	at Atlanta	W	34–13
January 4	Oklahoma BCS championship	at Sugar Bowl	W	21–14

Record: 13–1; **Total points:** 475–154
Ranking (AP): Preseason No. 14, Postseason No. 2 (No. 1 coaches)

Leaders
Rushing: Justin Vincent (1,001 yards, 154 carries)
Passing: Matt Mauck (229 of 358, 2,825 yards)
Receiving: Michael Clayton (78 catches, 1,079 yards)
Tackles: LaRon Landry (80)
Interceptions: Corey Webster (7)
Sacks: Chad Lavalais (7)

Lineup (National Championship Game)
Offense: Devery Henderson, split end; Andrew Whitworth, left tackle; Nate Livings, left guard; Ben Wilkerson, center; Stephen Peterman, right guard; Rodney Reed, right tackle; Eric Edwards, tight end; Matt Mauck, quarterback; Justin Vincent, running back; David Jones, H-back; and Michael Clayton, flanker.

Defense: Marcus Spears, defensive end; Kyle Williams, defensive tackle; Chad Lavalais, defensive tackle; Marquise Hill, defensive end; Eric Alexander, strong-side linebacker; Lionel Turner, middle linebacker; Cameron Vaughn, weakside linebacker; Corey Webster, cornerback; Travis Daniels, cornerback; Jack Hunt, strong safety; and Dave Peterson, linebacker.

Specialists: Skyler Green/Shyrone Carey, punt returns; Devery Henderson/Skyler Green, kick returns; Donnie Jones, punter; Ryan Gaudet/Chris Jackson, field goals; and Chris Jackson, kickoffs.

Honors
Major awards: Nick Saban, Paul W. "Bear" Bryant Coach of the Year

All-Americans: Chad Lavalais, defensive tackle; Corey Webster, cornerback

All-SEC: Michael Clayton, wide receiver; Chad Lavalais, defensive line; Corey Webster, defensive back. SEC Defensive Player of the Year: Chad Lavalais

2009

In terms of a football season, it was quite an ending.

The setting: the Rose Bowl, where the University of Alabama football program first made a name for itself in the 1920s and won its early national championships.

The opponent: Texas, which the Crimson Tide had never defeated before in eight attempts, including five bowl games.

The prize: much more than a crystal football.

At stake was an end to years of anxiety, wondering if the program's roller-coaster would ever stop, a lot of mediocrity, being two years removed from playing in back-to-back Independence Bowls, and lingering doubt as to whether one of the most storied programs in history would ever be able to reclaim its proud status.

"We back," sophomore running back Mark Ingram Jr. proudly said after the decisive 37–21 victory in the BCS National Championship Game. With five turnovers created by the defense, which also knocked Longhorns senior quarterback Colt McCoy out of the game with a shoulder injury, and both Ingram and freshman running back Trent Richardson tallying more than 100 rushing yards, the Crimson Tide celebrated in the same place where it won its first crown 84 years before in similar fashion against Washington.

But never before had an Alabama or Southeastern Conference team gone 14–0 to win the title, much less beat the previous three national champions along the way. The program's first Heisman Trophy and second Butkus Award (Derrick Thomas, 1988) were nice bonuses.

"I'll tell you what I told the team, that I've never been prouder of a group of guys for their resiliency, their buy-in, their hard work, the blood, sweat, and tears that they put forth to accomplish what they accomplished this season," said Nick Saban, who became the first coach in modern college football history to win national titles at two different schools. "I think most of us don't realize how difficult it is, the togetherness that it takes, the discipline and execution that it takes, and certainly the hard work that these guys did."

For that, Alabama won its 13th title by doing what it does best: playing physically, despite numerous players being limited. For example, Ingram was playing with a foot injury that caused him to miss some practice time and subsequently contributed to his cramping up. Quarterback Greg McElroy was playing through some painful cracked ribs, which combined with the Longhorns' defensive approach helped lead to the Crimson Tide attempting just 11 passes. Middle linebacker Rolando McClain had a digestive ailment that threatened to keep him from playing at all and he still had two IVs before the game and one at halftime.

Alabama also nearly handed the Longhorns six points before the fireworks smoke from the pregame festivities cleared, when the Crimson Tide tried to execute a fake punt at their own 20 only to be intercepted. Yet the subsequent goal-line stand helped set the defensive tone, and the pounding started soon after.

Ingram and Richardson gashed and grinded the nation's No. 1 defense against the run, with Alabama more than doubling in the first half what Texas had allowed per game (62.2 yards). Ingram got it going with carries of eight, nine, and nine yards to set up his first touchdown, a two-yard plunge when he ran into open space behind part-time fullback and full-time All-American nose tackle, Terrence Cody. Richardson took an even more direct route, bursting through the left side on a counter and outracing everyone 49 yards to the end zone midway through the second quarter.

But Alabama wasn't done. After Leigh Tiffin's 26-yard field goal, Texas took a timeout with 15 seconds remaining, with the subsequent shovel pass deflected, bobbled, and snared by defensive end Marcell Dareus, who made a spin move and ran over Texas freshman quarterback Garrett Gilbert en route to the end zone. "My first reaction was [to] grab the ball, and then after that I blanked out," said Dareus, who scored the 28-yard touchdown three seconds before halftime. "All I was thinking about is Mark Ingram and Javier [Arenas] and just doing moves I didn't think I could do."

Although Alabama had scored 24 unanswered points, Texas wasn't ready to concede and was able to pull within three points in the fourth quarter before the Tide got to Gilbert again. A fake blitz left senior linebacker Eryk Anders unblocked, and he caught the quarterback on his blind side to force the ball loose with sophomore linebacker Courtney Upshaw recovering the fumble at the Texas 3. With Ingram punching in the touchdown, and Richardson another, Alabama was again on top of college football. "It is really difficult to express just how proud I am," athletic director Mal Moore said. "This team, these coaches, and in particular Coach Saban, the effort he's put into this program in the three years he's been here, and to reach this level and this peak, and win the national championship, is quite remarkable. I think it's just so fitting that we were honored to play in the Rose Bowl for the national championship and win it here."

Texas outgained Alabama in yardage 276–263, was more successful on third downs, and notched five sacks against a unit that had yielded only 15 all season. None of that mattered. Ingram was named the game's offensive MVP, and Dareus took home the defensive award despite having just the interception and one tackle—when what appeared to be a routine hit ended McCoy's collegiate career. They, along with senior guard Mike Johnson, kissed and cradled the crystal football when it was handed to them on the victory platform.

"I feel like I've played an entire career, it's been one heck of a season," McElroy said. "This team is just so special. I've been a part of a lot of great things. I've been in a lot of football locker rooms, a lot of hockey locker rooms, and things like that, but this team has the heart. That's what it is, willingness to go the extra mile."

A few days later, the 2009 Crimson Tide gathered to celebrate one final time with 38,000 fans at Bryant-Denny Stadium. It featured tributes, speeches, and hardware—a whole lot of hardware—but it was also a final good-bye to more than 20 players. "This team, Coach Saban, and his staff, epitomized what a world-class program should be," university president Dr. Robert E. Witt proclaimed.

Moore also took the time to list many of the team's accomplishments, which took quite a while. He mentioned everything from the 22nd Southeastern Conference title to the record six first-team All-Americans and being the first team in history to beat 10 opponents that had finished with a winning record. They included No. 2 Texas, No. 3 Florida, No. 10 Virginia Tech, No. 17 LSU, and No. 20 Ole Miss, and the Crimson Tide also played South Carolina when it was ranked 22nd.

"It just shows that when you put in so much hard work and effort that things really do pay off for you," Johnson said. "I really honestly feel like we worked harder than any other team this year, and that's why we came out on top."

"What an unbelievable year," Moore said. "Thanks to every one of you and what you've done."

The loudest cheers came, though, when Saban asked for fans to stand and give the team its biggest ovation yet, which they gratefully obliged, but also when he set a new goal: for the Crimson Tide to have the most consistent winning program in the country. "I want everyone here to know this is not the end," Saban said. "This is the beginning."

2009 Alabama Crimson Tide

Assistant coaches: Burton Burns, Curt Cignetti, Bo Davis, Jim McElwain, Joe Pendry, Kirby Smart, Sal Sunseri, Bobby Williams, and James Willis. Strength and conditioning coach: Scott Cochran

Captains: Javier Arenas, Mike Johnson, and Rolando McClain

Date	Opponent	Location	W/L	Score
September 5	Virginia Tech	at Atlanta	W	34–24
September 12	Florida International	at Tuscaloosa	W	40–14
September 19	North Texas	at Tuscaloosa	W	53–7
September 26	Arkansas	at Tuscaloosa	W	35–7
October 3	Kentucky	at Lexington	W	38–20
October 10	Ole Miss	at Oxford	W	22–3
October 17	South Carolina	at Tuscaloosa	W	20–6

October 24	Tennessee	at Tuscaloosa	W	12–10
November 7	LSU	at Tuscaloosa	W	24–15
November 14	Mississippi State	at Starkville	W	31–3
November 21	Chattanooga	at Tuscaloosa	W	45–0
November 27	Auburn	at Auburn	W	26–21
December 5	Florida	at Atlanta	W	32–13
	SEC championship			
January 7	Texas	at Rose Bowl	W	37–21
	BCS championship			

Record: 14–0; Total points: 449–164
Ranking (AP): Preseason No. 5, Postseason No. 1

Leaders
Rushing: Mark Ingram Jr. (1,658 yards, 271 carries)
Passing: Greg McElroy (198 of 325, 2,508 yards)
Receiving: Julio Jones (43 catches, 596 yards)
Tackles: Rolando McClain (105)
Interceptions: Mark Barron (7)
Sacks: Marcell Dareus (6.5)

Regular Lineup
Offense: James Carpenter, left tackle; Mike Johnson, left guard; William Vlachos, center; Barrett Jones, right guard; Drew Davis, right tackle; Colin Peek, tight end; Julio Jones, wide receiver; Marquis Maze, wide receiver; Greg McElroy, quarterback; Preston Dial, H-back; Mark Ingram, running back.

Defense: Lorenzo Washington, defensive end; Terrence Cody, nose tackle; Brandon Deaderick, defensive end; Cory Reamer, linebacker; Rolando McClain, middle linebacker; Nico Johnson, linebacker; Eryk Anders, linebacker; Javier Arenas, cornerback; Mark Barron, safety; Justin Woodall, safety; Kareem Jackson, cornerback.

Specialists: Leigh Tiffin, kicker; P.J. Fitzgerald, punter; Javier Arenas punt/kick returns; Terry Grant, kick returns.

Honors

Major awards: Mark Ingram Jr., Heisman Trophy; Rolando McClain, Butkus Award.

All-Americans: First team—Mark Ingram Jr., running back; Mike Johnson, guard; Terrence Cody, defensive tackle; Rolando McClain, linebacker; Javier Arenas, cornerback/return specialist; and Leigh Tiffin, kicker. Third team—Mark Barron, safety.

Academic All-Americans: Colin Peek, tight end.

All-SEC: Mark Ingram Jr., running back; Mike Johnson, guard; Terrence Cody, defensive tackle; Rolando McClain, linebacker; Javier Arenas, cornerback/return specialist; Mark Barron, safety; and Leigh Tiffin, kicker. SEC Defensive MVP: Rolando McClain. SEC Special Teams MVP: Javier Arenas.

Heisman Trophy Voting

Player	School	Position	Votes
1. Mark Ingram Jr.	Alabama	RB	1,304
2. Toby Gerhart	Stanford	RB	1,276
3. Colt McCoy	Texas	QB	1,145
4. Ndamukong Suh	Nebraska	DT	815
5. Tim Tebow	Florida	QB	390

2011

When it comes to Nick Saban's third national championship, second with the Crimson Tide, there are two things that can't be avoided or overlooked. The first is Alabama's ability to overcome adversity, and we're not talking about sustaining a loss, the disappointment of the previous season, or dealing with the kinds of things that usually come up in a competitive environment. Instead, the team got an overdose of tragedy during the months building up to the 2011 season.

Mere days after the annual A-Day scrimmage in April and the unveiling of Saban's statue along the Walk of Champions for winning the 2009 national title, a series of horrific tornados struck the state, including one that went through the heart of Tuscaloosa. Then in May, reserve offensive lineman Aaron Douglas was found dead on a balcony the morning after attending a party in Jacksonville,

Florida; he was 21. The Nassau County Medical Examiner's Office eventually ruled the death an accident.

Despite all that and a 9–6 overtime loss to LSU at Bryant-Denny Stadium on November 5, Alabama managed to reach the BCS National Championship Game without playing for its own conference title.

The other thing the 2011 Crimson Tide will always be remembered for is its unbelievable defense. Although running back Trent Richardson was a Heisman Trophy finalist who set the Alabama single-season rushing record, and after moving from right guard to left tackle Barrett Jones became the third player in program history to win the Outland Trophy (college football's best interior lineman), the defense led the nation in nearly every statistical category. "I love competitors," Saban said. "I think that there's a lot of talent on this defensive team, but I tell you what, these guys are great competitors and they're warriors, and sometimes they can't practice very well all week, and I get mad at them. But, man, when they go to play, they play hard. They play well together. And they have a lot of pride in their performance, in what they do, and they've done it extremely well. Statistically, they've done it better than probably any group we've ever had."

He added, "You throw the ball out, they're going to go get it, because they are a hateful bunch and they are as competitive as you can ever imagine, and I think that's probably why they played really well in big games."

None was bigger than the rematch with LSU in New Orleans, where the Alabama defense dominated for a 21–0 victory and the only shutout in any BCS bowl. Led by the game's defensive MVP Courtney Upshaw, who had seven tackles and a sack, Alabama finished with a 21–5 edge in first downs, 69–44 in plays, and 384–92 in total yards. LSU's longest possession went just 23 yards, and the team's biggest play was for 19. They went three-and-out six times, with an interception by linebacker C.J. Mosley on the second play of a possession, and converted just two third-down opportunities.

LSU crossed the 50-yard line only once and then promptly went backward and fumbled away the ball. In comparison, Alabama failed to cross midfield only twice, one of which resulted in a punt from the 46, as it chiseled away its 14th national title. "I've never coached a team that was more determined, more dedicated to overcoming adversity than this group of guys," Saban said after getting another Gatorade treatment. "I've never seen a more dominant performance than what they did in the national championship game against LSU."

Meanwhile, with first-year starter AJ McCarron passing a lot on first down, he became the first sophomore quarterback to lead his team to victory in the BCS title game and was named its offensive MVP. "We knew coming into the game somebody else had to step up, and Coach just gave me an opportunity," said McCarron, who completed 23 of 34 attempts for 234 yards and had no turnovers. "I don't think I did anything special."

He was the only one.

"Tonight, he was on a whole other level; he actually blew me away," center William Vlachos said. "He talked to us at halftime, he talked to us at pregame, he's on the stage getting offensive MVP. The guy is unbelievable."

Nick Saban and his Alabama team celebrate the 21–0 victory against LSU to win the national title on January 9, 2012.

After making five field goals, with 4:36 remaining Alabama scored the one and only touchdown between the two teams in eight-plus quarters, when Richardson recorded his 21st rushing score of the season by bouncing outside on a 34-yard run. "That was probably the most fun touchdown I've ever scored," Jones said. "Two games of frustration, of not finding the end zone. Just to seal the deal, that was a great feeling."

In addition to the program winning its second crystal football in three years, Richardson captured the program's first Doak Walker Award (best running back), Jones collected the ACA Sportsmanship Award and Wuerffel Trophy, and Alabama was also presented with the Disney Spirit Award that annually goes to college football's most inspirational player, team, or figure. "It's awesome," Carson Tinker said between hugs from well-wishers and pieces of crimson and white confetti falling to the floor of the Mercedes-Benz Superdome. "There are no words that can describe this. Just a lot of work paid off. Everyone here faced some kind of adversity, and just to see how they all came out of that is a great thing."

But that didn't keep the Crimson Tide from relishing the finality of the moment and all it had accomplished. For example, after playing in his final game for Alabama, Vlachos refused to let go of the game ball, even in the locker room, while offensive coordinator Jim McElwain walked arm-in-arm with his family off the field and subsequently stepped into his new job as the head coach at Colorado State.

Everyone else headed back to Tuscaloosa, where the rebuilding continued, but another crown jewel would be prominently displayed, and a championship like none other celebrated. "It means a lot, we went through a lot this season, last year," Richardson said. "The tornado, we lost a teammate, it was big for our team. We needed this here, and we're glad to bring it back to Tuscaloosa and try and bring hope and faith back to our town. That accomplishment is big. You dream of stuff like that…[and] when stuff like that happens, it's incredible. That tells you about the program we have here and the kind of program we built here, and we're still building. We're not done yet."

2011 Alabama Crimson Tide

Assistant coaches: Burton Burns, Mike Groh, Jim McElwain, Jeremy Pruitt, Chris Rumph, Kirby Smart, Jeff Stoutland, Sal Sunseri, and Bobby Williams. Strength and conditioning coach: Scott Cochran

Captains: Mark Barron, Dont'a Hightower, and Trent Richardson

Date	Opponent	Location	W/L	Score
September 3	Kent State	at Tuscaloosa	W	48–7
September 10	Penn State	at State College	W	27–11
September 17	North Texas	at Tuscaloosa	W	41–0
September 24	Arkansas	at Tuscaloosa	W	38–14
October 1	Florida	at Gainesville	W	38–10
October 8	Vanderbilt	at Tuscaloosa	W	34–0
October 15	Ole Miss	at Oxford	W	52–7
October 22	Tennessee	at Tuscaloosa	W	37–6
November 5	LSU	at Tuscaloosa	L	9–6 OT
November 12	Mississippi State	at Starkville	W	24–7
November 19	Georgia Southern	at Tuscaloosa	W	45–21
November 26	Auburn	at Auburn	W	42–14
January 9	LSU	at New Orleans	W	21–0
	BCS championship			

Record: 12–1; Total points: 453–106
Ranking (AP): Preseason No. 2, Postseason No. 1.

Leaders
Rushing: Trent Richardson (1,679 yards, 283 carries)
Passing: AJ McCarron (219 of 328, 2,634 yards)
Receiving: Marquis Maze (56 catches, 627 yards)
Tackles: Dont'a Hightower (85)
Interceptions: Dee Milliner (3)
Sacks: Courtney Upshaw (9.5)

Regular Lineup

Offense: Barrett Jones, left tackle; Chance Warmack, left guard; William Vlachos, center; Anthony Steen/Alfred McCullough, right guard; D.J. Fluker, right tackle; Michael Williams, tight end; Marquis Maze, wide receiver; Darius Hanks, wide receiver; AJ McCarron, quarterback; Brad Smelley, H-back; Trent Richardson, running back.

Defense: Jesse Williams, defensive end; Josh Chapman, nose tackle; Damion Square, defensive end; Jerrell Harris, linebacker; Dont'a Hightower, middle linebacker; Nico Johnson/C.J. Mosley, linebacker; Courtney Upshaw, linebacker; Dre Kirkpatrick, cornerback; Mark Barron, safety; Robert Lester, safety; DeQuan Menzie, cornerback; Dee Milliner, nickel back.

Specialists: Cade Foster/Jeremy Shelley, kicker; Cody Mandell, punter; Marquis Maze, punt/kick returns; Carson Tinker, long-snapper.

Honors

Major awards: Trent Richardson, Doak Walker Award; Barrett Jones, Outland Trophy and Wuerffel Trophy.

All-Americans: First team—Mark Barron, safety; Dont'a Hightower, linebacker; Barrett Jones, offensive lineman; Dre Kirkpatrick, cornerback; DeQuan Menzie, cornerback; Trent Richardson, running back; Courtney Upshaw, linebacker. Second team—William Vlachos, center.

Academic All-American: Barrett Jones.

All-SEC: Mark Barron, safety; Dont'a Hightower, linebacker; Barrett Jones, offensive lineman; Dre Kirkpatrick, cornerback; DeQuan Menzie, cornerback; Trent Richardson, running back; Courtney Upshaw, linebacker; and William Vlachos, center. SEC Offensive Player of the Year: Trent Richardson. Jacobs Award: Barrett Jones.

Heisman Trophy Voting

Player	School	Position	Votes
1. Robert Griffin III	Baylor	QB	1,687
2. Andrew Luck	Stanford	QB	1,407
3. Trent Richardson	Alabama	RB	978
4. Montee Ball	Wisconsin	RB	348
5. Tyrann Mathieu	LSU	DB	327

2012

After the crystal football was awarded and the confetti cleared, all there was left to do was reflect, analyze, and put some perspective on what had happened.

That included even the Gatorade bath, which once again Nick Saban didn't see coming. "It's cold, it's sticky, but I appreciated not getting hit in the head with the bucket," he said. "That was an improvement. I really pride myself in being able to anticipate what's coming next, you know, anticipate what the next problem in the organization is, anticipate what we need to solve, what we need to focus on, what we need to work on, and I've never been able to anticipate the Gatorade coming. I don't know what's up with that."

Replay showed that when the team captains made their move, the player shielding them was none other than massive right tackle D.J. Fluker, giving the coach absolutely no chance. He had the final laugh on everyone else, though, by adding another ring to his already impressive collection, and told reporters, "I just put them on the coffee table for the recruits to look at."

With the 42–14 victory over Notre Dame in the BCS National Championship Game in Miami, Alabama became college football's first back-to-back consensus national champion since Nebraska in 1994–95, as well as the first school to win three national titles in the BCS era—never mind in four years. Outside of the Cornhuskers you had to go all the way back to the Fighting Irish in the late 1940s to find a comparison, and those Irish teams didn't play postseason games, or Minnesota, in the 1930s.

It was the Southeastern Conference's seventh straight championship, continuing an incredible run that's unprecedented in the sport, while Saban went from being the first coach to lift the crystal trophy a third time to enjoying the fourth (three at Alabama). In the modern era of the game, only Bear Bryant had won more national titles with six, five consensus. "Thank God he's on our side," athletic director Mal Moore said about Saban during the celebratory parade on campus, which fittingly concluded at the steps of Bryant-Denny Stadium and the Walk of Champions.

"I hope people really appreciate what this team has accomplished," Saban said. "To repeat and win back-to-back championships is maybe one of the most difficult things in sports, in any sport, for any team to do. Many times they say it's toughest to win your first championship, but really it's tougher to win the next one, because every day when you try and repeat and win the next championship, it's a test of your will to just be the best that you can be."

Saban credited the back-to-back titles as being the team's legacy, especially with there only being nine scholarship seniors on the roster. The Crimson Tide seniors went 49–5 during their careers, with two Southeastern Conference titles, four straight bowl wins, and three national championships. "We always seemed to be our best at crucial situations, and most importantly, we saved our best for last," team cocaptain Barrett Jones said. "We finished strong."

Alabama was especially known for its offensive line and ground game because, for the first time, the Crimson Tide had two 1,000-yard rushers with Eddie Lacy and T.J. Yeldon. Amari Cooper became the first freshman to record 1,000 receiving yards while also setting the program record for touchdown receptions, and quarterback AJ McCarron led the nation in passing efficiency thanks to having 30 touchdown passes and just three interceptions.

Outside of dominating Notre Dame, three games especially stood out:

1. LSU
Ten months after Les Miles called Alabama vs. LSU "big-boy football," it finally was, if not more. With a record crowd at Tiger Stadium that was so frenzied it literally shook the press box after the home team took a fourth-quarter lead, Alabama left fans on both sides stunned and lost for words after it capped a last-minute 72-yard drive for an incredible 21–17 victory.

Even a hoarse Saban said that Yeldon's 28-yard screen reception for the game-winning touchdown was something that he'll never forget.

"Those guys played their hearts out," Jones said, and he was talking about the other team.

2. Texas A&M
Just a week after barely surviving against LSU, a tired Crimson Tide team had numerous mistakes and missed opportunities, including a 20–0 deficit, three costly turnovers, and a potential game-winning drive that was stopped just two yards short of the end zone.

Johnny Manziel, who went on to win the Heisman Trophy, had 345 yards of total offense while senior wide receiver Ryan Swope grabbed 11 passes for 111 yards to pace the Aggies' quick-attack offense. McCarron nearly matched him by completing 21 of 34 passes for 309 yards but had his first two interceptions of the season.

Although the Aggies' 29–24 victory was arguably as big as any in that program's illustrious history, it very nearly derailed Alabama's run at another national championship and would have had the Crimson Tide not gotten some help from other teams pulling off upsets.

3. Georgia

Perhaps the best SEC Championship Game ever played came down to just five yards. That, after traveling almost the length of the field in less than a minute, was the distance Georgia was from the end zone when time ran out on its title dreams as Alabama pulled out a gut-wrenching 32–28 victory.

The game was hard-hitting, emotional, and had four lead changes in the second half. The Crimson Tide carved up the Bulldogs for 350 rushing yards, of which Lacy had 181 on 20 carries and scored two touchdowns to be named game MVP, and Yeldon tallied 153 yards on 25 carries.

Yet it still went down to the very last snap when, instead of spiking the ball to stop the clock and set up something, Georgia coaches watched helplessly when flanker Chris Conley caught a pass tipped by linebacker C.J. Mosley short of the end zone, killing any chance of the Bulldogs running another play.

Overall, it was the Crimson Tide's 15th national title. "This train is not stopping at all," senior defensive end Damion Square said. "They're just reloading. They're going to be even better next year."

The 2012 Crimson Tide

Assistant coaches: Burton Burns, Mike Groh, Doug Nussmeier, Jeremy Pruitt, Chris Rumph, Kirby Smart, Jeff Stoutland, Lance Thompson, and Bobby Williams. Strength and conditioning coach: Scott Cochran.

Captains: Barrett Jones, Damion Square, and Chance Warmack

Date	Opponent	Location	W/L	Score
September 1	Michigan Cowboys Classic	at Arlington	W	41–14
September 8	Western Kentucky	at Tuscaloosa	W	35–0

September 15	Arkansas	at Fayetteville	W	52–0
September 22	Florida Atlantic	at Tuscaloosa	W	40–7
September 29	Ole Miss	at Tuscaloosa	W	33–14
October 13	Missouri	at Columbia	W	42–10
October 20	Tennessee	at Knoxville	W	44–13
October 27	Mississippi State	at Tuscaloosa	W	38–7
November 3	LSU	at Baton Rouge	W	21–17
November 10	Texas A&M	at Tuscaloosa	L	29–24
November 17	Western Carolina	at Tuscaloosa	W	49–0
November 24	Auburn	at Tuscaloosa	W	49–0
December 1	Georgia SEC championship	at Atlanta	W	32–28
January 7	Notre Dame BCS championship	at Miami	W	42–14

Record: 13–1; Total points: 542–153
Ranking (AP): Preseason No. 2, Postseason No. 1.

Leaders
Rushing: Eddie Lacy (1,322 yards, 204 carries)
Passing: AJ McCarron (211 of 314, 2,933 yards)
Receiving: Amari Cooper (59 catches, 1,000 yards)
Tackles: C.J. Mosley (107)
Interceptions: Ha Ha Clinton-Dix (5)
Sacks: Adrian Hubbard (7)

Regular Lineup
Offense: Cyrus Kouandjio, left tackle; Chance Warmack, left guard; Barrett Jones, center; Anthony Steen, right guard; D.J. Fluker, right tackle; Michael Williams, tight end; Amari Cooper, wide receiver; Kevin Norwood, wide receiver; Christion Jones, wide receiver; AJ McCarron, quarterback; Eddie Lacy, running back.

Defense: Jesse Williams, nose tackle; Damion Square, defensive end; Ed Stinson, defensive end; Adrian Hubbard, linebacker; Nico Johnson/C.J. Mosley, weakside linebacker; Trey DePriest, middle linebacker; Xzavier Dickson, linebacker; Dee Milliner, cornerback; Robert Lester, safety; Ha Ha Clinton-Dix, safety; Deion Belue, cornerback.

Specialists: Cade Foster/Jeremy Shelley, kicker; Cody Mandell, punter; Christion Jones/Cyrus Jones, punt/kick returns; Carson Tinker, long-snapper

Honors

Major awards: Barrett Jones, William V. Campbell Trophy and Rimington Trophy.

All-American: Barrett Jones, center; Dee Milliner, cornerback; C.J. Mosley, linebacker; Chance Warmack, offensive lineman.

All-SEC: Chance Warmack, offensive lineman; D.J. Fluker, offensive line; Barrett Jones, center; Eddie Lacy, running back; C.J. Mosley, linebacker; Dee Milliner, cornerback.

★ ★ ★

How They Stack Up, Part II: Dynasties

While there's no doubt that Alabama has emerged to be college football's latest dynasty, and its place in history is already assured, what people can continue to debate is when Nick Saban's Crimson Tide achieved the distinction.

Was it after Alabama won the 2011 national championship, giving it two titles in three years and four straight 10-win seasons? Perhaps it was when Alabama edged No. 3 Georgia in the 2012 Southeastern Conference title game, guaranteeing another appearance in the BCS championship, where No. 1 Notre Dame awaited? How about when the Crimson Tide scored 69 unanswered points over seven-plus BCS championship quarters, stemming from the fourth quarter against Texas and concluding during the second half of Alabama's 42–14 dismantling of the Fighting Irish?

It caused ABC/ESPN announcer Brent Musburger to say in the spring of 2013: "Getting in the game is the first part of the challenge, and that in and of itself is not easy, so I have not seen a run like this. USC had a very strong run under Pete Carroll, but then they lost the championship game eventually to Texas in that great game in Pasadena. So I think in this particular era…it's very hard to compare eras for me, but in this particular era, I don't think there's a dynasty like this one. This is remarkable."

Saban's three championships at Alabama also came over just a six-year period, during which the Crimson Tide didn't just rise to the top of the college football world but was threatening to leave the stratosphere, while Saban essentially banned use of the *D* word around the football facilities.

Even though Alabama clearly is one, there are dynasties and there are *dynasties*, the likes of which may never be seen again on this continent. Teams like:

- The 1960s Green Bay Packers, who won five championships in seven years, including Super Bowls I and II.
- The New York Yankees from 1949 to 1964 won nine World Series and 14 pennants.
- The Boston Celtics from 1959 to 1966 captured eight straight NBA titles, and 16 from 1957 to 1986.
- The Montreal Canadiens won five straight Stanley Cups from 1956–60 and four straight from 1976–79.

In college sports John Wooden at UCLA won 10 NCAA basketball championships from 1964 to 1975.

For the most part, posting those kinds of numbers in college football appears to be pretty unrealistic, especially considering the growth of the sport and the financial stakes involved. John Gagliardi may have gone 489–138–11 at Division II St. John's University, and Larry Kehres went undefeated 21 times in 27 seasons while winning 11 national championships for Division III Mount Union, but at the game's premier level, even winning consecutive consensus titles is rare.

Not surprisingly, the game's most dominating programs all arguably came before the poll era began in 1936:

- **Yale (1874–1909):** The Bulldogs won 19 "titles" before most colleges thought of playing football or had even been founded. The first conference came into existence in 1896 (the Big Ten), and teams played anywhere from one or two games a season to 15-plus.
- **Michigan (1901–05):** Under the direction of Fielding Yost, his "Point-a-Minute" squads went 55–1–1, and outscored their opponents by a margin of 2,821–42. His 1901 team also beat Stanford 49–0 in the first postseason

game ever played, what became known as the Rose Bowl. However, the best players and teams were still thought to be in what would become known as the Ivy League. During Yost's 25 seasons in Ann Arbor, the Wolverines claimed six national championships and ten Big Ten conference titles while amassing a 165–29–10 record (.833 winning percentage).

- **Notre Dame (1918–30):** Knute Rockne had a winning percentage of .881 during his 13 seasons, with the Fighting Irish claiming three national championships and having two other non-consensus titles as well. Overall, his teams enjoyed five undefeated seasons, and Rockne won his lone post-season game 27–10 over Stanford in the Rose Bowl at the end of the 1924 season.

Since the advent of the Associated Press college football poll, there have been essentially four different types of dynasties over the years, with some obviously more legitimate than others.

1) **Core dynasties:** a team that dominated for multiple seasons or years.

Army (1944–50): During World War II many of the best athletes enlisted, and transfer rules were waived, which essentially allowed the military institutions to recruit players from colleges. Under the direction of Earl "Red" Blaik, Army had the Heisman Trophy–winning backfield of Glenn Davis and Doc Blanchard while winning consecutive titles in 1944 and 1945 and outscoring opponents 916–81. It finished second in the Associated Press poll in 1946 and 1950.

Florida State (1987–2000): At the height of Bobby Bowden's Hall of Fame career, the Seminoles had 14 straight 10-win seasons and never finished lower than fifth in the final Associated Press poll. During that span, his teams went 152–19–1 and claimed titles in 1993 and 1999.

Penn State (1967–70): Although the Nittany Lions' 31-game undefeated string is impressive, it's considered a bit of a reach to place it with other dynasties because they didn't win a national championship and faced just four ranked opponents during the streak. Coach Joe Paterno won titles in 1982 and 1986, but two of the three teams in between finished unranked.

Southern California (1962–72): John McKay won three national championships equally spaced five years apart and over a 16-year span went 127–40–8 while having six top-five finishes and nine conference titles. When he left to coach the NFL's Tampa Bay Buccaneers, John Robinson took over and kept winning but finished second in the final AP poll four times, including his split (and controversial) title in 1978.

2) **Asterisk dynasties:** influenced by NCAA penalties.

Miami (1983–94): Even though the Hurricanes had three different coaches during their reign—Howard Schnellenberger (1983), Jimmy Johnson (1984–88), and Dennis Erickson (1989–94)—they went 126–19. Schnellenberger laid the groundwork by harnessing the strong recruiting base in South Florida. Johnson put the run into overdrive by going 52–9 over five seasons and playing for two national championships, winning one, while Erickson subsequently captured two titles. However, in 1995 the NCAA charged Miami with lack of institutional control and issued severe sanctions for numerous infractions within the athletic department. The Hurricanes were forced to sit out postseason play for the 1995 season and docked 31 scholarships from 1996 to 1998, but they resurfaced from 2000 to 2003 when they won 34 straight games, had 17 first-round draft picks, and won another title.

Oklahoma (1971–80): Chuck Fairbanks began the run with a pair of No. 2 finishes in 1971–72 to help set up Barry Switzer's back-to-back titles in 1974–75. Combined, the two coaches finished in the top three of the final Associated Press poll eight times during the 10-year period. However, Oklahoma didn't play in a bowl game in 1973 or 1974 due to sanctions, and during the '74 split championship, its toughest opponent was No. 6 Nebraska, which finished 9–3. Switzer also won a national championship in 1985 but resigned in 1989 when the NCAA put Oklahoma back on probation due to numerous scandals.

Southern California (2002–08): After finishing 11–2 in just his second season with the Trojans, Pete Carroll appeared to have pieced together a juggernaut that would rewrite the history books and have an unprecedented collection of Heisman trophies. They arguably won a share of the 2003 national championship, went undefeated to defend the title, and only a shootout loss to Vince Young and Texas in the Rose Bowl kept USC from becoming the first modern program to claim a three-peat. But while the Trojans finished in the top five in each of the subsequent four seasons, in 2010 the NCAA issued heavy penalties, forcing the football team to vacate the final two wins of the 2004 national championship season and all of 2005. The Trojans subsequently gave up their claim on the 2004 title, and running back Reggie Bush was told to return his Heisman Trophy for accepting illegal benefits.

3) True dynasties: programs that can claim three championships over a span of six years or less.

Alabama (1961–66): Paul W. "Bear" Bryant won his first national championship with arguably his most dominant team in 1961. From the December 7, 1963, win against Miami until the January 1, 1968, loss to Texas A&M (and former Junction Boy Gene Stallings) in the Cotton Bowl, the Crimson Tide went 40–3–2. The stretch included back-to-back national championships followed by the undefeated 1966 season, when the polls snubbed undefeated Alabama, and for six straight years, it played in either the Orange or Sugar Bowl. However, in 1961 the Crimson Tide faced only one ranked team, No. 9 Arkansas, after already having been named national champions, and the 1964 season ended with a controversial loss to No. 5 Texas in the Orange Bowl (causing the Associated Press to move its final poll to after all bowl games had been played).

Alabama (1971–80): The Crimson Tide had seven 11-win seasons and won eight of nine SEC titles en route to three national championships. However, the 1973 title was the final year the coaches' poll held its final voting before the bowl games, and Alabama lost its Sugar Bowl showdown with Notre Dame, 24–23. After winning the 1978 title, the Crimson Tide repeated and outscored opponents 383–67 to give Bryant his last crown. This dynasty nearly had a three-peat as well with a No. 2 finish in the 1977 polls. (No. 5 Notre Dame leapfrogged the team with a 38–10 victory over No. 1 Texas in the Cotton Bowl while Alabama crushed No. 9 Ohio State 35–6 in the Sugar Bowl.) As a result, after recording college football's best record in the 1960s—85–12–3 (.865 winning percentage)—the Crimson Tide had the most wins in the 1970s: 103–16–1 (.863).

Nebraska (1993–97): Tom Osborne's incredible 25-year coaching run peaked with back-to-back national titles in 1994–95 and the controversial '97 split championship with Michigan. The 1995 Cornhuskers outscored opponents 638–174 and scored at least 41 points against each of the four top 10 teams it faced, including a 62–24 victory against No. 2 Florida in the Fiesta Bowl. Over a four-year stretch, Nebraska scored 2,257 points in 49 games, averaging 46. Thanks to a 42–17 victory against No. 3 Tennessee in the Orange Bowl, Osborne's final game, the coaches' poll voted to leapfrog the Cornhuskers over the Wolverines, which was the only time in history a No. 1 team won its bowl game and subsequently was dropped by voters.

Oklahoma (1948–58): Being a veteran was the secret to Bud Wilkinson's success as he heavily recruited military personnel coming out of World War II, many of whom still had four years of collegiate eligibility remaining. Not only did it give his teams a physical advantage over younger opponents, but almost overnight Oklahoma went from being a mediocre program to national power. After winning 31 straight games from 1948 to 1950, Wilkinson topped that with 47 consecutive wins from 1953 to 1957. Wilkinson won his first title during just his third season, 1950, and won two more in 1955 and 1956, but he didn't face a ranked opponent during the latter season.

4) **Pure dynasties:** programs that can claim three consensus championships over a span of six years or less and at least tied a top-five opponent during each season.

Minnesota (1934–41): Although the legendary run began before the Associated Press poll was created, the Gophers were named national champions by various organizations in 1934, 1935, 1936, 1940, and 1941 (the last three by the AP), all consensus. Coach Bernie Bierman enlisted in the marines in January 1942 to serve during World War II and returned to Minnesota, but only two of his last six teams finished ranked.

Notre Dame (1941–49): Frank Leahy was able to claim a national title in 1943 before serving in the navy during World War II, and when he returned in 1946, the Fighting Irish went 36–0–2 over the next four seasons, posting 12 shutouts over a 38-game span and claiming three more championships. However, two of them are considered among the most controversial in college football history.

The 1946 season featured a marquee matchup with Army at Yankee Stadium with both teams undefeated. Six times Army had the ball inside the Notre Dame 30-yard line, only to be rebuffed, with the Fighting Irish crossing midfield three times, as the game ended in a 0–0 tie. Army remained at No. 1 and beat No. 5 Penn 34–7 the following week, but after Notre Dame topped No. 16 Southern

California 26–6 to close the season, the Irish narrowly surpassed Army in the final Associated Press poll.

In 1947 Michigan and Notre Dame switched places three times atop the Associated Press rankings, and at the conclusion of the regular season both teams were 9–0. They had two common opponents, Pittsburgh and Northwestern. The Fighting Irish won 40–6 and 26–19, respectively, while the Wolverines also beat both teams, in the same order, 69–0 and 49–21. In the final poll, Notre Dame was listed first, and its season was complete because for 44 years (1925–68) the school rejected all bowl invitations.

Michigan, however, had no such policy, and Fritz Crisler's team agreed to play No. 3 Southern California (7–1–1) in the Rose Bowl. The game was a slaughter, with the Wolverines celebrating a crushing 49–0 victory, at that point the worst loss in USC history.

Due to the outcry, on January 6, 1948, the Associated Press held a special non-binding postseason poll that had "1. Michigan, 2. Notre Dame," by a vote total of 226–119, only it didn't supersede the final regular-season poll. Thus many consider Notre Dame, which earlier in the season defeated Southern California 38–7, the official national champion and Michigan the consensus national champion.

Alabama (2009–12): Under Saban, the Crimson Tide became the first program to join this illustrious club in 60-plus years. It's also the only program during the sport's modern era to win three clear, concise championships with no split consideration or significant controversy.

Even though there was some talk about Alabama's path to the 2012 national championship and how the Crimson Tide faced Auburn, Arkansas, and Tennessee all on down years, when it was all said and done, Alabama still ended up playing three top-five-ranked teams.

By defeating No. 5 LSU, No. 3 Georgia, and No. 1 Notre Dame, the 2012 Crimson Tide became one of just 12 national championship teams to face that many since the creation of the Associated Press poll in 1936. It's also the only time one of Saban's title teams had to face that many, while each had to play at least five ranked opponents during the course of the respective seasons.

Nevertheless, not all championships are created equal, and with the advent of the Bowl Championship Series on top of a 12-game regular seasons and conference title games, there have been progressively more marquee matchups. The last

Quarterback AJ McCarron barks out the play during Alabama's 42–14 drubbing of Notre Dame, which gave Nick Saban his fourth national championship.

time a consensus national champion didn't have to face any top-five opponents was Georgia in 1980. The only time one didn't have to face any ranked teams at all was Oklahoma in 1956.

To gauge how much tougher it's become, the following is every consensus national champion during the poll era, along with the number of ranked opponents each faced, and those ranked in the top five of the AP poll. (Note: from 1962 to 1967 the poll only ranked 10 teams.) Previous to when the Bowl Championship Series began in 1998, the team atop the AP poll is listed, with one exception: 1947.

Year	Coach	Team	Ranked Opponents	Top Five
2013	Jimbo Fisher	Florida State	5	2
2012	Nick Saban	Alabama	6	3
2011	Nick Saban	Alabama	5	2
2010	Gene Chizik	Auburn	6	1
2009	Nick Saban	Alabama	6	2
2008	Urban Meyer	Florida	6	3
2007	Les Miles	LSU	8	1
2006	Urban Meyer	Florida	5	1
2005	Mack Brown	Texas	4	2
2004	Pete Carroll	USC (vacated)	3	1
2003	Nick Saban	LSU	5	2
2002	Jim Tressel	Ohio State	5	1
2001	Larry Coker	Miami	5	1
2000	Bob Stoops	Oklahoma	6	3
1999	Bobby Bowden	Florida State	5	2
1998	Phillip Fulmer	Tennessee	6	2
1997	Lloyd Carr	Michigan	7	2
1996	Steve Spurrier	Florida	6	3
1995	Tom Osborne	Nebraska	4	1
1994	Tom Osborne	Nebraska	5	2
1993	Bobby Bowden	Florida State	7	3
1992	Gene Stallings	Alabama	4	1
1991	Dennis Erickson	Miami	4	1
1990	Bill McCartney	Colorado	7	2
1989	Dennis Erickson	Miami	4	1
1988	Lou Holtz	Notre Dame	4	3
1987	Jimmy Johnson	Miami	6	2
1986	Joe Paterno	Penn State	2	2
1985	Barry Switzer	Oklahoma	4	2
1984	LaVell Edwards	Brigham Young	1	1
1983	Howard Schnellenberger	Miami	3	1
1982	Joe Paterno	Penn State	6	4

1981	Danny Ford	Clemson	3	2
1980	Vince Dooley	Georgia	3	0
1979	Paul W. "Bear" Bryant	Alabama	3	0
1978	Paul W. "Bear" Bryant	Alabama	5	1
1977	Dan Devine	Notre Dame	4	2
1976	Johnny Majors	Pittsburgh	3	1
1975	Barry Switzer	Oklahoma	7	3
1974	Barry Switzer	Oklahoma	2	0
1973	Ara Parseghian	Notre Dame	3	1
1972	John McKay	USC	6	2
1971	Bob Devaney	Nebraska	3	2
1970	Bob Devaney	Nebraska	4	2
1969	Darrell Royal	Texas	3	1
1968	Woody Hayes	Ohio State	4	3
1967	John McKay	USC	3	3
1966	Ara Parseghian	Notre Dame	4	1
1965	Paul W. "Bear" Bryant	Alabama	1	1
1964	Paul W. "Bear" Bryant	Alabama	4	1
1963	Darrell Royal	Texas	2	2
1962	John McKay	USC	3	1
1961	Paul W. "Bear" Bryant	Alabama	1	0
1960	Murray Warmath	Minnesota	3	2
1959	Ben Schwartzwalder	Syracuse	3	1
1958	Paul Dietzel	LSU	2	0
1957	Shug Jordan	Auburn	3	0
1956	Bud Wilkinson	Oklahoma	0	0
1955	Bud Wilkinson	Oklahoma	3	1
1954	Woody Hayes	Ohio State	6	1
1953	Jim Tatum	Maryland	3	1
1952	Biggie Munn	Michigan State	3	0
1951	Bob Neyland	Tennessee	3	1
1950	Bud Wilkinson	Oklahoma	4	2
1949	Frank Leahy	Notre Dame	3	1
1948	Bennie Oosterbaan	Michigan	4	1

1947	Fritz Crisler	Michigan	3	1
1946	Frank Leahy	Notre Dame	3	1
1945	Red Blaik	Army	5	2
1944	Red Blaik	Army	2	2
1943	Frank Leahy	Notre Dame	5	4
1942	Paul Brown	Ohio State	3	1
1941	Bernie Bierman	Minnesota	2	1
1940	Bernie Bierman	Minnesota	3	1
1939	Homer Norton	Texas A&M	2	1
1938	Dutch Meyer	Texas Christian	1	0
1937	Jock Sutherland	Pittsburgh	4	0
1936	Bernie Bierman	Minnesota	2	2

Here's the decade-by-decade breakdown:

Decade	Ranked Opponents	Top Five	Ratio
2010s (X)	22	8	5.5/2.0
2000s	53	17	5.3/1.7
1990s	55	19	5.5/1.9
1980s	36	18	3.6/1.8
1970s	40	14	4.0/1.4
1960s	28	15	2.8/1.5
1950s	30	7	3.0/0.7
1940s	33	15	3.3/1.5
1930s (Y)	9	3	2.25/.75

X-through 2013; Y-just four years

Consequently, one could make the argument that Saban's Crimson Tide is already the greatest dynasty in college football history, especially when you factor in the different eras and quality of the game today. Alabama's 2012 senior class finished with 49 wins, tying the 1997 Cornhuskers (49–2) for the most ever, and if you included the 2008 season when Alabama was a Tim Tebow rally away from playing for that title as well, it had 60 over a five-year period, one more than 1993–97 Nebraska for the most ever (the previous SEC record was 58 by Florida, in 2005–09).

During Alabama's three titles over four seasons, the Crimson Tide played in six postseason games, four bowls, and two Southeastern Conference championships. Three of those opponents were ranked No. 1, while the others were No. 2, No. 3, and No. 9, and they had a combined record of 72–2. Alabama outscored them 213–82 for an average outcome of 35.5–12.5. The Crimson Tide faced 24 ranked opponents, of which 11 were in the top 10, contributing to the SEC's unparalleled run of seven straight national titles.

In comparison, when the Fighting Irish won three titles between 1946 and 1949, it didn't play in a conference title game or even a bowl.

Regardless, should Alabama and Saban win another championship, say before 2016, there will be no argument that he's led the greatest dynasty that college football has ever seen.

★ ★ ★

The Mount Rushmore of College Football: Knute Rockne

★ ★ ★ ★ ★ ★ ★

"There are a lot of guys who can draw up defenses in the dirt and draw X's and O's. The question is, what little things can you find to help each player play his position? That's one thing Nick is good at."
—Baltimore Ravens defensive coordinator Dean Pees, a former assistant coach for Nick Saban

He coached only 13 years at Notre Dame, but Knute Rockne left the legacy of a lifetime. Actually, Rockne's influence on college football started to be felt before he became a coach, when he was a player.

Born in Norway, his family moved to the Chicago area, and after high school he took a job as a mail dispatcher with the Chicago post office for four years until he had enough money to enroll at Notre Dame. Rockne continued to work during the summer and in 1913 he and his roommate, quarterback Gus Dorais, were janitors and busboys for a beachfront hotel in Cedar Point, Ohio. During their downtime they worked on a new weapon that had been legalized in 1906: the forward pass.

Their pass patterns and timing routes caught Army by surprise for a 35–13 victory to key an undefeated season.

But that was nothing like what was to come, with Rockne's coaching prowess possibly only exceeded by his abilities as a showman and motivator. His "Notre Dame shift," a quick, pre-snap movement by his backfield, was so successful that it was banned (and is why only one player can go in motion).

After graduating with a degree in pharmacy, Rockne was hired as an assistant coach at Notre Dame and continued to play on the side through the 1917 season with the Akron Indians and Massillon Tigers. When Jesse Harper stepped down after five seasons as head coach, with a 34–5–1 record and 86.3 winning percentage, Rockne was promoted. It was a tough act to follow, but he got through a 3–1–2 rookie season shortened by World War I and came back to go 9–0 in 1919.

One of his star players that year was George Gipp, perhaps the greatest player in Notre Dame history. The halfback is still high on the school's all-time rushing list with 2,341 yards, and he also passed for 1,769 yards, scored 156 points, and punted and returned kicks. But most people know him from Rockne's inspirational "Win just one for the Gipper" speech in 1928, even through Gipp had died from strep throat and pneumonia in 1920.

Rockne considered the 1924 national champions his favorite team. Notre Dame outscored the opposition 258–44 during its nine-game regular season and then crushed Stanford 27–10 in the Rose Bowl. It was the last bowl game the Irish would play for 45 years, but the team was best known for the backfield, including Harry Stuhldreher, Don Miller, Jim Crowley, and Elmer Layden. "I think I sensed that the backfield was a product of destiny," Rockne said. "At times they caused me a certain amount of pain and exasperation, but mainly they brought me great joy."

Here's the more famous quote about the backfield: "Outlined against a blue, gray October sky, the Four Horsemen rode again," Grantland Rice wrote in the *New York Herald-Tribune* on October 19, 1924. "In dramatic lore, they are known as famine, pestilence, destruction and death. Those are only aliases. Their real names at Stuhldreher, Miller, Crowley and Layden."

Nick Saban vs. Knute Rockne

Category	Saban	Rockne
Seasons	18	13
Consensus national titles	4	3
Top five finishes	4	NA
Top 25 finishes	11	NA
Overall record (%)	165–57–1 (74.2%)	105–12–5 (88.1%)
Losing seasons	0	0
Bowl record (%)	8–7 (53.3%)	1–0 (100%)
Conference titles	5	NA
Conference record	101–39–1	NA
Consensus All-Americans	23	11
First-round draft picks (through 2013)	19	NA
Record against ranked teams (%)	51–35 (59.30%)	NA
Record against top 10 teams (%)	27–17 (61.61%)	NA
Ratios/percentages		
National title seasons	One every 4.5 seasons	4.3
Consensus All-Americans	1.28 every season	.85
First-round draft picks (through 2013)	1.12 every season	NA
Average wins vs. ranked teams	2.83 each season	NA
Wins over top 10 teams per year	1.50 every season	NA

The program was at an all-time high when it won back-to-back national championships in 1929 and 1930 with undefeated seasons. The 1929 Fighting Irish, with guard Bert Metzger, helmetless guard Jack Cannon, and quarterback Frank Carideo, played every game on the road with Notre Dame Stadium under construction. Despite Rockne describing his team's prospects as "fair," it finished 9–0 and then successfully defended its title in 1930 (10–0).

Incidentally, the stadium was designed by Rockne and built by the same company that constructed Yankee Stadium, the Osborn Engineering Company of Cleveland. Rockne also served as Notre Dame's athletic director, business manager, ticket distributor, track coach, and equipment manager. He wrote a newspaper column once a week, authored three books (one fiction for young adults), and even "Fighting Irish" became the nickname of Notre Dame during his time there, with university president Rev. Matthew Walsh making it official in 1927 (many had been calling them Rockne's Ramblers, which Walsh didn't especially like).

However, right at the peek of his success, Rockne died in a plane crash at the age of 43. He had a remarkable record of 105–12–5, with the 88.1 winning percentage still the best in Division I college football history.

While celebrities, prominent figures, and even some foreign dignitaries like the King of Norway attended Rockne's funeral on campus, thousands had to be turned away, and it was estimated that more than 100,000 people lined the procession route from Rockne's house to the Cathedral of the Sacred Heart. "It was almost the size of President Kennedy's impact," Layden said of the funeral years later. "It was amazing. They turned out on the train and at the funeral. He was a national hero."

Even humorist and social commentator Will Rogers paid tribute: "Notre Dame was Knute Rockne's address, but every gridiron in America was his home."

Part III

"He's driven. He works very hard. His teams are very disciplined. They're well coached, and he wins at everything he touches. I just think when you see what he does, you just admire the way he handles his business, the way he runs his program."

—Former Texas coach Mack Brown

★ ★ ★

Saban vs. His Peers

Major League Baseball, the National Football League, the National Basketball Association, and the National Hockey League all use the same standard when it comes to their version(s) of immortality, and the same holds true for college football. For an athlete or coach to be considered among the best at something, he or she first has to be considered one who defined and dominated his or her particular era.

It's a common argument that's especially being heard around baseball circles these days in regards to the Hall of Fame—who should be elected or left out. Complicating the matter in baseball has been trying to evaluate those who were part of the steroid era. That's why in 2013 the voting members of the Baseball Writers' Association of America didn't select anyone for the game's highest honor, even though the ballot included the game's home-run king, Barry Bonds, and only seven-time Cy Young winner, Roger Clemens.

Before this deteriorates into a Pete Rose debate, the premise is applicable here for our purposes because before weighing Nick Saban's coaching career against the all-time greats, one must examine if and how he's separated himself from his contemporaries. That's the aim of this part of the book, which focuses on the coaches of the Bowl Championship Series era, so Pete Carroll and Jim Tressel are listed here and not in the subsequent section.

As a reminder, with previous head coaching stops at Toledo (1990), Michigan State (1995–99), and LSU (2000–04), Saban finished the 2013 season with a 165–57–1 record and having never experienced a losing season—although the

NCAA vacated a handful of his wins from 2007 due to playing ineligible players from an inherited situation.

Specifically, Saban's on-the-field record in 2007 was 7–6 (4–4 SEC), until the NCAA ruled Alabama must vacate 21 victories due to sanctions stemming from textbook-related infractions that had began under previous coach Mike Shula and were anything but limited to football. The widespread rule violation was discovered midway through Saban's first season with the Crimson Tide and included 201 student-athletes from 16 sports. Although Saban was the first to act and suspend his players involved, the penalties included three years probation, vacation of records, and a $43,900 fine. The vacated games are not included here.

Saban therefore had a winning percentage of 74.2, and just two of his teams missed playing in a bowl game (one being Toledo after a 9–2 season). The 2000 Citrus Bowl is not included in his bowl record, as Saban had already left Michigan State for LSU. The Spartans still defeated Florida 37–34.

All of the designations for the other coaches are explained at the end of each chart.

Frank Beamer

Although Frank Beamer was first the head coach at Murray State, and from 1981 to 1986 compiled a 43–23–2 record with the then–Division I-AA program, to give an idea of what he's meant to Virginia Tech, consider that the first time the team finished ranked in the Associated Press poll was 1954, and the second time was 1986.

That was the season before Beamer took over for Bill Dooley in 1987. While it took a few years for things to click, he finished the 2013 season leading all active coaches in wins with 266 if you count his years at Football Championship Subdivision Murray State (1981–86) and 224 leading the Hokies.

In 1993 he began an impressive run of postseason games, including regular appearances in the Orange and Sugar Bowls. It peaked over the 1999–2000 seasons, when Virginia Tech went 22–2 and came within a sniff of a national championship.

The game that served notice to the nation that the Hokies were for real was a nationally televised Thursday night contest against Clemson, which Virginia Tech won 31–11. The buzz regarding quarterback Michael Vick only grew louder with

Nick Saban vs. Frank Beamer

Category	Saban	Beamer
Seasons	18	27
Consensus national titles	4	0
Record in BCS title games	4–0	0–1
Record in conference title games	4–1	3–2
Top five finishes	4	1
Top 25 finishes	11	16
Overall record (%)	165–57–1 (74.2%)	224–109–2 (67.2%)
Losing seasons	0	4
Bowl record (%)	8–7 (53.3%)	9–12 (42.9%)
Conference titles	5	7 (Z)
Conference record	101–39–1	119–41
Consensus All-Americans	23	6
First-round draft picks (through 2013)	19	7
Record against ranked teams (%)	51–35 (59.30%)	43–50–1 (46.28%)
Record against top 10 teams (%)	27–17 (61.63%)	7–32 (17.95%)

Record against Saban: 1–3

Ratios/percentages

National title seasons	One every 4.5 seasons	None
Consensus All-Americans	1.28 every season	.22
First-round draft picks (through 2013)	1.12 every season	.27
Average wins vs. ranked teams	2.83 each season	1.59
Wins over top 10 teams per year	1.50 every season	.26

Z-Beamer has four ACC titles (2004, 2007, 2008, 2010), and three Big East (1995, 1996, 1999). He also won one at the Football Championship Subdivision level.

a 62–0 win against No. 16 Syracuse and a 43–10 win vs. powerhouse Miami, ranked 19th. "No one can tell this team any longer that it doesn't belong," Beamer said after a 38–14 victory against Boston College.

At 11–0 the No. 2 Hokies earned a place in the 1999 national championship game and had a 29–28 lead after three quarters but were subsequently outscored 18–0 by No. 1 Florida State in the Sugar Bowl for a 46–29 final score.

Virginia Tech came back to match the 11–1 record in 2000 and was making another title run in 2002 when a 28–21 comeback win by Pittsburgh began a three-game tailspin. When the Atlantic Coast Conference split into divisions after the 2003 season, Tech placed first or second in the Coastal Division and finished ranked each year through 2011.

The first time Beamer and Nick Saban met as head coaches was in 2002, when the host Hokies were ranked 16th and the Tigers 14th, and the game helped define Beamer as being extremely opportunistic. Virginia Tech managed just 231 offensive yards but yielded only 214. A blocked punt, an interception return, and a nice 17-yard punt return at midfield by DeAngelo Hall set up Tech's touchdowns. "If you can play defense and get a few points off your kicking game and let your offense keep getting better, that's a good plan," Beamer said after just his fourth victory against a top 15 team in 25 tries. "We've won a lot of ballgames like that around here."

It was the second game of the season for Tech but the opener for LSU, which subsequently won six straight and eventually managed to tie for the SEC West Division title. Saban didn't make the same mistake again when the teams agreed to open the 2009 season against each other in the neutral-site Chick-fil-A Kickoff Game at the Georgia Dome.

For three-plus hours, the Crimson Tide experienced mostly frustration while making numerous mistakes against the No. 7 Hokies. Then, as if someone flipped a switch, No. 5 Alabama dominated the last 15 minutes to pull out the 34–24 victory. "If we don't kill ourselves, the game isn't close," said former standout running back Shaun Alexander (1996–99), who was sweating out the game with every other Alabama fan at the Georgia Dome. "This team is going to do very, very well. Any time you have a defense like this you have a shot—and a shot is all you want."

What turned things around was a short stretch at the start of the fourth quarter, beginning with a holding penalty by Virginia Tech, nullifying a two-yard carry on third-and-1. Instead, the Hokies punted, and on Alabama's subsequent play, quarterback Greg McElroy, making his first start, executed a play-action and nailed streaking sophomore receiver Marquis Maze down the middle of the field for a 48-yard completion. "That changed the entire momentum of the game," McElroy said.

Running back Mark Ingram Jr. reached the end zone from the 6 on the following snap, and Chris Rogers ripped the ball out and recovered the fumble on the following kickoff (resulting in another field goal). Ingram finished with 150 yards on 26 carries (5.8 average), 64 of which came in the fourth quarter. "It's been a long time since a guy got that many yards against us," Beamer said.

"You have to create six seconds of hell each play, and we did that tonight," said Saban, who went on to win his first national championship at Alabama while Ingram won the program's first Heisman Trophy.

When the teams met again under similar circumstance in 2013, Alabama won 35–10.

Mack Brown

It was simply one of the best and most exciting college football games ever played, highlighted by possibly the biggest play in University of Texas history.

Down by five points with only seconds remaining at the Rose Bowl and the 2005 national championship at stake, the Longhorns had fourth down with five yards to go on the Southern California 8-yard line. All game long the Trojans had struggled to stop quarterback Vince Young, who would finish with 200 rushing yards and 267 passing yards, yet no one knew what to expect.

After taking the snap in shotgun formation, Young bounced on his toes while scanning the field for an open receiver. Finding none he took off toward the right pylon, and on its last offensive play of the season, Texas won the title when the quarterback scored his third touchdown of the game. "Do whatever it takes," Young said after the dramatic 41–38 victory.

With the victory Texas snapped Southern California's 34-game winning streak and deprived the Trojans of a claim on their third straight national championship (one of which has since been vacated). Instead, the Longhorns won their first title since 1970 after developing a reputation for having a powerhouse program with seemingly endless talent that couldn't win big games.

For example, Texas had played in only three Big 12 Championship Games (dating back to 1996) and lost the two times it was ranked before crushing Colorado 70–3 in 2005 to secure its place in Pasadena. "Well, there was a tremendous amount of pressure on them," coach Mack Brown said. "Even though we had not won a national championship for many years, that streak is a difficult thing."

Prior to Brown's arrival, Texas had managed to win 10 games just three times over its previous 15 seasons. During his 16 years, his Longhorns did so nine times, including 11 wins six times. At one point his team finished in the top 15 of the Associated Press poll in 10 straight years.

Previously Brown coached at North Carolina, where the Tar Heels enjoyed a string of eight winning seasons and six straight bowl appearances. His final two seasons, UNC combined to go 20–3 with final rankings of No. 10 and No. 4 in the Associated Press polls. From the 1997 team, three players went in the top 19 picks of the 1998 NFL Draft, defensive end Greg Ellis (No. 8, Dallas Cowboys), linebacker Brian Simmons (No. 17, Cincinnati Bengals), and defensive tackle Vonnie Holliday (No. 19, Green Bay Packers).

Mack Brown and Nick Saban shake hands prior to the 2010 BCS National Championship Game in which Saban's Crimson Tide defeated Brown's Longhorns 37–21. (AP Images)

Nick Saban vs. Mack Brown

	Saban	Brown
Seasons	18	29
Consensus national titles	4	1
Record in BCS title games	4–0	1–1
Record in conference title games	4–1	2–2
Top five finishes	4	5
Top 25 finishes	11	17
Overall record (%)	165–57–1 (74.2%)	238–117–1 (67.0%)
Losing seasons	0	5
Bowl record (%)	8–7 (53.3%)	13–8 (61.9%)
Conference titles	5	2
Conference record	101–39–1	138–68–1
Consensus All-Americans	23	25
First-round draft picks (through 2013)	19	21
Record against ranked teams (%)	51–35 (59.3%)	45–61–1 (42.52%)
Record against top 10 teams (%)	27–17 (61.63%)	11–32 (25.58)

Record against Saban: 1–1

Ratios/percentages

National title seasons	One every 4.5 seasons	.29
Consensus All-Americans	1.28 every season	.86
First-round draft picks (through 2013)	1.12 every season	.73
Average wins vs. ranked teams	2.83 each season	1.55
Wins over top 10 teams per year	1.50 every season	.38

Brown and Nick Saban met twice as head coaches, the first being at the Cotton Bowl at the end of the 2002 season, when Saban was still at LSU. With Roy Williams having 181 total yards and two touchdowns, including 142 receiving yards on just four receptions, Texas pulled out a 35–20 victory.

However, in a key game for both programs, Alabama and Texas met in the 2009 national championship, played at the site where the Crimson Tide won its first titles at the end of the 1925 and 1926 seasons, the Rose Bowl.

Although Greg McElroy was playing with cracked ribs, the story ended up being with the other quarterback, as defensive lineman Marcell Dareus sidelined

Colt McCoy—the NCAA's all-time winningest quarterback who had never missed a game with an injury—with a numb shoulder on what appeared to be a pretty normal hit. Mark Ingram Jr. and Trent Richardson both had 100-yard rushing performances, and Dareus intercepted a shovel pass and returned it 28 yards for a touchdown just before halftime; Alabama won 37–21.

"I told the guys that they had a great run, 17 straight, 26 out of 28," Brown said afterward. "They came into this game, I thought [that] they were prepared. I thought they worked really hard. After Colt got hurt, obviously we were limited in some of the things we could do, and the play before the half they tried to throw a little shovel pass and tried to take a shot in the end zone because we knew points would be hard, that one went against us."

What was surprising, though, was what happened to Texas after that season. The team went 5–7 in 2010, Brown's only losing season with the Longhorns, 8–5 in 2011, and 9–4, and 8–5. Along with the 9–5 finish in 1999, they were the worst seasons he'd had in Austin.

In 2013 athletic director DeLoss Dodds had to quell rumors that Brown might be replaced or that Texas would make a big push to try and hire Saban away from Alabama, telling the *Daily Texan* that stability and continuity were the best course: "If somebody tells me we need to change, I say, 'Okay, but who should we hire? Saban? Well, Saban isn't going to come here.'"

However, before the calendar year ended, Dodds announced that he would retire, and Brown stepped down.

Pete Carroll

Pete Carroll and Nick Saban have never opposed one another as head coaches, but a lot of people wish they had in 2003. For most of that season, Oklahoma was considered the team to beat, the preseason No. 1 selection that rattled off 12 straight wins. Led by quarterback Jason White, it had the nation's top offense while the defense didn't allow a touchdown during its final three games of the regular season.

It just had to beat No. 13 Kansas State in the Big 12 Championship Game to assure a spot in the Sugar Bowl, where it would face either LSU or Southern California for the national championship, but the Wildcats had other ideas and pulled off an impressive 35–7 victory to send the title picture into disarray.

Although the Associated Press poll and the coaches' poll both had Southern California at No. 1 and LSU second, the computers saw it differently, and when the final BCS standings came out, the pairing was Oklahoma vs. LSU, with the Trojans shut out and left to beat up on No. 4 Michigan in the Rose Bowl.

Saban, of course, went on to win his first title as LSU topped Oklahoma 21–14, but it was the only split BCS National Championship as the Associated Press kept USC at No. 1 while LSU took home the crystal football.

However, in the long run that didn't end up defining Carroll's legacy at Southern California. During the "Leave No Doubt" season, the Trojans went undefeated to capture the 2004 national championship. They were poised to claim dynasty status in 2005 by again running the table en route to a No. 1–vs.– No. 2 pairing with Texas in the title game, only to lose one of the most dramatic games in college football history at the Rose Bowl, 41–38 to Texas.

That turned out to be the beginning of USC's troubles, as it finished No. 3 or lower the next three years while major cracks began to manifest themselves in college football's version of the Roman Empire. While the NCAA's investigation of Reggie Bush for receiving illegal benefits gained more momentum and assistant coaches started jumping ship, Stanford coach Jim Harbaugh was quoted in 2007 as saying, "[Pete Carroll will] be there one more year. That's what I've heard. I heard it inside the staff."

Carroll, who in 2008 thumbed his nose even more at the NCAA by hiring more coaches than allowed, left after the 2009 season to take over the Seattle Seahawks. In 2010 the NCAA issued heavy sanctions on the USC athletic program, with the football team forced to vacate the final two wins of the 2004 national championship season and all of 2005. The Trojans gave up their claim on the 2004 title, and Bush was told to return his Heisman Trophy.

"I'm absolutely shocked and disappointed in the findings of the NCAA," Carroll said through the Seahawks, while *Los Angeles Times* columnist Bill Plaschke wrote, "He goes from a coach who presided over the greatest days in USC football history to one who was in charge of its biggest embarrassment. He goes from saint to scallywag. Carroll says he didn't know about the Bush violations. That now seems impossible, given that apparently everyone from here to San Diego knew, including Carroll's loyal running backs coach [Todd] McNair. I will forever believe he went to Seattle because of the money and opportunity

Nick Saban vs. Pete Carroll

Category	Saban	Carroll
Seasons	18	9
Consensus national titles	4	1 (Z)
Record in BCS title games	4–0	0–1 (Z)
Record in conference title games	4–1	NA
Top five finishes	4	7
Top 25 finishes	11	8
Overall record (%)	165–57–1 (74.2%)	83–19 (Z) (81.4%)
Losing seasons	0	0
Bowl record (%)	8–7 (53.3%)	6–2 (Z) (75.0%)
Conference titles	5	5 (Z)
Conference record	101–39–1	53–14 (Z)
Consensus All-Americans	23	17
First-round draft picks (through 2013)	19	14
Record against ranked teams (%)	51–35 (59.3%)	29–9 (Z) (76.3%)
Record against top 10 teams (%)	27–17 (61.63%)	12–4 (Z) (75.0%)

Ratios/percentages

Category	Saban	Carroll
National title seasons	One every 4.5 seasons	9
Consensus All-Americans	1.28 every season	1.89
First-round draft picks (through 2013)	1.12 every season	1.56
Average wins vs. ranked teams	2.83 each season	3.2
Wins over top 10 teams per year	1.50 every season	1.3

Record against Saban: 0–0

Z–Due to NCAA sanctions, two 2004 victories—including the national championship win over Oklahoma—were vacated, along with all 12 wins from 2005. Among them were six wins against ranked teams, two against top 10 opponents.

because Carroll never thought the NCAA could nail the Trojans. Nonetheless, he made $33 million from violations that will cost his old school its reputation, and folks here will never look at him the same."

For purposes of this book, we will consider Carroll's record after the penalties, and there's obviously a sort of asterisk that has to be applied, so readers can judge for themselves.

On one hand, the Trojans had two national titles, three Heisman Trophy winners, seven consecutive Pac-10 championships, and made nine consecutive BCS bowl appearances. That has to be weighed against a two-year bowl suspension, 30 lost scholarships, 14 vacated wins, and both a national title and Heisman subtracted.

Additionally, while Carroll's numbers remain impressive, it has to be noted that while most successful college coaches cut their teeth at smaller schools, Carroll went a different route, which sort of skews his numbers even more. One of the few coaches who served as both an offensive coordinator (Pacific, 1983) and defensive coordinator (North Carolina State, 1980–82) at the collegiate level, he subsequently climbed the ranks in the National Football League and became the head coach of the New York Jets (1994) and New England Patriots (1997–99).

So while Carroll had 14 first-round draft picks with the Trojans, giving him an average of 1.6 per season, consider the following: if you only counted Saban's average at Alabama, his average would shoot up from 1.12 to 2.33 (through the 2013 draft). He also won three national titles during his first six years and averaged 2.71 All-Americans per season, four wins over ranked teams, and 2.3 against top 10 opponents.

Jimbo Fisher

When it comes to rising coaches in college football, there are numerous people worth mentioning.

For example, after helping Gene Chizik win the 2010 national title as Auburn's offensive coordinator, Gus Malzahn left the Plains to become a head coach, only to return a year later as his replacement. During his first two seasons as a head coach at Arkansas Sate and Auburn, Malzahn went 21–5 and led the Tigers all the way to the BCS National Championship Game. Combined, his teams were 6–3 against ranked opponents.

Meanwhile, Chris Petersen went 92–12 over eight years at Boise State, including 8–4 against ranked opponents and 2–0 against top 10 opponents, before he moved on to Washington at the end of the 2013 season. Four of his Broncos teams finished in the top 10 with the 2009 squad fourth as he led Boise State to its first two Bowl Championship Series games.

After a 35–17 record at Houston, including a 12–1 season in 2011, Kevin Sumlin went to Texas A&M and along with Heisman Trophy–winning quarterback Johnny Manziel essentially made the Aggies an instant force in the Southeastern Conference. His teams went 0–2 in the Conference USA Championship Game, and he had an 8–3 record against ranked teams, 2–1 versus top 10 opponents, before going 1–4 and 0–2, respectively, in 2013.

Chip Kelly was 46–7 at Oregon and finished ranked in the top five three of his four seasons before he left for the Philadelphia Eagles in 2013. Former Saban assistant Mark Dantonio led Michigan State to three seasons of 11 or more wins, including a 13–1 No. 3 finish in 2013, and two Big Ten titles. David Shaw was 34–7 during his first three seasons leading Stanford.

But Jimbo Fisher gets the entry here after winning the 2013 national championship. Led by Heisman Trophy winner Jameis Winston, the Seminoles went 14–0 and came back from an 18-point deficit to score a touchdown with 13 seconds remaining to win the title game against Auburn 34–31.

Perhaps it was only fitting that when Nick Saban's attempt to become the first coach in the modern era to win three straight national championships came up short, it was one of his former assistant coaches who came through.

Fisher's coaching career began at his alma mater, Samford (where the former quarterback still holds many passing records), and was Auburn's quarterbacks coach (1993–98) until Terry Bowden resigned. He coached quarterbacks for one season at Cincinnati before joining Nick Saban's staff at LSU in 2000 as offensive coordinator and quarterbacks coach. Together they won the 2003 title, but when Saban left to try his hand in the National Football League, Fisher didn't follow.

Following the 2006 season, Fisher interviewed for the head coaching position at UAB, only to have the board of trustees veto the contract offer, which was probably the best thing that could have happened to him. He subsequently turned down an offer to rejoin Saban at Alabama and instead signed on to be Florida State's "head coach in waiting" behind Bobby Bowden. After three years as offensive coordinator, he took over the Seminoles. "Empowered, confident athletes are winners," he said during his introductory press conference.

After capturing the crystal football, he sat next to his former boss on the ESPN set at the Rose Bowl, and among his comments were: "We have a really great coaching staff." Said staff included defensive coordinator Jeremy Pruitt, whom

Nick Saban vs. Jimbo Fisher

Category	Saban	Fisher
Seasons	18	4
Consensus national titles	4	1
Record in BCS title games	4–0	1–0
Record in conference title games	4–1	2–1
Top five finishes	4	1
Top 25 finishes	11	4
Overall record (%)	165–57–1 (74.2%)	45–10 (81.8%)
Losing seasons	0	0
Bowl record (%)	8–7 (53.3%)	4–0 (100%)
Conference titles	5	2
Conference record	101–39–1	26–6
Consensus All-Americans	23	6
First-round draft picks (through 2013)	19	4
Record against ranked teams (%)	51–35 (59.3%)	9–5 (64.29%)
Record against top 10 teams (%)	27–17 (61.63%)	4–3 (57.14%)

Record against Saban: 0–0

Ratios/percentages

National title seasons	One every 4.5 seasons	4.0
Consensus All-Americans	1.28 every season	1.50
First-round draft picks (through 2013)	1.12 every season	1.33
Average wins vs. ranked teams	2.83 each season	2.25
Wins over top 10 teams per year	1.50 every season	1.00

Saban gave his big break to and was grooming to eventually replace Kirby Smart; defensive ends coach Sal Sunseri, who had been an assistant coach for Saban at both Alabama and LSU; and wide receivers coach Lawrence Dawsey, who had been a Saban graduate assistant at LSU.

"Nick, to me, is a tremendous friend to me, he always has been," Fisher said the next day. "I've learned a lot from him. He's a great guy. He has a great heart. His wife, Terry, she's reached out to me. I talked to her this morning. They were happy. They were very influential in myself and Candi and how we go about our businesses as leaders of an organization. Nick and Terry do it first-class. They're great people. Nick and I talked about this, a couple of old hillbillies from those coalmines that came on and became football coaches. We shared a few moments. Like I say, I have the utmost respect for Nick. I think he's a tremendous coach and a tremendous guy, and he and I will always stay close friends."

Brian Kelly

Even though they had never been on the same coaching staff or opposed each other, Nick Saban and Brian Kelly had been in many of the same coaching circles.

Although Kelly was raised in Massachusetts and his father was a Boston politician, both made their mark in the Midwest with ties to Ohio and head coaching gigs in Michigan. Kelly's first head coaching job was at Division II Grand Valley State, where over 13 years he was 118–35–2, and the Lakers won two national championships, five conference titles, and made six playoff appearances. He was 11–4 in the postseason. "I certainly knew of Coach Kelly when he was at Grand Valley because of the success that he had there and [I] certainly had a lot of respect for that," Saban said before their first meeting, the BCS National Championship Game at the end of the 2012 season. "We never really played each other, but we were in the same state, and I had a tremendous amount of respect for that, and because of that, sort of wherever he's gone, we've sort of followed that path. We have a tremendous amount of respect for his coaching but also the overall organization that he must have to develop successful programs because he's been successful everywhere he's been."

After reaching the Division II Championship Game three straight years, Kelly decided to make the leap into Division I and accepted the job at Central Michigan, which had won more than three games only once over the previous four seasons. The Chippewas went 9–4 in 2006, won the Mid-American title, and were invited to the Motor City Bowl. Kelly accepted the job at Cincinnati before the 31–14 victory against Middle Tennessee State University.

During his three seasons with the Bearcats, their worst season was 10–3, which was even more impressive considering that UC's last 10-win season had been in 1951. The team won its first outright Big East title and appeared in two BCS bowls with the 2009 team finishing No. 4 in the final Associated Press poll after an undefeated regular season.

Nick Saban vs. Brian Kelly

Category	Saban	Kelly
Seasons	18	10
Consensus national championships	4	0
Record in BCS title games	4–0	0–1
Record in conference title games	4–1	1–0
Top five finishes	4	1
Top 25 finishes	11	5
Overall record (%)	165–57–1 (74.2%)	90–37 (70.9%)
Losing seasons	0	1
Bowl record (%)	8–7 (53.3%)	4–3 (57.1%)
Conference titles	5	3 (Z)
Conference record	101–39–1	32–13
Consensus All-Americans	23	3
First-round draft picks (through 2013)	19	3
Record against ranked teams (%)	51–35 (59.30%)	15–11 (57.69%)
Record against top 10 teams (%)	27–17 (61.63%)	2–6 (25.0%)

Record against Saban: 0–1

Ratios/percentages

National title seasons	One every 4.25 seasons	0
Consensus All-Americans	1.28 every season	.30
First-round draft picks (through 2013)	1.12 every season	.44
Average wins vs. ranked teams	2.83 each season	1.50
Wins over top 10 teams per year	1.50 every season	.20

Z-Two Big East titles and one Mid-American Conference title

Once again, though, he was lured away, this time by Notre Dame. In 2012 he led the Fighting Irish to their first undefeated regular season in 24 years (since 1988), and a spot in the BCS title game. Consequently, he became the first two-time winner of the Home Depot Coach of the Year Award (2009, 2012).

However, it wasn't all smooth sailing. A 20-year-old student, Declan Sullivan, died in a practice accident after wind gusts made conditions unsafe for videographers to be in lifts filming practice. Further, there were accusations that the cover-up of a football player being accused of sexual assault helped lead to the victim's suicide. During the 2012 season, reporters were captivated by linebacker Manti Te'o's inspirational play following the death of his grandmother and girl-friend, en route to becoming one of the most decorated players in college football history, only to have it eventually revealed that the girlfriend didn't exist.

Of course, none of those things mattered to Saban when he was preparing to face the Fighting Irish in Miami. "Notre Dame is a very good offensive team," he said. "I think they have a really well-conceived system. I think…I'm sure they'll do some things that are a little different in this game. We have looked at their history of what they've done at Notre Dame, but I think what Coach Kelly does probably as well as anybody that we've played all year is utilize the personnel that he has extremely well, and I think that's why they've been very, very successful."

They weren't on January 7, 2013, as Alabama completely manhandled Notre Dame, 42–14. Coming in, the Fighting Irish hadn't given up long drives, red-zone touchdowns, or rushing scores all season. They also hadn't seen an offensive line like the Crimson Tide's. Alabama had five drives of 70 yards or more, scored touchdowns on all five possessions inside the 20, and notched more rushing touchdowns in the first half (three) than Notre Dame had yielded all season (two). To steal a line from the movie *The Usual Suspects*, Alabama "showed those men of will what will really was."

"We've got to get physically stronger, continue to close the gap there, and just overall you need to see what it looks like," Kelly said afterward. "Our guys clearly know what it looks like. When I say 'know what it looks like,' a championship football team. They're back-to-back national champs. So that's what it looks like. Measure yourself against that, and I think it was pretty clear across the board what we have to do."

Urban Meyer

Nick Saban's departure into the National Football League for the 2005 and 2006 seasons coincided with the arrival of Urban Meyer, who may have immediately replaced him as the toughest coach to beat in the Southeastern Conference.

Meyer had been a fast riser as a head coach, with Bowling Green going from 2–9 to 8–3 his first year. After a combined 17–6 record over two seasons, he headed to Utah. With Alex Smith at quarterback, the Utes became not only the first team from a non-automatically qualifying BCS conference to play in a BCS Bowl, but won, dominating Pittsburgh 35–7 in the Fiesta Bowl.

Following Utah's first perfect season since 1930, however, both Notre Dame and Florida came calling, and to the surprise of some, Meyer chose the Gators and a lucrative seven-year contract that would pay $14 million over one of the places he had been an assistant coach (1996–2000) and had repeatedly called his "dream job." That Meyer also had to deal with former Florida coach Steve Spurrier being in the same division was problematic until he beat out Alabama for the player who would become the face of college football, Tim Tebow.

In 2006 the Gators survived the toughest schedule in the country to win the SEC championship and, thanks to UCLA upsetting Southern California in the regular-season finale, played Ohio State for the national title. Although the Buckeyes scored on the opening kickoff, the Gators crushed them 41–14. "Honestly, we played a lot better teams than them," defensive end Jarvis Moss said. "I could name four or five teams in the SEC that could probably compete with them and play the same type of game we did against them."

Due to the defense being depleted by graduation and departures to the NFL, the Gators stumbled in 2007, losing three games and failing to return to the conference championship, but they were once again considered the team to beat in 2008. A one-point loss led to "the Speech" by Tebow, who promised fans, "You'll never see a team play harder than we will the rest of this season."

Florida went on to crush every subsequent opponent, with the closest score 42–14 at Vanderbilt, until it faced No. 1 Alabama and Saban in the SEC championship. The game went back and forth until Florida finally pulled away in the fourth quarter for a 31–20 victory and went on to beat Oklahoma 24–14 for the national title. "I'm not sure I enjoyed that last one enough," Meyer said. "I'm going to enjoy this one."

The 2009 team looked like it could be even better, and after running the table in the regular season, the rematch in the SEC Championship Game was billed not only as being the exclamation point to Tebow's career, but he was on the doorstep of going down as the greatest player in college football history while Florida became a dynasty. However, Alabama's focus over the off-season was on beating the Gators, and it showed.

Nick Saban vs. Urban Meyer

Category	Saban	Meyer
Seasons	18	12
Consensus national championships	4	2
Record in BCS title games	4–0	2–0
Record in conference title games	4–1	2–2
Top five finishes	4	5
Top 25 finishes	11	9
Overall record (%)	165–57–1 (74.2%)	128–25 (83.7%)
Losing seasons	0	0
Bowl record (%)	8–7 (53.3%)	7–2 (77.8%)
Conference titles	5	4 (Z)
Conference record	101–39–1	76–18
Consensus All-Americans	23	9
First-round draft picks (through 2013)	19	9
Record against ranked teams (%)	51–35 (59.30%)	25–12 (67.57%)
Record against top 10 teams (%)	27–17 (61.63%)	12–5 (70.59%)

Record against Saban: 1–2

Ratios/percentages		
National title seasons	One every 4.5 seasons	6.0
Consensus All-Americans	1.28 every season	.75
First-round draft picks (through 2013)	1.12 every season	.82
Average vs. ranked teams	2.83 each season	2.08
Wins over top 10 teams per year	1.50 every season	1.00

Z-Meyer won two SEC titles and two Mountain West titles.

The Crimson Tide arrived at the Georgia Dome with a mile-wide chip on its collective shoulder and took it out on the Gators in a game that wasn't as close as the 32–13 score indicated. Overall, Alabama pummeled Florida nearly across the board statistically, including first downs (26–13), rushing yards (251–88), time of possession (39:27–20:23), and third-down conversions (11 of 15 vs. 4 of 11). The Tide never trailed, scored on six of its first seven possessions (minus running out the clock before halftime), and pulled up in the fourth quarter.

Tebow's last-gasp pass wound up being intercepted in the end zone by cornerback Javier Arenas, reducing the quarterback to tears on the sideline. Alabama fans refer to it as "Tebow wept."

"He's a great player," said receiver Julio Jones, "but man, we're tired of him."

Mark Ingram Jr. rushed for 113 yards and three touchdowns, and Greg McElroy, who landed at Alabama after it got beaten out for Tebow, threw for 239 yards and a touchdown to claim the MVP award.

Although a great rivalry appeared to be brewing between the coaches, their regular-season rematch in 2010 turned out to be a dud as Alabama easily won at home, 31–6. It was the first of three straight losses for Florida, and after a lackluster 8-4 season, Meyer shocked the college football world by announcing that he was stepping away from coaching due to health concerns and to spend more time with his family.

In six seasons the Gators had won 65 games, two Southeastern Conference championships, and two national titles. But the team also had 31 players arrested from 2005 to 2010—a stigma that would stick with the coach for years.

Meyer ended up working for ESPN for a year and then got back into coaching at Ohio State in 2012. Previously he had called himself an "organizational freak," who had a speed-based spread offense that was particularly difficult to counter, but the real secret of his success wasn't too difficult to figure out. "Back as a player, I was always the hardest-working guy," he said. "I would be so upset with myself if I wasn't. Was I the best? I was average, but I outworked everybody. As a coach, am I the smartest? No. But I believe that in a lot of areas I outwork a lot of guys."

With the Buckeyes ineligible for the postseason due to NCAA penalties, they went 12–0 during Meyer's first season in Columbus and rekindled the idea of another potential postseason matchup with Saban—hoping next time it would be for a national title.

Les Miles

There's no way to deny that Les Miles was in a difficult situation. After taking over for Nick Saban at LSU, he inherited an extremely talented and deep roster and, following his 28–21 stint at Oklahoma State (3–12 against ranked opponents), posted back-to-back 11-win seasons in Baton Rouge when Saban decided to return to the collegiate game at rival Alabama.

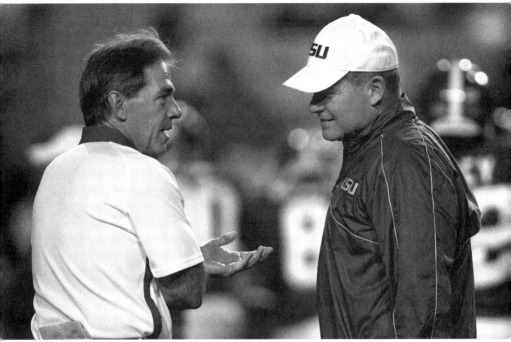

Les Miles, who succeeded Nick Saban at LSU, greets the Alabama coach before Alabama's 21–17 victory against the Tigers on November 3, 2012. (AP Images)

Naturally, that didn't sit too well with the Tigers faithful, who were already comparing everything Miles did to what Saban had done and kept hearing rumors that their coach was about to bolt for his alma mater, Michigan. They loved it, though, when Miles was addressing the Bayou Bash in Baton Rouge after National Signing Day and said, "We're looking forward to playing Florida. We're looking forward to playing Auburn. But we have a new rival in f—ing Alabama!"

He later apologized…to LSU fans…and had a much different take at SEC Media Days a few months later: "We really have enjoyed the accomplishments that Coach had while he was at LSU. He left, went by way of another stop, now is back in the conference. I can tell you that's one game on our schedule, no more than one. I can tell you that we really have not changed anything. There will be no bearing on what we do that's different. We look forward to getting to that game."

Regardless, it was "game on" between the schools, and each meeting was the sport's equivalent of a knock-down-drag-out fight from which both sides needed weeks to recover.

While Saban was busy rebuilding the Crimson Tide in 2007, Miles led the Tigers on a wild season that included two triple-overtime losses—43–37 at No. 17 Kentucky and 50–48 to Arkansas at home—that had LSU ranked fifth heading into the SEC Championship Game.

With Tennessee quarterback Erik Ainge having two passes intercepted in the fourth quarter, LSU won 21–14 and then watched as No. 1 Missouri and No. 2 West Virginia both lost later that night, and No. 4 Georgia was idle after not reaching the SEC title game. The subsequent pairing was LSU vs. Ohio State in New Orleans, where Matt Flynn threw four touchdown passes as LSU scored 31 unanswered points to turn a 10-point deficit into a 38–24 victory. "Certainly there will be some argument as to who's the best team. But I think the national champion has been crowned tonight," Miles said. "I have to give great credit to some divine intervention that allows us to be in this position."

But Saban vs. Miles was just getting started. After LSU scored two touchdowns during the final three minutes to take the first meeting 41–34, Alabama answered a year later by coming out on top in Baton Rouge, 27–21 in overtime. Safety Rashad Johnson tied the Crimson Tide record with three interceptions, and Julio Jones set up the winning touchdown with a 24-yard catch in which he dragged a defender to the 1-yard line. "This one is bitter. It's painful," Miles said during his postgame press conference. "But as a competitor, when you play your tail off, there's a comfort in that."

It got less comfortable for him.

The Saban Bowl

Year	Location	Winning Team	Score
2007	Tuscaloosa	LSU	41–34
2008	Baton Rouge	Alabama	27–21 OT
2009	Tuscaloosa	Alabama	24–15
2010	Baton Rouge	LSU	24–21
2011	Tuscaloosa	LSU	9–6 OT
	New Orleans	Alabama	21–0
2012	Baton Rouge	Alabama	21–17
2013	Tuscaloosa	Alabama	38–17

Nick Saban vs. Les Miles

Category	Saban	Miles
Seasons	18	13
Consensus national championships	4	1
Record in BCS title games	4–0	1–1
Record in conference title games	4–1	2–1
Top five finishes	4	3
Top 25 finishes	11	8
Overall record (%)	165–57–1 (74.2%)	123–45 (73.2%)
Losing seasons	0	1
Bowl record (%)	8–7 (53.3%)	7–5 (58.3%)
Conference titles	5	2
Conference record	101–39–1	68–36
Consensus All-Americans	23	9
First-round draft picks (through 2013)	19	14
Record against ranked teams (%)	51–35 (59.30%)	40–31 (56.33%)
Record against Top 10 teams (%)	27–17 (61.63%)	16–17 (48.48%)

Record against Saban: 3–5

Ratios/percentages		
National title seasons	One every 4.25 seasons	13
Consensus All-Americans	1.28 every season	.69
First-round draft picks (through 2013)	1.12 every season	1.17
Average wins vs. ranked teams	2.83 each season	3.08
Wins over top 10 teams per year	1.50 every season	1.23

In 2009 Jones turned a short gain into a 73-yard touchdown to lead a 24–15 win that clinched the SEC West. Alabama went on to win the national championship. "It was a tough, physical game," Saban said. "Man, those games are fun to be a part of."

The following year the Mad Hatter's gutsy play-call of a reverse on fourth-and-1 helped lead to a 24–21 victory in Baton Rouge, and LSU also won the regular-season meeting in 2011, a No. 1–vs.–No. 2 "Game of the Century" showdown that resulted in a hard-hitting 9–6 win in overtime.

However, Alabama didn't lose again that season and, combined with a couple of key upsets in other games, landed a spot in the BCS National Championship Game for a rematch. Although LSU had defeated eight ranked teams and was being touted as possibly having one of the best teams in college football history, the Tigers didn't cross midfield until there were eight minutes remaining (and then fumbled after being pushed back); they were outgained 348–92. Alabama kicker Jeremy Shelley hit five field goals and Trent Richardson capped the scoring with a 34-yard touchdown run.

"We didn't get it going offensively at all," Miles said. "Defense was on the field a long time. I give credit to our opponent. Great playing. They kept the ball, and it became very difficult to get first downs. And with time, certainly, it spoke to victory for them. I told my team that it should hurt. Quality people. We fight like hell and we finished second. It's…supposed to be painful. And the good news is that there will be more resolve. We've had a nice run here. We won a lot of games. We've got to the back end of the season and won bowl games and won championships, and you cannot enjoy it any more than we have. In the same vein, it was [as] painful as anything we've been through."

Yet as if to add even more salt to the wound, Alabama again came out on top in 2012 back in "Death Valley," this time thanks to a last-minute drive. With quarterback Zach Mettenberger having the best game of his career at that point, completing 24 of 35 for 298 yards, LSU scored its first touchdown in 11 quarters against Alabama. When it scored again, the Crimson Tide trailed in the fourth quarter for the first time since 2010 before the team rallied to win 21–17 at probably the most difficult venue in college football. "I'm really, really pleased with that last drive," Saban said. "That's something I'll never forget."

Mark Richt

Strange but true: the decision that could have had the greatest impact on Mark Richt's coaching career may have been when Nebraska didn't recruit him. Richt was actually born in the Cornhusker State, moved to Colorado when he was seven years old, and later to Boca Raton, Florida, where he became a top quarterback prospect and agreed to play at Miami under Howard Schnellenberger. Richt still has family in Nebraska, who call themselves "CornDawgs" due to the dual allegiances.

"I figured I'd start my first year, be an All-American my second year, win the Heisman Trophy my third year, and then go pro after that," Richt said. Obviously that didn't happen as Richt instead spent most of his college career backing up future NFL Hall of Fame quarterback Jim Kelly, and Bernie Kosar was another teammate.

Instead, he began his coaching career in 1985 as a volunteer quarterbacks coach for Florida State and Bobby Bowden. He ended up leaving twice—1989 to be the offensive coordinator at East Carolina for a season, only to be hired back for the same role with the Seminoles, and 2001 as head coach at Georgia.

Richt won two national championships with Bowden, coached two Heisman Trophy winners in Charlie Ward and Chris Weinke, and the worst final ranking the Seminoles had while he was offensive coordinator was fifth, during his last season.

In 2002 Georgia advanced to play in its first SEC Championship Game, where the team dominated Arkansas 30–3 to win its first conference title in 20 years. As part of the Bowl Championship Series, Georgia was fittingly paired against Florida State in the Sugar Bowl. Running back Musa Smith rushed for 145 yards, cornerback Bruce Thornton returned an interception 71 yards for a touchdown, and Billy Bennett kicked four field goals as the Bulldogs won 26–13. "To beat Florida State is a great feeling, since I have a great respect for the Florida State program," Richt said. "I'm so proud of these kids. They deserve to go out like this."

However, more than 10 years later, it still may have been Richt's biggest win as a head coach. During his first 12 years guiding the Bulldogs, he essentially averaged 10 wins a season (9.8), and Georgia played in a bowl game each and every year. In 2005 Georgia topped Les Miles and LSU in the SEC Championship Game, and in 2007 the team beat Hawaii in one of the most unusual pairings in Sugar Bowl history to finish second in the rankings.

But like with so many others, Nick Saban proved to be quite a nemesis, though Richt does have a pair of wins against him. In 2004 his Bulldogs ended reigning national champion LSU's hopes of repeating with a 45–16 victory, keyed by David Greene throwing five touchdown passes. "This was a curveball to me," Saban said at the time. "When things like this happen, you must dig deep down inside."

Nick Saban vs. Mark Richt

Category	Saban	Richt
Seasons	18	13
Consensus national titles	4	0
Record in BCS title games	4–0	0–0
Record in conference title games	4–1	2–3
Top five finishes	4	3
Top 25 finishes	11	10
Overall record (%)	165–57–1 (74.2%)	126–45 (73.7%)
Losing seasons	0	1
Bowl record (%)	8–7 (53.3%)	8–5 (61.5%)
Conference titles	5	2
Conference record	101–39–1	72–32
Consensus All-Americans	23	8
First-round draft picks (through 2013)	19	11
Record against ranked teams (%)	51–35 (59.30%)	34–31 (52.31%)
Record against top 10 teams (%)	27–17 (61.63%)	11–16 (40.74%)

Record against Saban: 2–3

Ratios/percentages

National title seasons	One every 4.5 seasons	0
Consensus All-Americans	1.28 every season	.62
First-round draft picks (through 2013)	1.12 every season	.92
Average wins vs. ranked teams	2.83 each season	2.62
Wins over top 10 teams per year	1.50 every season	.85

In 2007, Saban's first year at Alabama, Georgia visited Tuscaloosa and barely escaped with a 26–23 overtime victory on a 25-yard touchdown pass from Matthew Stafford to Mikey Henderson. "A game like this makes it all worthwhile," Richt said. "Rings and trophies are nice, but the memories we made tonight are going to last a lifetime."

However, Saban has three much bigger wins against Richt, the first being the 2003 SEC Championship Game. It was the second time the Tigers beat the Bulldogs that season, the first being a close 17–10 result. Justin Vincent ran all over the Bulldogs, setting a championship game record with 201 rushing yards for the 34–13 victory. "There's not much to say," Richt said. "We just got whipped."

In 2008 Georgia hosted Alabama and called for a "black out," with the team wearing special jerseys for the No. 8–at–No. 3 showdown. Strength and conditioning coach Scott Cochran told the Crimson Tide that it meant they were going to a funeral, and he turned out to be right.

With a large contingency of national media on hand, Alabama raced out to a stunning 31–0 lead in the second quarter that made Sanford Stadium as quiet as a morgue—aside from the celebrating Crimson Tide section. Georgia came back to score 30 points in the second half of the 41–30 loss, but the game signaled what was to come with Saban at Alabama. "We just got whipped," Richt said. "There's no excuses, and don't expect any from me."

The really heartbreaking loss, though, came in 2012, again at the SEC Championship Game in Atlanta. In a No. 2–vs.–No. 3 matchup with the winner getting a shot at No. 1 Notre Dame for the national championship, AJ McCarron hit Amari Cooper for a 45-yard touchdown pass with 3:15 to go, and Aaron Murray's last-minute drive got all the way down to the 5-yard line when the clock expired. "It's disappointing," Richt said after the 32–28 classic. "Hurts a lot. I mean, we prepared hard all week, all season, all off-season to get back to the [Georgia] Dome, and to win. And so I mean, we came up short against an outstanding football team. They played well. We played well. Clock ran out. You know, what are you going to do?"

While Alabama went on to win its third national championship in four years, Richt got a sort of homecoming game against Nebraska in the Capital One Bowl, a 45–31 Bulldogs victory that gave Georgia 12 wins for the third time in school history.

Bill Snyder

When Bill Snyder retired as Kansas State's coach in 2005, he was not only the winningest coach of a program that was once described by *Sports Illustrated* as "Futility U," but the school named the stadium after him.

"He is to K-State everything that Dean Smith is to North Carolina," former Kansas State athletic director Tim Weiser said to *USA TODAY*. "He's *the* guy."

But retirement didn't stick, and despite being gone for just three seasons, Snyder still had to rebuild the program again after returning in 2009. "There's no dark tint to it whatsoever," he joked about the difference in his hair the second go-around. "It's kind of that old adage: If you're around it every single day, you don't see the changes; when you're away from it and come back, you see the changes. Well, I see myself every day. Not that I enjoy it, but I see myself every day. If I'm a little different, I'm not sure I know exactly where the difference lies. You know, I feel like I'm basically the same individual. I feel like I'm not approaching this endeavor any differently than I have before. But when you see a difference, let me know so I'll know as well."

When Snyder initially took over the program in 1989, it was about as bad as any in the country. Since 1937 the Wildcats had enjoyed only four winning seasons, compared to 27 with eight losses or more. The highlights had been one conference championship (in 1934), one bowl appearance (a 14–3 loss to Wisconsin in the 1982 Independence Bowl), and linebacker Gary Spani (1974–77), the first Wildcat to be inducted into the College Football Hall of Fame.

Among the major lowlights was a 30-game winless streak—including 27 failed attempts at the program's 300th all-time win—which was still ongoing when Snyder was hired. To put it into further perspective, it took Kansas State 51 seasons (1938–88) to total just 130 wins, while the 12 head coaches prior to Snyder's arrival in Manhattan combined to win just 116 games from 1945 to 1988.

Athletic director Steve Miller told him beforehand that not only was Kansas State "flat on its back," but "You may have heard it's one of the toughest jobs in the country. It's not. It's the toughest." Snyder, who had been the offensive coordinator at Iowa, still took the job and he finished 1–10 that first season. Four years later Kansas State played in the 1993 Copper Bowl and defeated Wyoming 52–17. From 1997 to 2003 the Wildcats won at least 11 games every season except one and finished in the Associated Press top 10 five out of seven seasons.

In 1998 Kansas State defeated Nebraska for the first time in 30 attempts (after being outscored 1,234–337 in the previous 29 losses), and the Wildcats reached No. 1 in the coaches' poll (No. 2 in the Associated Press poll) for the first time in program history. Quarterback Michael Bishop finished second in Heisman

Nick Saban vs. Bill Snyder

Category	Saban	Snyder
Seasons	18	22
Consensus national titles	4	0
Record in BCS title games	4–0	0–0
Record in conference title games	4–1	1–2
Top five finishes	4	0
Top 25 finishes	11	12
Overall record (%)	165–57–1 (74.2%)	178–90–1 (66.4%)
Losing seasons	0	5
Bowl record (%)	8–7 (53.3%)	7–8 (46.7%)
Conference titles	5	2
Conference record	101–39–1	102–69–1
Consensus All-Americans	23	9
First-round draft picks (through 2013)	19	2
Record against ranked teams (%)	51–35 (59.30%)	21–42–1 (33.59%)
Record against top 10 teams (%)	27–17 (61.63%)	4–29 (12.12%)

Record against Saban: 0–0

Ratios/percentages		
National title seasons	One every 4.5 seasons	0
Consensus All-Americans	1.28 every season	0.41
First-round draft picks (through 2013)	1.12 every season	0.10
Average wins vs. ranked teams	2.83 each season	0.95
Wins over top 10 teams per year	1.50 every season	.18

Trophy voting, but the Wildcats blew a 27–12 lead against Texas A&M in the Big 12 Championship Game and subsequently lost 37–34 to Purdue in the Alamo Bowl.

In 2003 Kansas State turned the tables on Oklahoma, which was being praised as potentially the best Sooners team ever. The Wildcats won the Big 12 Championship Game in a 35–7 rout.

To the surprise of no one, Snyder's second run has been as impressive as his first. During his third year back, the Wildcats went 10–3 while finishing second in the Big 12. In 2012 Kansas State tied for the league title and was back in a BCS bowl, where it faced No. 5 Oregon in the Fiesta Bowl.

But *comeback* isn't the word the most fans associate with Snyder, rather it's *family*. When school officials decided to honor him with the stadium name, he insisted it be called Bill Snyder Family Stadium, and the word *family* is always listed among the team's 16 season goals. "Family is the one that is most prevalent," Snyder said about the goals. "You'll see it week in and week out through our fan base."

Steve Spurrier

Steve Spurrier has never really been known for biting his tongue, much to the delight of sportswriters everywhere. Some of his gems over the years include:

"You can't spell Citrus without UT," about rival Tennessee playing the game that became the Capital One Bowl and features the SEC's best division runner-up.

"In 12 years at Florida, I don't think we ever signed a kid from the state of Alabama…Of course, we found out later that the scholarships they were giving out at Alabama were worth a whole lot more than ours."

"But the real tragedy was that 15 hadn't been colored yet," about an Auburn dorm fire in which numerous books were destroyed.

"You know what FSU stands for, don't you? Free Shoes University."

There's nothing in college football like a Spurrier zinger to get under the skin of opposing fans, but his career has been nothing short of stellar, including as a player.

Against visiting Auburn on October 29, 1966, the quarterback essentially assured Florida of its first Heisman Trophy when, facing fourth down in the closing moments, he waved off the kicker to attempt the 40-yard game-winning field goal himself. Spurrier had thrown for 259 yards—and to give you an idea of how times have changed, he finished with 2,012 passing yards that season—and averaged 47 yards a punt. When he cleared the crossbar by about a foot, coach Ray Graves could only smile. Auburn coach Ralph "Shug" Jordan called him "Steve Superior."

As a coach he turned the Gators into a national powerhouse, and over the span of 12 seasons, they won seven SEC titles, one national championship, and finished ranked in the nation's top 10 nine times.

Florida became only one of six schools in major college football history, and one of two in SEC history, to win 100 games during a decade (100–22–1 in the 1990s). The Gators were also the first team in the conference to win at least 10 games in six straight seasons and the third school ever to be ranked for 200 consecutive weeks.

Spurrier even slapped the "Swamp" nickname on Ben Hill Griffin Stadium, saying, "Only Gators can survive a trip to the swamp." Easily one of the loudest stadiums in the country, Florida was 70–5 there under his direction.

Although Spurrier has never won one of the major national Coach of the Year awards, he did become the first Heisman Trophy winner to coach another Heisman winner: Danny Wuerffel in 1996.

"He was a little different," said Tommy Tuberville, who at Ole Miss and Auburn lost his first four games against Spurrier. "He was outspoken. You can be pretty much outspoken when you're kicking everybody's butt like he was."

"If people like you too much, it's probably because they're beating you," Spurrier said.

Despite their impressive résumés, Spurrier and Nick Saban have opposed each other only four times, with Spurrier holding a 3–1 advantage, and sadly have never met with a championship on the line. Saban came up empty his first two years at LSU when Spurrier was still at Florida, 41–9 and 44–15, and they've split their two Alabama–South Carolina meetings.

The Crimson Tide won a pretty sloppy 20–6 game in Tuscaloosa during their 2009 national championship season, but Spurrier's Gamecocks pulled off an emotional 35–21 home victory the following year. While Alabama was playing its third consecutive ranked SEC team and had won 19 straight games, it was South Carolina's first win ever against a No. 1–ranked opponent. "I think that this game was meant to be," said Spurrier, who in the process earned his 107th SEC victory to move into second for the all-time lead behind only Paul W. "Bear" Bryant (159). I gave myself a game ball for that one."

Although both Spurrier and Saban won a national championship before giving the NFL a two-year shot, Spurrier with the Washington Redskins (12–20, 2002–03), their careers have been very different after returning to the SEC.

Spurrier has been solid at South Carolina, going 77–39 from 2005 to 2013, but his team didn't finish ranked in the final Associated Press poll during his first

Nick Saban vs. Steve Spurrier

Category	Saban	Spurrier
Seasons	18	24
Consensus national titles	4	1
Record in BCS title games	4–0	1–1
Record in conference title games	4–1	5–3
Top five finishes	4	7
Top 25 finishes	11	16
Overall record (%)	165–57–1 (74.2%)	219–79–2 (73.3%)
Losing seasons	0	1
Bowl record (%)	8–7 (53.3%)	10–10 (50.0%)
Conference titles	5	7
Conference record	101–39–1	139–52–1
Consensus All-Americans	23	16
First-round draft picks (through 2013)	19	16
Record against ranked teams (%)	51–35 (59.30%)	63–52–1 (54.74%)
Record against top 10 teams (%)	27–17 (61.63%)	26–31–1 (45.69%)

Record against Saban: 3–1

Ratios/percentages

National title seasons	One every 4.5 seasons	24
Consensus All-Americans	1.28 every season	0.67
First-round draft picks (through 2013)	1.12 every season	0.70
Average wins vs. ranked teams	2.83 each season	2.63
Wins over top 10 teams per year	1.50 every season	1.08

five seasons. When the Gamecocks finally broke through and won the Eastern Division in 2010, they lost 56–17 to Auburn in the program's first appearance in the SEC Championship Game.

South Carolina went 11–2 in 2011–13 to post its first back-to-back top 10 finishes in program history, but the Gamecocks have yet to appear in a BCS bowl.

As for Saban…Yeah, you knew it was coming: "He's got a nice little gig going, a little bit like [Kentucky basketball coach John] Calipari," Spurrier told ESPN. com in 2012. "He tells guys, 'Hey, three years from now, you're going to be a first-round pick and go.' If he wants to be the greatest coach or one of the greatest coaches in college football, to me, he has to go somewhere besides Alabama and win because they've always won there at Alabama." (Spurrier, of course, was first a head coach at Duke, where from 1987 to 1989 the Blue Devils went 20–13–1 and won the 1989 Atlantic Coast Conference championship before returning to his alma mater in 1990.)

Four months later, Saban responded with, "LSU wasn't winning when I went there. Michigan State wasn't winning when I went there. Toledo wasn't winning when I went there. And Alabama really wasn't winning when I came here. I guess I gotta go someplace else. I don't know. I think it's great, I love Steve. I'm always anxious to hear what he has to say—it's always funny."

Of course, he couldn't help but needle the "old ball coach" a little himself. "You know, there are other coaches in this league, like Steve Spurrier, who are older than me, that I look up to, that are my mentors, that I really learn a lot from, that I really want to try to be like," Saban said at the next SEC Media Days. "In fact, I was even going to consider wearing a visor on the sidelines this year. I was afraid I'd throw it."

Bob Stoops

Like so many others in the coaching profession, Bob Stoops grew up with football, and it's never left his life. His father was a high school coach at Cardinal Mooney High School in Youngstown, Ohio, where he and his three brothers all played, and his own path included being a defensive back at Iowa, an assistant coach at Kent State, and defensive coordinator for Bill Snyder and Steve Spurrier.

"It is something that I've always enjoyed, without ever having it forced upon me," Stoops said. "It's something that we would always ask our dad: 'Can I go, can I go, can I go?' And he always said yes and he threw us in the car and [drove] up to practice, and we would spend the entire day up there. So when it comes time when you're a junior or senior in college, and you're figuring out—my degree is in marketing and business—and you start envisioning what you are going to do with your life, to me [being] with some company [and] sitting behind a desk and working a business job didn't fire me up a whole lot.

Nick Saban vs. Bob Stoops

Category	Saban	Stoops
Seasons	18	15
Consensus national titles	4	1
Record in BCS title games	4–0	1–3
Record in conference title games	4–1	7–1
Top five finishes	4	5
Top 25 finishes	11	13
Overall record (%)	165–57–1 (74.2%)	160–39 (80.4%)
Losing seasons	0	0
Bowl record (%)	8–7 (53.3%)	8–7 (53.3%)
Conference titles	5	8
Conference record	101–39–1	99–24
Consensus All-Americans	23	23
First-round draft picks (through 2013)	19	13
Record against ranked teams (%)	51–35 (59.30%)	50–23 (68.49%)
Record against top 10 teams (%)	27–17 (61.63%)	18–13 (58.06%)

Record against Saban: 1–1

Ratios/percentages

National title seasons	One every 4.5 seasons	15
Consensus All-Americans	1.28 every season	1.53
First-round draft picks (through 2013)	1.12 every season	0.93
Average wins vs. ranked teams	2.83 each season	3.33
Wins over top 10 teams per year	1.50 every season	1.20

"I look out every day. I loved practice, even as a player, I loved the X's and O's, strategies of the game, and I loved the excitement and challenge and the competition. And that…you know, that pretty much convinced me, and I started to realize, 'Hey, I need to stick around football,' and I'm fortunate that Hayden Fry and Bill Frazier was my defensive coordinator and defensive back field coach at Iowa, wanted me as a graduate assistant and really was a guy who's been a big influence on my coaching and defense. [I] really learned a great deal from Bill Frazier."

Following his impressive success at Kansas State and Florida, other programs tried to lure Stoops away, including Minnesota, but he held out for the right coaching job to come along and was rewarded by Oklahoma in 1999.

The turnaround was swift, going 7–5 the first season with the Sooners and making their first bowl appearance in five years. The next year Oklahoma ran the table in the regular season and edged Kansas State in the Big 12 Championship Game 27–24 for a spot in the Orange Bowl to face Florida State for the national championship.

The Sooners had already defeated two top-five teams, but with Florida State making its third straight appearance in the title game, the Seminoles were considered at least 12-point favorites. With Oklahoma able to turn it into a defensive struggle, it pulled out a 13–2 victory. "There was never a day where we were just happy to be here," Stoops said. "We wanted to win this football game and we fully expected to. There was no hoping about it. We expected to win this game. I think now it is easy to say that Oklahoma is officially back."

But getting back to that point has been more than difficult.

Over the next 10 years Oklahoma played in seven BCS bowls and three national championship games, but Stoops still only had the one crystal football.

In 2003 Oklahoma got to face LSU in the Sugar Bowl for the national championship, even though it lost the Big 12 title game 35–7 to Kansas State. While Associated Press voters had Southern California at No. 1, the computers that helped compose the BCS standings flipped the top three teams, resulting in the controversial pairing and leaving the Trojans out.

LSU blitzed the daylights out of the Sooners, who led the nation in scoring by averaging 45.2 points, but managed just 102 passing yards and 52 rushing yards in the 21–14 loss. "Sometimes it just, you know, it doesn't work out, and another team plays better, another coach coaches better than me and all of us, and that's what happens," Stoops said.

That coach, of course, was Nick Saban, who won his first national title. "You don't really want to know what I'm thinking," Saban said during the postgame press conference, "What I'm thinking is, 'How are we going to get this done next year?' Because this year's accomplishments are next year's expectations. Dealing with success and all that kind of stuff." He then compared his emotions to that of winning a high school state championship back in West Virginia and added, "So I'm going to be proud for a long time about this."

In 2004 Oklahoma came up short 55–19 against Southern California in a game that was also the first meeting between Heisman Trophy winners Matt Leinart and Jason White.

"I think they're great, and they sure proved it," Stoops said. "We just got whupped."

The 2008 team went 12–1 before running into Florida in the BCS National Championship Game, which was billed as a showdown between Tim Tebow and Sam Bradford. Although Tebow had a career-high two interceptions, he led the offense to the clinching score, jumping and throwing a four-yard touchdown pass to David Nelson with 3:07 remaining for the 24–14 victory. "In the end, I'll be glad to try again next year," Stoops said. "If that's the biggest burden I have to bear in my life, I'm a pretty lucky guy."

Jim Tressel

The story, at least the way Jim Tressel tells it, is that after he won his first national championship, the coach was asked before even leaving the field if he could do it again. His response was, "I'm going to keep the tradition alive."

It was 1991, and Tressel was at Youngstown State, which defeated Marshall to capture the Division I-AA title. He became part of the only father-son pair to win national championships at the collegiate level, as Lee Tressel—Jim's father—coached Baldwin Wallace University in Berea, Ohio, when it won the Division III championship in 1978.

He did win two more national championships over the next three years with Youngstown State, defeating Marshall again in 1993 and Boise State in 1994. His fourth I-AA title came in 1997 with a 10–9 victory against McNeese State before moving on to Columbus after the 2001 season.

"I can assure you that you will be proud of your young people in the classroom, in the community, and most especially in 310 days in Ann Arbor, Michigan, on the football field," Tressel said after being introduced to fans at an Ohio State basketball game. The Buckeyes did dominate the rivalry during Tressel's tenure, only losing once, and played for the BCS title in just his second season, when they faced juggernaut Miami in the Fiesta Bowl. The reigning champion Hurricanes had won 34 straight games, while Ohio State was trying to win its first championship in the same number of years: 34.

The game lived up to expectations, but the electric finish more than exceeded them. Tied at 17 the game went to overtime, and Miami scored on a seven-yard touchdown pass from Ken Dorsey to tight end Kellen Winslow Jr. to put the pressure on Ohio State. OSU converted a fourth-and-14 to stay in the game but then faced fourth-and-3 at the 5 when quarterback Craig Krenzel threw to the right corner of the end zone for Chris Gamble, who was being covered by Glenn Sharpe.

Gamble got his hands on the ball but couldn't complete the catch, which seemed to end the game, but moments later as Miami players and fans began racing onto the field in celebration, field judge Terry Porter threw a flag from the back of the end zone. "He was holding me," Gamble said afterward. "He was in my face mask and my shoulder pads. I was waiting for the flag, but he kind of hesitated. I didn't see him going for the flag, and I thought, *He ain't going to throw it.* Luckily, he did, and I'm like, 'Whew.'"

Armed with a first down, Krenzel scored from the 1 to send the game into a second overtime, when Maurice Clarett ran in a five-yard touchdown. Miami, which had been playing without running back Willis McGahee, saw Dorsey get drilled by linebacker Matt Wilhelm, which sidelined the quarterback for a play. He returned, but on fourth-and-goal at the 1, he threw up a desperation ball that was batted down to end the game for real. "Miami played their hearts out," Tressel said. "That's what the national championship should look like, double overtime."

Tressel got two more shots at the national title, in 2006 and 2007, but lost to Florida and LSU, respectively, as the Southeastern Conference started to put a vice grip on the championship.

In 2006 the Buckeyes were undefeated and considered seven-point favorites, and they opened the BCS National Championship Game with a 93-yard kick return for a touchdown by Ted Ginn Jr. However, the rest of the game belonged to Florida, which cruised to a 41–14 victory. "We scored on the first play of the game and from that point on really couldn't keep the pressure where we needed it to be," Tressel said. "Ohio State didn't get it done."

Nick Saban vs. Jim Tressel

Category	Saban	Tressel
Seasons	18	10
Consensus national titles	4	1
Record in BCS title games	4–0	1–2
Record in conference title games	4–1	NA
Top five finishes	4	7
Top 25 finishes	11	9
Overall record (%)	165–57–1 (74.2%)	94–21* (81.7%)
Losing seasons	0	0*
Bowl record (%)	8–7 (53.3%)	5–4* (55.6%)
Conference titles	5	6
Conference record	101–39–1	59–14
Consensus All-Americans	23	14
First-round draft picks (through 2013)	19	14
Record against ranked teams (%)	51–35 (59.3%)	31–15* (67.39%)
Record against top 10 teams (%)	27–17 (61.63%)	9–8* (52.94%)

Record against Saban: 0–0

Ratios/percentages

National title seasons	One every 4.5 seasons	10
Consensus All-Americans	1.28 every season	1.40
First-round draft picks (through 2013)	1.12 every season	1.40
Average wins vs. ranked teams	2.83 each season	3.1
Wins over top 10 teams per year	1.50 every season	.90

*Ohio State vacated all 12 wins from 2010, including the Sugar Bowl win against Arkansas, due to ineligible players. The Buckeyes were 3–1 against ranked teams and 1–0 against top 10 teams.

The Buckeyes did a little better a year later against LSU, but with the same result. Ohio State jumped out to a 10–0 lead and promptly gave up 24 unanswered points before halftime. With Matt Flynn having four touchdown passes, the Tigers won 38–24.

"We just didn't do the things you need to do to win a ballgame of this nature," Tressel said. "We're very aware that LSU's a deserving champion."

Tressel had top 10 teams in each of the three subsequent seasons, giving the Buckeyes eight appearances in BCS bowls over a span of nine years, only to see everything collapse after reports began to surface that the Department of Justice had informed the coach a number of his players, including quarterback Terrelle Pryor, had been trading team memorabilia for tattoos or cash at a local parlor—the owner of which was under investigation by the FBI for drug trafficking.

Yahoo! Sports broke the story in March 2011, and as the scandal unfolded, Tressel was initially suspended for two games, and the school was fined $250,000. Then the suspension was increased to five games. Finally, after *Sports Illustrated* reported that it had found evidence the memorabilia-for-tattoos scandal dated back to at least the 2002 national championship season, and as many as 28 players were involved, Tressel was asked for his resignation on Memorial Day.

The NCAA determined that eight players, including Pryor, were involved, receiving some $14,000 in cash and tattoos, but Tressel's dismissal was primarily due to his failing to report the transgressions after he found out and essentially covering it up.

But it also wasn't the lone issue.

SI's investigation uncovered additional allegations, including that Tressel had potentially broken NCAA rules when he was a Buckeyes assistant coach in the mid-1980s. Also, in 1998 former Youngstown State quarterback Ray Isaac admitted to accepting extensive benefits from Mickey Monus, founder of Phar-Mor and former chairman of the school's board of trustees. Youngstown State admitted to a lack of institutional control but was also allowed to keep its 1991 title since the NCAA's statute of limitations had already expired.

In 2003 the NCAA investigated and concluded that running back Maurice Clarett received improper benefits while in school, but the organization never sanctioned Tressel or Ohio State.

★ ★ ★
How They Stack Up, Part III: All-Americans and the NFL Draft

When Casper Whitney named the first All-American team in 1889, in his *This Week's Sports*, it included 11 players from three different Ivy League schools: Harvard, Yale, and Princeton. Among them were both the player who is credited as being the first professional football player, William "Pudge" Heffelfinger, and an end who would become one of the most legendary coaches in American sports: Amos Alonzo Stagg.

Stagg had been a standout at Yale and went on to coach Chicago from 1892 to 1932 and the University of the Pacific from 1933 to 1946. Chicago won seven Big Ten titles between 1899 and 1924, which has been topped by only four coaches in the league's illustrious history: Woody Hayes (13), Bo Schembechler (13), Fielding Yost (10), and Henry Williams (eight).

Nowadays to be considered a consensus All-American selection, a player has to be named first-team by the majority of the services the NCAA uses for determining unanimous status: the American Football Coaches Association, Walter Camp Foundation, Associated Press, Football Writers Association of America, and *Sporting News*.

Through Saban's first seven seasons at Alabama, the Crimson Tide had 17 players named consensus All-American, with two repeating, for an average of 2.7 per season. Overall, he's had 23 consensus All-Americans, for an average of 1.27 per season.

Total All-Americans, Active Coaches
Nick Saban 23
Bob Stoops 23
Steve Spurrier 16
Urban Meyer 9
Les Miles 9
Bill Snyder 9
Mark Richt 8
Frank Beamer 6
Brian Kelly 3

Over the length of their head coaching careers, here's how it averages out per season:
Bob Stoops 1.53
Nick Saban 1.28
Urban Meyer .75
Les Miles .69
Steve Spurrier .67
Mark Richt .62
Bill Snyder .41
Brian Kelly .30
Frank Beamer .22

Incidentally, Jim Tressel had 14 consensus All-Americans during his 10 years at Ohio State (1.4 average), and Pete Carroll had 17 consensus All-Americans at Southern California (also a 1.4 average) before their programs were hit hard by NCAA penalties.

Of course, while most successful college coaches cut their teeth at smaller schools, like Tressel, Carroll went a different route, first becoming a head coach in the NFL, where he's returned to lead the Seattle Seahawks. Meanwhile, Stoops has had only one head coaching job, at Oklahoma.

Going back to Stagg, you may have wondered how many consensus All-American players he had during his 56 years as a head coach when he compiled an incredible record of 314–199–35. The answer is 10, which averaged out to .17 per season.

Total Consensus All-Americans, Retired Coaches (Minimum 15 Years)

Joe Paterno 33
Bobby Bowden 31
Tom Osborne 30
Barry Switzer 28
Woody Hayes 26
Mack Brown 25
Bo Schembechler 25
Paul W. "Bear" Bryant 23
Frank Leahy 23
Ara Parseghian 23
Pop Warner 23
Lou Holtz 21
Howard Jones 21
John McKay 19
Earl Blaik 16
Bud Wilkinson 15
Bob Devaney 14
Darrell Royal 14
Bernie Bierman 13
Knute Rockne 11
Amos Alonzo Stagg 10
Shug Jordan 9
Bob Neyland 9
Wallace Wade 3

Their averages:
Frank Leahy 1.77
Barry Switzer 1.75
Tom Osborne 1.20
John McKay 1.19
Ara Parseghian .96
Bo Schembechler .93
Bob Devaney .88
Bud Wilkinson .88
Woody Hayes .87
Mack Brown .86
Knute Rockne .85
Bobby Bowden .78
Howard Jones .75
Joe Paterno .72
Earl Blaik .64
Lou Holtz .64
Paul W. "Bear" Bryant .61
Darrell Royal .61
Bernie Bierman .54
Pop Warner .52
Bob Neyland .43
Shug Jordan .36
Amos Alonzo Stagg .17
Wallace Wade .13

At his current pace at Alabama, Saban will surpass Paterno's total of 33 in 2017, but Leahy's career average probably isn't within reach.

Saban has had 23 consensus All-Americans, and entering the 2014 NFL Draft, he'd had 19 players selected in the first round. And that doesn't include the seven former players selected in the first round within three years after he left LSU and Michigan State. On face value the explanation seems simple, that the best players in the nation should correspond to those being selected first for the NFL.

It also makes sense that the coach who recruits the most talent would have the most draft picks, though Saban's staff has been highly proficient at developing players as well. For example, defensive lineman Marcell Dareus, who went on to be the third overall selection of the 2011 NFL Draft, was considered a three-star recruit. So was guard Chance Warmack, the 10th overall pick in 2013. Alabama's impressive list of consensus All-Americans also doesn't include the likes of wide receiver Julio Jones, a five-star prospect who was the sixth overall selection in the 2011 NFL Draft, or tackle D.J. Fluker, who went 11th in 2013. "I think that anybody who comes out of Coach Saban's program is a little ahead of the curve because of how he develops his players physically, mentally, and as men," Heisman Trophy winner Mark Ingram Jr. said.

A number of high-profile coaches had similar ratios between consensus All-Americans and first-round draft selections. Woody Hayes had 26 of both, Joe Paterno 33, and Bobby Bowden 31. Lou Holtz had 21. John McKay had 19 consensus All-Americans and 18 first-round draft selections, while Paul W. "Bear" Bryant had 23 and 19, respectively.

However, for every coach with similar numbers, there's another in which they're not close. Nebraska's Bob Devaney had 14 consensus All-Americans but just seven first-round selections, and his replacement, Tom Osborne, had 30 and 21. Frank Leahy had 23 consensus All-Americans compared to just 16 first-rounders. Similarly, Darrell Royal's numbers were 14 and seven, Barry Switzer was 28 and 16, Bo Schembechler was 25 and 16, and Bud Wilkinson 15 and nine, respectively.

From 2009 to 2013, Alabama led all teams with 14 first-round selections after not having any between 2000 (Chris Samuels and Shaun Alexander) and 2009 (Andre Smith), and no draft picks at all in 2008.

First-Round Draft Selections, Active Coaches (through 2013)

Nick Saban 19
Steve Spurrier 16
Les Miles 14
Bob Stoops 13
Mark Richt 11
Urban Meyer 9

Frank Beamer 7
Brian Kelly 3
Bill Snyder 2

Average First-Round Draft Selections (Per Season), Active Coaches
Les Miles 1.17
Nick Saban 1.12
Bob Stoops .93
Mark Richt .92
Urban Meyer .82
Steve Spurrier .70
Brian Kelly .44
Frank Beamer .27
Bill Snyder .10

Carroll had 14 first-round draft picks, giving him an average of 1.6 per season, and Tressel had 14 for a 1.4 average. As a reminder, Saban's average at Alabama was 2.33 heading into the 2014 NFL Draft

First-Round Draft Picks, All-Time (Minimum 15 Years)
Joe Paterno 33
Bobby Bowden 32
Woody Hayes 27
Mack Brown 21
Lou Holtz 21
Tom Osborne 21
Paul W. "Bear" Bryant 19
Nick Saban 19
John McKay 18
Frank Leahy 16
Steve Spurrier 16
Barry Switzer 16
Ara Parseghian 14
Bo Schembechler 14

Bob Stoops 13
Bud Wilkinson 9
Shug Jordan 8
Bob Devaney 7
Darrell Royal 7

Their career averages per season:
John McKay 1.13
Nick Saban 1.12
Barry Switzer 1.00
Woody Hayes .90
Bob Stoops .92
Tom Osborne .84
Bobby Bowden .80
Mack Brown .75
Joe Paterno .72
Steve Spurrier .70
Earl Blaik .64
Lou Holtz .64
Ara Parseghian .58
Bud Wilkinson .53
Bo Schembechler .52
Paul W. "Bear" Bryant .50
Bob Devaney .38
Shug Jordan .32
Darrell Royal .30

★ ★ ★

The Mount Rushmore of College Football: Bobby Bowden

★ ★ ★ ★ ★ ★ ★

"I always wished I had an opportunity to work with him. Maybe I could have learned something."

—Former Florida State coach Bobby Bowden

One of the most memorable phone calls that Nick Saban ever received was shortly after his father died in 1973, when he was a graduate assistant at Kent State. "This is Bobby Bowden," said the voice on the other end, from West Virginia, located roughly 25 minutes away from where Saban grew up. The Mountaineers' football coach had known Saban's father, knew that his mother was having a bit of a tough time, and offered more than just condolences. "If you need to come home, if you want to be a coach, I'll create a graduate assistant position for you so you can do what you need to and be around your mother," Saban recalled Bowden saying.

It's a story that both have told numerous times, including 37 years later when Saban won the inaugural Bobby Bowden Coach of the Year Award, and two of the subsequent three. "His rise in coaching is just unsurpassed," Bowden said.

That's coming from someone who enjoyed a meteoritic progression of his own. Bowden's first head coaching job was at South Georgia Junior College (1956–58), which led to a four-year stint at Howard, now known as Samford University (31–6, 1959–62), and then West Virginia (42–26, 1970–75).

Meanwhile, Florida State, which until the late 1940s was a women's school, didn't start playing football until 1947, when Ed Williamson was appointed the first coach weeks before the inaugural season, and there was no stadium, scholarships, budgeted salaries, or nickname. The program wasn't ranked in an Associated Press poll until 1964, when it lasted two weeks at No. 10 until a 20–11 loss at Virginia Tech. It occurred during Bill Peterson's reign, when from 1960 to 1970 the Seminoles went 62–42–11 and played in four bowl games, including a 36–19 victory against Oklahoma in the 1965 Gator Bowl.

But in the three seasons before Bowden arrived in 1976, Florida State was 4–29, including a horrendous 0–11 in 1973 that prompted talk of dropping the program. "I tell you, everything's changed so much from when I started, we had nothing," Bowden said about first arriving at Florida State in 1976. At the time, it was $500,000 in debt, fans weren't attending games, and he had to sell Seminoles football to everyone.

In addition to recruits, Bowden set up a speaking tour throughout the state of Florida to raise money and he continually worked the media. He wrote in his autobiography, *Bound for Glory*, that at the time he thought of only two jobs that could have been worse: being elected mayor of Atlanta shortly after Sherman's March or being the general who volunteered to replace George Custer during the last siege of the Little Big Horn. "At West Virginia, they sold bumper stickers that said 'Beat Pitt.' When I came to Florida State, they sold bumper stickers that said 'Beat Anybody,'" he quipped.

But Bowden went from believing Florida State to be a stepping-stone for him to turning it into a program similar to the ones he hoped to someday run like Alabama.

Over 34 years he coached more than 1,000 Seminoles and notched 300-plus wins, to easily outdistance the seven previous Florida State coaches combined.

Bobby Bowden, the all-time winningest NCAA football coach, congratulates Nick Saban upon receiving the National Collegiate Coach of the Year Award in 2010. (AP Images)

His teams won two consensus national championships, 1993 and 1999 (after numerous near-misses), two Heisman Trophies (quarterbacks Charlie Ward and Chris Weinke in 1993 and 2000, respectively), and at least a share of 12 Atlantic Coast Conference titles, despite FSU being an independent during Bowden's first 16 years in Tallahassee.

The 1993 championship was somewhat controversial in that Florida State had lost a No. 1–vs.–No. 2 regular-season meeting at Notre Dame 31–24 a week before the Fighting Irish lost 41–39 to No. 17 Boston College. Although West Virginia was undefeated (and went on to lose 41–7 to Florida in the Sugar Bowl), FSU played No. 2 Nebraska for the national championship at the Orange Bowl

Nick Saban vs. Bobby Bowden

Category	Saban	Bowden
Seasons	18	40
Consensus national titles	4	2
Top five finishes	4	15
Top 25 finishes	11	27
Overall record (%)	165–57–1 (74.2%)	346–123–4 (73.6%)
Losing seasons	0	2
Bowl record (%)	8–7 (53.3%)	22–10–1 (68.2%)
Conference titles	5	12
Conference record	101–39–1	105–27 (Z)
Consensus All-Americans	23	31
First-round draft picks (through 2013)	19	32
Record against ranked teams (%)	51–35 (59.30%)	79–65–1 (54.48%)
Record against top 10 teams (%)	27–17 (61.63%)	38–44–1 (46.39%)

Record against Saban: 1–0

Ratios/percentages		
National title seasons	One every 4.5 seasons	20
Consensus All-Americans	1.28 every season	.78
First-round draft picks (through 2013)	1.12 every season	.80
Average wins vs. ranked teams	2.83 each season	1.98
Wins over top 10 teams per year	1.50 every season	.95

Z-West Virginia was independent, and Florida State was until 1992.

and won 18–16. The final rankings had Florida State at No. 1 and 11–1 Notre Dame, which defeated Texas A&M 24–21 at the Cotton Bowl, second.

In 1999 Bowden recorded his only perfect season when Florida State defeated No. 2 Virginia Tech 46–29 in the Sugar Bowl. Wide receiver Peter Warrick caught a 64-yard touchdown pass from Weinke in the first quarter, returned a punt 59 yards for another score in the second quarter, and made a sensational catch of a 43-yard bomb to put the game away. "Right before that play, I asked the offense, 'Do you want me to finish them off?'" Warrick said. "They said, 'Yeah.'"

"We had to make a decision to win the game right here or sit on the ball," Bowden said. "He called about four guys over, and he really said it to them."

Bowden's the only coach to ever lead his team to 10 or more wins over 14 straight seasons (1987–2000), during which the Seminoles finished in the top five of the Associated Press poll each year and were the preseason No. 1 team five times. During that string FSU went 152–18–1. For the 1990s decade, Florida State finished 109–13–1 for an .890 winning percentage. Bowden also had an amazing 14-game unbeaten streak in bowl games (1982–95), though there was a 17–17 tie to Georgia in the 1984 Citrus Bowl.

"We've always told our players, 'You're the only team living in a dynasty,'" Bowden said prior to the 2001 Orange Bowl against Oklahoma, which was the national championship (the Seminoles lost 13–2). "'Bama was in a dynasty, Notre Dame was in a dynasty, Miami was in a dynasty, so-and-so was in a dynasty. We hope we keep it alive."

Overall, Bowden won 411 games, with 12 vacated by an infractions ruling and the NCAA not counting his junior college record, giving him a final record of 377–129–4, which, when Florida State did not let him go out on his own terms, placed him second to Joe Paterno in Division I wins (346 at major schools). However, sanctions handed down by the NCAA on the Penn State coach vacated all of his wins from 1998 to 2011, making Bowden the all-time career leader.

On September 25, 2004, FSU honored him with a bronze statue in front of the Moore Athletics Center on campus.

"There's not a gentleman in this business who has more dignity and class, and honesty and integrity [than] Coach Bowden," said Saban, who faced Bowden as a position coach, coordinator, and head coach and lost all three meetings. "I never heard him say a bad word about anyone in our profession, or anybody anywhere, anytime. In a day and age where everyone negatively recruits and tries to kill everybody else, [he] never did it once. [He] always won, [was] always classy when he won, and was always classy if he wasn't fortunate enough to win. There's no one in our profession I have more respect for than Bobby Bowden."

Part IV

"He's been a class act. When you watch their teams play, there's not a lot of junk going on. They play hard. They play tough. They play all out. They're disciplined. Nick's a fine football coach, a good guy, good family guy, and the whole bit."

—Former Penn State coach Joe Paterno on September 6, 2011

★ ★ ★

Saban vs. History

When trying to get a fix on Nick Saban's place in college football history, it's extremely difficult to draw comparisons with colleagues from different eras and not just because the game has evolved so much over the years.

Teams play more games now, and schedules have become more difficult. Conferences used to be smaller and didn't have championship games until recently. Before the Bowl Championship Series began in 1998, No. 1 almost never played No. 2 in the postseason and rarely during the regular season. With various organizations naming national champions, most seasons ended with multiple teams claiming at least a share of the title.

The NFL Draft was first held in 1936, but at the time, there were only nine teams participating. The same year the first Associated Press poll was held and listed just 20 teams. From 1962 to 1967, only 10 teams were ranked. The poll didn't go to the top 25 until 1989. In 1940 there were just five bowl games. For the most part their growth has been steady, as there were eight in 1960, 16 in 1980, 25 in 2000, and 35 in 2010.

Nevertheless, here goes…

Bernie Bierman

Only two coaches in the history of college football have won five consensus national championships, yet there's little talk these days about Bernie Bierman because his run began before the first Associated Press poll was held in 1936.

Bierman enjoyed a dynasty with his alma mater, Minnesota, but it wasn't the first powerhouse he coached. Following his first tour of duty with the marines in World War I, he took over as head coach at the University of Montana in 1919 and after two years of selling bonds in Minneapolis he returned to coaching as an assistant to Clark Shaughnessy at Tulane in 1923. It only took two years for him to land another head coaching job, at Mississippi State (then Mississippi A&M), and in 1927 he succeeded Shaughnessy at Tulane. Over the next five seasons, the Green Wave went 36–10–2, and the 1929 team finished a perfect 9–0 to receive an invitation to the Rose Bowl, only to have it turned down by school officials.

Tulane came back to go 8–1 and 11–0 in 1931 to receive another Rose Bowl bid, which this time was accepted. Led by halfback Bill Banker, receiver Jerry Dalrymple, and a defense that shut out eight opponents during the regular season, Tulane was riding an 18-game winning streak when it was paired against Southern California in Pasadena. However, the Trojans jumped out to a 21–0 lead, and despite outgaining them the rest of the game, Tulane could pull no closer than 21–12.

"When I was coaching at Texas A&M, we played Tulane's 1931 Rose Bowl team, and I never forgot the ice-water poise they had and the unexcited way they went about their business," SMU coach Matty Bell once recalled. "I told myself that if I ever had a great team, I'd try to keep them in the same frame of mind."

Bierman took that mentality back to Minnesota, where he created a dynasty that was interrupted by another stint with the marines, this time during World War II (when he coached the Iowa Pre-Flight school to a 7–3 record, as it was believed that the rigors of college football were ideal preparation for combat). From 1933 to 1941, the Gophers went undefeated five times and won seven Big Ten titles and five national championships—two before the start of the poll era. "If I found that four or five plays were doing the job, we stuck with them," the low-key Bierman said. "Still, we probably had more plays than our opponents. I always figured that ball control with good execution is the best thing you can have."

Arguably, his best team was Bierman's Monsters of 1934. Led by players like Bill Bevan, the last Big Ten player not to wear a helmet, and future Oklahoma coach Bud Wilkinson, the Gophers averaged 33.8 points while allowing just 4.8 points and 103 yards per game.

Nick Saban vs. Bernie Bierman

Category	Saban	Bierman
Seasons	18	24
Consensus national titles	4	5
Top five finishes	4	4 (I)
Top 25 finishes	11	7 (I)
Overall record (%)	165–57–1 (74.2%)	144–56–9 (71.1%)
Losing seasons	0	5
Bowl record (%)	8–7 (53.3%)	0–1(0.0%)
Conference titles	5	10 (Y)
Conference record	101–39–1	84–43–8
Consensus All-Americans	23	13
First-round draft picks (through 2013)	19	7 (I)(Z)
Record against ranked teams (%)	51–35 (59.30%)	13–18–1 (I) (42.19%)
Record against top 10 teams (%)	27–17 (61.63%)	6–12 (I) (33.33%)

Ratios/percentages

National title seasons	One every 4.5 seasons	4.8
Consensus All-Americans	1.28 every season	.54
First-round draft picks (through 2013)	1.12 every season	NA
Average wins vs. ranked teams	2.83 each season	NA
Wins over top 10 teams per year	1.50 every season	NA

I-The first Associated Press poll and NFL Draft were held in 1936.
Y-Bierman won seven Big Ten titles and three Southern Conference titles.
Z-Minnesota had three first-round selections in 1942–43 when Bierman was in the military.

Highlighting that season was a 48–12 victory at Iowa in which all 514 offensive yards came on the ground and the 34–0 destruction of Wisconsin in the season finale after the Badgers gave up just 50 points all season.

Minnesota matched the 8–0 record in 1935, when SMU also had a good claim on the title, and after a 7–1 season in 1936 was voted No. 1 in the first Associated Press final poll. The Gophers had a rare losing season in 1939 but rebounded to record another perfect fall in 1940 for another national championship.

UM was the preseason No. 1 team heading into 1941, when coming off narrow wins against No. 3 Michigan (7–0) and No. 9 Northwestern (8–7), the Gophers were bypassed in the Associated Press poll by Texas, following the Longhorns' impressive 34–0 victory against No. 20 SMU. But a week later when Texas only managed a 7–7 tie against Baylor, Minnesota, led by Heisman Trophy winner Bruce Smith and halfback George "Sonny" Franck, was back on top and, after finishing 8–0, voted the undisputed champion.

Incidentally, Bierman was also a standout player himself and, along with end Bert Baston and Pudge Wyman's passing, helped lead Minnesota to a 6–0–1 record in 1915 and a 6–1 season in 1916, when the Gophers averaged 49.7 points per game.

Overall, Bierman had a career record of 144–56–9 (71.1 winning percentage), including a 93–35–6 mark at Minnesota. Some of his other top players included Pug Lund, Leo Nomellini, Clayton Tonnemaker, Ed Widseth, and Dick Wildung, who are all in the College Football Hall of Fame.

Earl "Red" Blaik

Although Earl "Red" Blaik is primarily known for his football prowess, he was also a military man. In addition to being part of the United States Cavalry for two years, he was an All-American end as a player (1919) and returned to West Point for two coaching stints at the United State Military Academy, the first as an assistant from 1927 to 1933.

His first head coaching job was at Dartmouth, which went undefeated in 1925 and received some national title consideration (although Alabama is generally considered the consensus champion for that year). He led the then-named Indians (because Dartmouth was founded in 1769, in part to educate Native Americans) for seven seasons and compiled a record of 45–15–4, which included a 22-game unbeaten streak from 1934 to 1937. The 1937 season saw the program's best finish in the Associated Press poll at No. 7, following a 7–0–2 season.

In 1941 Blaik inherited a 1–7–1 team but immediately turned the program around and went 121–33–10 over the next 18 years with just one losing season. Among his assistants, 15 of whom went on to become head coaches, were Sid Gillman (line coach, 1948) and Vince Lombardi (backs coach, 1949–53).

Under his direction, Army, aided by numerous top-end players enlisting to fight in World War II, had one of the most impressive runs in college football history. The Black Knights enjoyed a 32-game unbeaten streak from 1944 to

Nick Saban vs. Earl "Red" Blaik

Category	Saban	Blaik
Seasons	18	25
Consensus national titles	4	2
Top five finishes	4	6 (I)
Top 25 finishes	11	16 (I)
Overall record (%)	165–57–1 (74.2%)	166–48–14 (75.9%)
Losing seasons	0	1
Bowl record (%)	8–7 (53.3%)	0–0 (0.0%)
Conference titles	5	NA
Conference record	101–39–1	NA
Consensus All-Americans	23	16
First-round draft picks (through 2013)	19	4 (I)
Record against ranked teams (%)	51–35 (59.30%)	27–19–7 (I) (57.55%)
Record against top 10 teams (%)	27–17 (61.63%)	13–12–6 (I) (51.61%)
Ratios/percentages		
National title seasons	One every 4.5 seasons	12.5
Consensus All-Americans	1.28 every season	.64
First-round draft picks (through 2013)	1.12 every season	NA
Average wins vs. ranked teams	2.83 each season	NA
Wins over top 10 teams per year	1.50 every season	NA

I-The first Associated Press poll and NFL Draft were conducted in 1936.

1947, won consecutive national titles in 1944 and 1945, and finished with a controversial No. 2 ranking after tying Notre Dame at Yankee Stadium in 1946.

The 1944 team averaged 56 points per game while yielding a total of 35, thanks in part to four shutouts. It also boasted six first-team All-Americans, who caused Blaik to once proclaim that the best game he saw his team play that season was a practice scrimmage. (Note: four years later he became one of the first college coaches to implement a two-platoon system, using players strictly for offense or defense.) After finishing undefeated the coach received a 17-word telegram: "The greatest of all Army teams—STOP—We have stopped the war to celebrate your magnificent success. MacArthur." With another perfect record in 1945 and going 9–0–1 in 1946, Blaik received his only national Coach of the Year honor, from the American Football Coaches Association.

During his 1941–58 reign, the Cadets had three Heisman Trophy winners: Doc Blanchard (1945), Glenn Davis (1946), and Pete Dawkins (1958). While in the same backfield, Blanchard and Davis were known as Mr. Inside and Mr. Outside. Ed McKeever, while coaching Notre Dame during the 1944 season, said, "I've just seen Superman in the flesh. He wears number 35 and goes by the name of Blanchard."

However, Blaik was also the head coach during a cheating scandal that resulted in the dismissal of 90 cadets, including 37 football players. Among them was Blaik's son, Bobby, who was also Army's quarterback. Blaik had to be talked out of resigning by General Douglas MacArthur, who said, "Don't leave under fire."

Blaik rebuilt the program and retired after an 8–0–1 season with a record of 121–33–10, 166–48–14 overall. Among his other accomplishments, Blaik was awarded the Presidential Medal of Freedom from President Reagan in 1986, wrote the book *You Have to Pay the Price* with sportswriter Tim Cohane (foreword by General MacArthur), and also wrote a syndicated newspaper column published twice a week during football season with the proceeds earmarked to graduate scholarships for football players.

Bob Devaney

When Bob Devaney was first contacted by Nebraska about possibly becoming its next head coach, he was more than a little hesitant. It wasn't so much that he had gone 35–10–5 in five seasons at Wyoming, at least tying for first place in the Skyline Conference during four of them, but despite a pretty proud tradition, the Cornhuskers had fallen on hard times.

Nebraska was coming off a 3–6–1 year, 2–5 in the Big 8 and over the previous two decades had enjoyed just three winning seasons. Needing a replacement for William Jennings, who had gone 15–34–1, athletic director Tippy Dye had offered the job to Utah's Ray Nagel, Utah State's John Ralston, and Michigan State's Duffy Daugherty, only to be turned down. However, Daugherty recommended Devaney and then talked his former assistant coach into taking the job by claiming that he could potentially win a national championship at Nebraska but

Nick Saban vs. Bob Devaney

Category	Saban	Devaney
Seasons	18	16
Consensus national titles	4	2
Top five finishes	4	4
Top 25 finishes	11	9
Overall record (%)	165–57–1 (74.2%)	136–30–7 (80.6%)
Losing seasons	0	0
Bowl record (%)	8–7 (53.3%)	7–3 (70.0%)
Conference titles	5	12
Conference record	101–39–1	89–18–4
Consensus All-Americans	23	14
First-round draft picks (through 2013)	19	7
Record against ranked teams (%)	51–35 (59.30%)	12–13–2 (48.15%)
Record against top 10 teams (%)	27–17 (61.63%)	6–11–1 (36.11%)
Ratios/percentages		
National title seasons	One every 4.5 seasons	8
Consensus All-Americans	1.28 every season	.88
First-round draft picks (through 2013)	1.12 every season	.44
Average wins vs. ranked teams	2.83 each season	.75
Wins over top 10 teams per year	1.50 every season	.38

not at Wyoming. Cornhuskers fans have been grateful ever since that Devaney accepted the job, which came with a $19,000 annual salary.

The turnaround was immediate, as Nebraska went 9–2 in 1962, including a 36–24 victory over Miami in the Gotham Bowl at Yankee Stadium—just the program's third postseason game. The Cornhuskers didn't see another losing season until 2004, and Devaney followed up his initial season with a 10–1 year that included a conference title and Orange Bowl win over Auburn.

Although he had top 10 finishes from 1963 to 1966, it wasn't until the next decade that Daugherty's words proved to be true. Riding a 32-game unbeaten streak, Nebraska won back-to-back national championships in 1970–71.

During the 1970 season, Nebraska had an early season 21–21 tie at No. 3 Southern California, and after defeating No. 16 Missouri, the team came back from a 10-point deficit against Kansas to win 41–20, prompting the coach to tell his team, "You learned you can come back. Remember that. That is the lesson of life." The Cornhuskers subsequently went on to win the first of three consecutive Orange Bowls 17–12 against No. 5 LSU.

With Johnny Rodgers at halfback and Rich Glover leading the defense, the 1971 team was simply dominating, finishing 13–0 and scoring 507 points. The marquee game that season was a 35–31 victory against No. 2 Oklahoma, though Nebraska went on to defeat No. 2 Alabama 38–6 in the Orange Bowl. Consequently, the final Associated Press poll had three Big 8 teams at the top: 1. Nebraska; 2. Oklahoma; 3. Colorado. "We're the only undefeated team," Devaney said at the time. "I can't see how the Pope himself would vote for Notre Dame."

Devaney (101–20–2 from 1962 to 1972), had a winning record all 11 seasons at Nebraska—with nine bowl games, winning six, and eight conference titles—but decided that the time was right for assistant Tom Osborne to take over while he concentrated on being the Cornhuskers' athletic director. Devaney had been doing both jobs since 1967 and kept the AD title until 1993, when he then became athletic director emeritus, concerned primarily with fund-raising. "I have never looked at coaching or athletic administration as a job," he said when stepping down in 1996, a year before his death. "It has always been a lot of fun for me, and that's why I never really wanted to retire."

Woody Hayes

Strangely enough, the football program that may have been most responsible for Woody Hayes getting hired at Ohio State was none other than its biggest rival, Michigan. When they were scheduled to play in 1950, the temperature in Columbus was 10 degrees with winds up to 40 mph blowing snow everywhere. As school officials met before kickoff to discuss the idea of postponing, Michigan's Fritz Crisler supposedly said, "We're here and we're not coming back down next week."

In front of the 50,000-plus fans who somehow managed to show up, the two sides combined for 68 total yards with Michigan scoring a touchdown and safety off blocked punts to pull out a 9–3 victory. After going 0–3–1 against the

Wolverines (but 21–10–2 against everyone else), Buckeyes coach Wes Fesler was subsequently fired despite having a ranked team and Heisman Trophy winner Vic Janowicz.

Hayes, who had posted a 19–6 record at his alma mater, Denison, and 14–5 at Miami (Ohio)—with the 1950 Redskins winning the Mid-American Conference and defeating Arizona State in the Salad Bowl in Phoenix—was hired over the likes of former Ohio State coach Paul Brown, assistant coach Harry Strobel, and Missouri coach Don Faurot. It was just the first of many controversies surrounding Hayes at Ohio State.

Hayes lost his first game against Michigan 7–0, which led to arguably the best rivalry in college football, peaking from 1969 to 1978, a period known as the "Ten Year War." That particular stretch began when No. 1 Ohio State, which had destroyed its first eight opponents that season 371–69 and was riding a 22-game winning streak, lost 24–12 at Michigan—which was coached by former Hayes assistant Bo Schembechler.

However, Hayes, one of the most successful coaches in college football history, needed just four years to win his first national title in 1954. During his 28 years, he won 205 games, 13 Big Ten titles, and two consensus national championships, with the Buckeyes on the doorstep for three more.

Hayes' best team was probably the 1968 Buckeyes, who started five sophomores on offense and six on defense, including safety Jack Tatum, nicknamed "the Assassin." Ohio State upset No. 1 Purdue 13–0, finished the regular season 9–0, and defeated Southern California 27–16 in the Rose Bowl for the national title. A total of 11 players from the team earned All-American honors during their careers, and six became first-round draft selections.

Hayes also had two players win the Heisman Trophy, the first being halfback Albert "Hopalong" Cassady, who led the Buckeyes to the 1954 national title and captured the Heisman in 1955. Despite lining up both ways, he had 2,374 career rushing yards and scored 37 touchdowns. Hayes once said Cassady "was the most inspirational player I have ever seen."

The other may have been the most famous Heisman winner in history, Archie Griffin, the only player to win it twice (1974 and 1975). Although he was just 5'9" and 180 pounds, Griffin accumulated 5,589 rushing yards, including an NCAA-record 100 or more in 31 consecutive games. Despite this, in 1975 Griffin

Nick Saban vs. Woody Hayes

Category	Saban	Hayes
Seasons	18	30
Consensus national titles	4	2
Top five finishes	4	10
Top 25 finishes	11	18
Overall record (%)	165–57–1 (74.2%)	219–66–10 (74.7%)
Losing seasons	0	2
Bowl record (%)	8–7 (53.3%)	6–6 (50.0%)
Conference titles	5	14
Conference record	101–39–1	159–38–7
Consensus All-Americans	23	26
First-round draft picks (through 2013)	19	27
Record against ranked teams (%)	51–35 (59.30%)	41–31–5 (56.49%)
Record against top 10 teams (%)	27–17 (61.63%)	23–21–4 (52.08%)
Ratios/percentages		
National title seasons	One every 4.5 seasons	.50
Consensus All-Americans	1.28 every season	.87
First-round draft picks (through 2013)	1.12 every season	.90
Average wins vs. ranked teams	2.83 each season	1.37
Wins over top 10 teams per year	1.50 every season	.77

cast the deciding vote among teammates to name quarterback Cornelius Greene the team's MVP. Hayes, who once said, "You win with people," called Griffin "a better young man than he is a football player, and he's the best football player I've ever seen."

Griffin is also the only player to start in four Rose Bowls and was named Big 10 MVP twice (1973 and 1974) but not in 1975 when he won his second Heisman. As a sophomore in 1973, Griffin had 1,428 rushing yards (more than he had as a senior, 1,357) and finished fifth in Heisman voting behind winner John Cappelletti of Penn State, while teammate John Hicks, a tackle, was second.

As for his enigmatic coach, the former lieutenant commander in the navy once declared, "All good commanders want to die in the field," but his emotions got the best of him in the 1978 Gator Bowl when he punched Clemson nose guard

Charlie Bauman after his interception sealed the Tigers' 17–15 victory. Hayes, who had been a part of numerous incidents before but never with a player, was fired the next day.

Earle Bruce replaced him and went 81–26–1 with the Buckeyes from 1979 to 1987. While Bruce couldn't recapture Hayes' level of success, his coaching tree is one the greatest ever developed, including luminaries like Pete Carroll, Dom Capers, Urban Meyer, Jim Tressel, and Nick Saban.

Lou Holtz

In 2012 Lou Holtz accepted an invitation to be one of the featured speakers at Nick Saban's annual coaching clinic, which was always held in conjunction with the football team's spring practices.

Although he no longer attends many clinics, Holtz was still a motivational speaker and had authored 10 books. His primary message at Alabama was that someone can give you the title of coach, but that doesn't automatically make you the leader.

He then watched Saban put the reigning national champions through practice. "I'm good, I don't have to play Alabama," Holtz quipped to reporters. "They really have some fine athletes, and you have to be impressed with the coaching and how they do things. I think it's good he doesn't let the opponents come in and watch them practice; they would really intimidate you. You can see they do the little things the right way. They get better and are fundamentally sound."

Holtz didn't see anything changing at the Capstone, either. "I've coached against Coach Saban. I have the utmost respect for him as a person, as a coach. I love being around him, but he's a greedy sucker. Some people get you first-and-10, second-and-12, third-and-9, and they're content at fourth-and-5. Not Nick. He wants it first-and-10, second-and-12, third-and 14, fourth-and-19. He wants to move you back, he doesn't want to give you a yard. You can see it the way they practice out there. They just don't want you to make a yard. Some people don't want you to make a first down, not Nick."

Although Saban and Holtz were at Michigan State and Notre Dame at the same time for two years, they didn't oppose one another as head coaches until their next stops in the Southeastern Conference. With South Carolina and LSU

Nick Saban vs. Lou Holtz

Category	Saban	Holtz
Seasons	18	33
Consensus national titles	4	1
Top five finishes	4	5
Top 25 finishes	11	18
Overall record (%)	165–57–1 (74.2%)	249–132–7 (65.1%)
Losing seasons	0	8
Bowl record (%)	8–7 (53.3%)	12–8–2 (59.1%)
Conference titles	5	3
Conference record	101–39–1	88–66–3
Consensus All-Americans	23	21
First-round draft picks (through 2013)	19	21
Record against ranked teams (%)	51–35 (59.30%)	51–64–4 (44.54%)
Record against top 10 teams (%)	27–17 (61.63%)	26–42–2 (38.57%)
Ratios/percentages		
National title seasons	One every 4.5 seasons	33
Consensus All-Americans	1.28 every season	.64
First-round draft picks (through 2013)	1.12 every season	.64
Average wins vs. ranked teams	2.83 each season	1.55
Wins over top 10 teams per year	1.50 every season	.79

each hosting the other in 2002 and 2003, Saban came out on top both times, 38–14 and 33–7.

Holtz, who is already in the College Football Hall of Fame, went 249–132–7 as a head coach from 1969 to 2004. Best known for winning 100 games at Notre Dame and the 1988 national championship, he also coached at William & Mary, North Carolina State, Arkansas, Minnesota, and finally South Carolina. Although nearly all had some issues with the NCAA by the time he departed, Holtz is the only coach in college football history to lead six different programs to bowl games and the only one to guide four to top 20 final rankings.

Incidentally, he also came up with the "Play like a champion today" sign at Notre Dame, which players touch on their way to the field, but they didn't heed the advice in the BCS National Championship Game at the end of the 2012 season, when Alabama destroyed the Fighting Irish 42–14.

"I think he already has a dynasty," Holtz foreshadowed in the spring. "He hasn't lost on the road in a long time, but I don't think Nick Saban or his staff has gotten near the credit that he truly deserves year in and year out. You think, *Yeah, they have great recruiting years*, but I tell you, you cannot win without talent. You can lose with it, and he doesn't lose with talent."

Howard Jones

Howard Jones, who during 29 years went 194–64–21 for a 73.3 winning percentage and captured essentially three consensus national championships, is one of the most successful, yet somewhat overlooked, coaches in college football history. While Nick Saban became the first coach during the modern era to win consensus national titles at different schools, Jones did it 78 years previous, before the poll era.

The first was at Yale in 1909. Although the Bulldogs were an incredible powerhouse during the sport's early years (they claim 27 championships, but many weren't consensus and some were before Walter Camp became coach and was considered the "Father of American Football"), the 1909 team that didn't give up a single point is thought by most to be the best in program history. While Jones played for Yale teams that went 28–0–2 from 1905 to 1907, the Bulldogs capped the season with a highly anticipated finale with undefeated Harvard and won 8–0 on a pair of field goals and a blocked punt for a safety.

Two other things stood out about that season. First, when Yale defeated Syracuse 15–0 it was the first time that brothers faced each other as opposing head coaches (so much for Jim and John Harbaugh, head coaches of the 49ers and Ravens in Super Bowl XLVII in 2013). The other was that Yale had a whopping six All-Americans: Ted Coy, Carroll Cooney, Hamlin Andrus, Henry Hobbs, John Kilpatrick, and Stephen Philbin.

In addition to one-year stints at Syracuse and Trinity (which was later renamed Duke), Jones led Iowa's first two title chases as the 1921 and 1922 squads both went 7–0. The 1921 team outscored opponents 225–36 and snapped Notre Dame's 20-game winning streak, but the Hawkeyes didn't play in their first bowl game until the 1956 season. Jones went 42–17–1 from 1916 to 1923 but

Nick Saban vs. Howard Jones

Category	Saban	Jones
Seasons	18	29
Consensus national titles	4	3
Top five finishes	4	1 (I)
Top 25 finishes	11	2 (I)
Overall record (%)	165–57–1 (74.2%)	194–64–21 (73.3%)
Losing seasons	0	5
Bowl record (%)	8–7 (53.3%)	5–0 (100.0%)
Conference titles	5	9 (Z)
Conference record	101–39–1	86–35–12
Consensus All-Americans	23	21
First-round draft picks (through 2013)	19	NA
Record against ranked teams (%)	51–35 (59.30%)	6–5–2 (I) (53.85%)
Record against top 10 teams (%)	27–17 (61.63%)	5–4–2 (I) (54.55%)
Ratios/percentages		
National title seasons	One every 4.5 seasons	9.3
Consensus All-Americans	1.28 every season	.75
First-round draft picks (through 2013)	1.12 every season	NA
Average wins vs. ranked teams	2.83 each season	NA
Wins over top 10 teams per year	1.50 every season	NA

I-incomplete. The NFL Draft and Associated Press poll both started in 1936.
Z-Duke, Yale, and Syracuse were all independent.

didn't get another shot at a national title until he brought Southern California to prominence.

After an impressive 11–2 debut in 1925, Jones made a run for the title in 1928 by posting a 9–0–1 record. (Georgia Tech was the popular champion.) But USC left no doubt in 1931 and 1932 as part of a 27-game unbeaten streak, when the Trojans were overwhelmingly named national champions.

Although the 1931 team boasted Hall of Famers John Baker, Raymond "Tay" Brown, Aaron Rosenberg, and Ernie Smith blocking for the "Thundering Herd" backfield featuring Erny Pinckert, the 1932 team was even better. The Trojans went 10–0, outscored opponents 201–13, and destroyed Pittsburgh 35–0 in the

Rose Bowl. Five times Jones had a team play in Pasadena and he won them all by a combined score of 124–29.

Although Jones was considered extremely intense, he was the opposite of the outgoing Knute Rockne, who played to the media and was considered quite the self-promoter. However, one famous story about Jones that was included in Mal Florence's 1980 book *The Trojan Heritage: A Pictorial History of USC Football*, centered around the 1930 Stanford game when Indians halfback Phil Moffat sustained a twisted knee on the first play. Jones apparently went to the Stanford locker room and asked Moffat if he had taken a clean hit, promising that if he hadn't the tackler would be kicked off his team. The stunned Moffat eventually responded that it had been a fair hit. "We don't want to win any other way on that field," Jones was quoted as saying.

He was named to the College Football Hall of Fame's inaugural class in 1951.

Ralph "Shug" Jordan

From 1951 to 1975, Ralph "Shug" Jordan compiled a record of 176–83–6 and recorded the most wins in Auburn history, but there was a lot more to him than football. After being a three-sport star, he joined the Army Corps of Engineers, became a major during World War II, and took part in the invasions of Northern Africa, Sicily, Normandy, and Okinawa. Regardless, Jordan had the misfortune of coaching in the state of Alabama at the same time as another legend, Paul W. "Bear" Bryant.

Jordan arrived first, in 1951, and six years later won the program's first national title. After opening the season with a 7–0 victory against Tennessee, Auburn jumped up to No. 7 but didn't claim the top ranking until its season-ending 40–0 domination of the Crimson Tide.

With Jimmy "Red" Phillips averaging 23.8 yards per reception, the Tigers ran the table, and despite not being bowl eligible due to improper recruiting inducements, the Southeastern Conference champions were still voted No. 1 by the Associated Press (No. 2 by United Press International to 9–1 Ohio State). They outscored opponents 207–28, of which only seven points were tallied by an SEC opponent (Mississippi State), and shut out their two biggest rivals thanks to two goal-line stands against Georgia. "We went undefeated last year," Jordan said. "It's going to be awful difficult to improve on our record."

Nick Saban vs. Ralph "Shug" Jordan

Category	Saban	Jordan
Seasons	18	25
Consensus national titles	4	1
Top five finishes	4	4
Top 25 finishes	11	13
Overall record (%)	165–57–1 (74.2%)	176–83–6 (67.5%)
Losing seasons	0	3
Bowl record (%)	8–7 (53.3%)	5–7 (41.7%)
Conference titles	5	1
Conference record	101–39–1	98–63–4
Consensus All-Americans	23	9
First-round draft picks (through 2013)	19	8
Record against ranked teams (%)	51–35 (59.30%)	33–45–2 (42.50%)
Record against top 10 teams (%)	27–17 (61.63%)	16–28 (36.36%)

Ratios/percentages		
National title seasons	One every 4.5 seasons	25
Consensus All-Americans	1.28 every season	.36
First-round draft picks (through 2013)	1.12 every season	.32
Average wins vs. ranked teams	2.83 each season	1.32
Wins over top 10 teams per year	1.50 every season	.64

That was especially true after Alabama responded by hiring Bryant away from Texas A&M, which he had been turning into a national power. Instead, he did the same with the Crimson Tide, bringing the Iron Bowl rivalry to new heights in terms of intensity.

In 1971 quarterback Pat Sullivan led the nation with 2,856 yards, set an NCAA record for most yards per play with 8.57, and tied another with 71 career touchdowns. What he did best, though, was throw to Terry Beasley, with the passing combination accounting for more than 2,500 yards and nearly 30 touchdowns from 1969 to 1971.

But the Jordan game a lot of Auburn fans cherish was the 1972 Iron Bowl. Alabama had a 16–3 lead when Bill Newton burst into the backfield and blocked a punt, which bounced into the hands of David Langner, who returned it for a 25-yard touchdown. Following the Tide's subsequent possession, Newton and Langner did the exact same thing, this time with 20 yards on the return, for a 17–16 victory. "Always remember that Goliath was a 40-point favorite over little David," Jordan once said.

Frank Leahy

You may not have known that in addition to his illustrious football career, Frank Leahy was credited with the now-cliché quote: "When the going gets tough, let the tough get going."

He also had a lot of success before becoming one of the most accomplished head coaches in Notre Dame and college football history.

As a tackle, Leahy played on Knute Rockne's last three teams, two of which went undefeated and claimed national championships. As an assistant coach, Leahy had one-year stints at Georgetown and Michigan State before he created the famous Seven Blocks of Granite line at Fordham, which included future NFL legendary coach Vince Lombardi.

As a head coach, Leahy first made his mark at Boston College, where during his two seasons there the Golden Eagles only lost two games. The 1939 team earned the program's first postseason invitation (it lost to Clemson 6–3 in the Cotton Bowl), and the undefeated 1940 squad included future College Football Hall of Fame inductees center Chet "the Gentle Giant" Gladchuk, end Gene Goodreault, fullback Mike Holovak, guard George "The Righteous Reject" Kerr, and halfback Charlie O'Rourke.

Although Minnesota was considered the national champion and Stanford also finished undefeated, when Boston College capped the season with a 19–13 victory in the Sugar Bowl against No. 4 Tennessee, which hadn't lost a regular-season game in three years under Robert Neyland, the team was greeted by an estimated 100,000 fans in downtown Boston. "To me, this is the best football program in the world," Leahy said at the time.

However, that didn't prevent him from leaving for his alma mater, where Leahy created Notre Dame's second dynasty. Although he shocked fans by switching the offense from the Notre Dame box to the T formation due to the greater scoring

Nick Saban vs. Frank Leahy

Category	Saban	Leahy
Seasons	18	13
Consensus national titles	4	3 (Z)
Top five finishes	4	9
Top 25 finishes	11	11
Overall record (%)	165–57–1 (74.2%)	107–13–9 (86.4%)
Losing seasons	0	0
Bowl record (%)	8–7 (53.3%)	1–1 (50.0%)
Conference titles	5	NA
Conference record	101–39–1	NA
Consensus All-Americans	23	23
First-round draft picks (through 2013)	19	16
Record against ranked teams (%)	51–35 (59.30%)	32–5–4 (82.93%)
Record against top 10 teams (%)	27–17 (61.63%)	22–3–1 (86.54%)

Ratios/percentages

National title seasons	One every 4.5 seasons	4.3
Consensus All-Americans	1.28 every season	1.77
First round draft picks (through 2013)	1.12 every season	1.23
Average wins vs. ranked teams	2.83 each season	2.46
Wins over top 10 teams per year	1.50 every season	1.69

Z-For the purpose of this book, Michigan is considered the national champion in 1947 as discussed elsewhere.

possibilities, his first three teams won 24 games while losing three and tying three and captured the 1943 national title.

While Angelo Bertelli won the program's Heisman Trophy despite enlisting for the military before season's end, Creighton Miller topped the nation in rushing with 911 yards despite skipping every day of spring practice to play golf. Leahy later admitted, "He was the best halfback I ever coached." To give an idea of how high praise that was, Leahy said of the 1949 team, which went on to win the national championship, "We'll have the worst team Notre Dame has ever had." Red Grange said about that same squad, "It's the greatest college team I've ever seen."

After spending two years in the navy during World War II, Leahy returned to Notre Dame in 1946 and immediately had the Fighting Irish back in the title hunt. With Johnny Lujack leading the team, Notre Dame won controversial titles in 1946 and 1947 when the quarterback took home the Heisman Trophy and it was the consensus choice in 1949 when Leon Hart captured the award.

In Leahy's final season, 1953, Notre Dame went 9–0–1 to claim another title, only the coach collapsed due to a pancreas attack at halftime of the Georgia Tech game. He announced his retirement on January 31, 1954.

All but two of his 13 teams finished ranked in the final Associated Press poll with eight in the top three and three more between No. 5 and No. 11. Consequently, he has the second-best winning percentage in Division I history, trailing only the man who was his mentor, Rockne. They're the only two coaches with 10-plus years of experience who have no more losses than seasons coached.

John McKay

Although Southern California has had an impressive lineup of coaches over the years, John McKay is viewed as having the strongest legacy. From 1960 to 1975, the Trojans won three consensus national titles, were on the doorstep of at least two more, played in eight Rose Bowls, and won two Heisman Trophies (Mike Garrett in 1965 and O.J. Simpson in 1968).

The coach was also one of college football's true characters. "I told my team it doesn't matter," he said after a 51–0 loss to Notre Dame in 1966. "There are 750 million people in China who don't even know this game was played. The next day, a guy called me from China and asked, 'What happened, Coach?'"

"Well, gentlemen, I guess I wasn't so stupid today," McKay said after a 21–20 victory against UCLA in 1967.

When asked why he gave the ball to Simpson so much in a game, McKay said, "Why not? It's not heavy, and he doesn't belong to a union."

(His most famous quote came while coaching the expansion Tampa Bay Buccaneers. When a reporter asked about the execution of his offense, McKay quipped that he was in favor of it. Also, one of his quarterbacks in 1976 was Steve Spurrier.) "He knew when to loosen a team up and he knew how to get after you," former USC quarterback Craig Fertig (1961–64) once said. "You'd never have to worry about him slapping a player. He could do it with his tongue."

Nick Saban vs. John McKay

Category	Saban	McKay
Seasons	18	16
Consensus national titles	4	3 (Z)
Top five finishes	4	6
Top 25 finishes	11	12
Overall record (%)	164–57–1 (74.2%)	127-40-8 (74.9%)
Losing seasons	0	2
Bowl record (%)	8-7 (53.3%)	6-3 (66.7%)
Conference titles	5	9
Conference record	101-39-1	70-17-3
Consensus All-Americans	23	19
First-round draft picks (through 2013)	19	18
Record against ranked teams (%)	51-35 (59.30%)	34-20-4 (62.07%)
Record against top 10 teams (%)	27-17 (61.63%)	21-15-3 (57.69%)

Ratios/percentages		
National title seasons	One every 4.5 seasons	5.3
Consensus All-Americans	1.28 every season	1.19
First-round draft picks (through 2013)	1.12 every season	1.13
Average wins vs. ranked teams	2.83 each season	2.13
Wins over top 10 teams per year	1.50 every season	1.31

Z-Oklahoma was on probation in 1974, which excluded it from consideration for the final coaches' poll, but the Sooners were No. 1 in the final Associated Press poll.

McKay compiled a 127–40–8 record, including just 17 conference losses during those 16 seasons. Over his last nine years, USC went 18–3 against its two biggest rivals, UCLA and Notre Dame.

The 1974 game against the Fighting Irish, dubbed "the Comeback," is still talked about in Los Angeles. Despite a 24–0 deficit in the second quarter, tailback Anthony Davis (with Ricky Bell at fullback before he had 1,875 yards the following year to finish second for the Heisman) sparked the Trojans with a 102-yard kickoff return to open the second half, and USC went on to score 55 points in just less than 17 minutes. "We turned into madmen," Davis said.

The 1972 team, though, was considered one of the best in college football history. It went 12–0, beat six ranked teams by an average of 20.2 points, and never trailed. "USC's not the No. 1 team in the country," Washington State coach Jim Sweeney said after his team lost 44–3. "The Miami Dolphins are better."

McKay also coached offensive standouts like Sam Cunningham, Pat Haden, Lynn Swann, and Ron Yary, but it was under his direction that the "Tailback U" moniker emerged with the Trojans' trademark I-formation attack. Simpson became the school's second Heisman winner in 1968 when he set the NCAA single-season rushing record with 1,709 yards. He also equaled or set 19 NCAA, conference, and USC records before going on to establish the NFL single-season rushing record of 2,003 yards in 1973.

McKay's also the father of former Buccaneers general manager and current Atlanta Falcons president Rich McKay, and his son J.K. played for him twice as a wide receiver, first for the Trojans (1972–75) and then with the Buccaneers (1976–79). McKay quipped, "I had a rather distinct advantage. I slept with his mother."

Bob Neyland

The biggest name in Tennessee football history is undoubtedly General Robert Neyland, who transformed the Volunteers into a national power after taking the job in 1926. Due to his military duties and obligations, the West Point graduate who served in France during World War I ended up coaching Tennessee at three different times. He was also called upon for a peacetime tour in Panama followed by another tour of duty as a brigadier general in the Pacific theater during World War II.

Known for his discipline and hard-nosed approach, Neyland was originally hired because of rival Vanderbilt, to which Tennessee had lost 18 of 22 games (with two ties). The turnaround was all but immediate, eventually prompting dean Nathan Daugherty, the faculty chairman of athletics, to call Neyland's hiring the best move he ever made. Led by quarterback Bobby Dodd, Tennessee went 27–1–2 from 1928 to 1930.

During his three stints, Neyland compiled an amazing record of 173–31–12. In those 216 games, the opponent failed to score 112 times, including all 10 regular-season opponents in 1939. His 71 consecutive scoreless quarters is still an NCAA record. "If Neyland could score a touchdown against you, he had you beat," claimed Herman Hickman, one of Neyland's players who went on to join the original staff of *Sports Illustrated*. "If he could score two, he had you in a rout."

An 11–0 finish in 1938 led to a No. 2 ranking in the final Associated Press poll, which the team matched a year later. (The Vols went 10–1 after a 14–0 loss to Southern California in the Rose Bowl.) However, Neyland's Volunteers were the consensus national champions in 1951, though they went on to lose 28–13 to Maryland in the Sugar Bowl.

One of Neyland's biggest games was on October 20, 1928, when he approached Alabama coach Wallace Wade before kickoff in Tuscaloosa and asked if the game could end early if things got out of hand. The gamesmanship worked. Halfback Norm McEver returned the opening kickoff 98 yards for a touchdown, and the

Nick Saban vs. Robert Neyland

Category	Saban	Neyland
Seasons	18	21
Consensus national titles	4	1
Top five finishes	4	5
Top 25 finishes	11	9
Overall record (%)	165–57–1 (74.2%)	173–31–12 (82.9%)
Losing seasons	0	0
Bowl record (%)	8–7 (53.3%)	2–5 (28.6%)
Conference titles	5	7
Conference record	101–39–1	103–17–10
Consensus All-Americans	23	9
First-round draft picks (through 2013)	19	3 (I)
Record against ranked teams (%)	51–35 (59.30%)	16–8 (I) (66.67%)
Record against top 10 teams (%)	27–17 (61.63%)	9–6 (I) (60.00%)
Ratios/percentages		
National title seasons	One every 4.5 seasons	21
Consensus All-Americans	1.28 every season	.43
First-round draft picks (through 2013)	1.12 every season	NA
Average wins vs. ranked teams	2.83 each season	NA
Wins over top 10 teams per year	1.50 every season	NA

I-The first Associated Press poll and NFL Draft were conducted in 1936.

defense frustrated the heavily favored Crimson Tide for a 15–13 victory. The two sides have been fierce rivals since, with their matchups each season now known as the "Third Saturday in October."

Perhaps that's why Knute Rockne once called Neyland "football's greatest coach."

"The general was not the easiest guy to work with Monday through Friday, but on Saturday he was a fatherly figure," Neyland tailback Herky Payne said. "On Saturday he was a warm man who gave you a lot of confidence."

Tom Osborne

Nick Saban will never, ever forget what it was like to face a Tom Osborne team. It was 1995, his first game as Michigan State's head coach, and Nebraska was the reigning national champion. "They beat us 55–14 [actually 50–10], and the score did not indicate how bad they beat us," Saban said. "I hadn't been in college football for four or five years, being in the NFL. I'm thinking we're never going to win a game. We'll never win a game here at Michigan State. I must have taken a bad job, wrong job, no players, something. I remember Coach Osborne when we shook hands after the game, he put his arm around me and whispered in my ear, 'You're not really as bad as you think.' So I think he knew he had a pretty good team, and we actually ended up winning six games, so we weren't really probably as bad as I thought."

Actually, Nebraska was in the early stages of a dynasty, during which it won back-to-back consensus national championships, secured a split title in 1997, went 49–2, and had nine All-Americans. The Cornhuskers won two Outland Trophies, one Lombardi, and a Johnny Unitas Golden Arm Award for best quarterback, even though Nebraska wasn't known for its passing.

Osborne too had a little bit of a rocky start after he replaced Bob Devaney in 1973 and he developed a reputation for being unable to win big games after losing his first five and eight of nine against rival Oklahoma. Once he cleared that hurdle, though, and finally played for the national championship at the end of the 1983 season, the coach came up short after making one of the gutsiest calls in college football history.

After a fierce comeback in the Orange Bowl against hometown No. 4 Miami, top-ranked Nebraska scored on Jeff Smith's fourth-down 24-yard run with 48 seconds remaining. With No. 2 Texas, the only other undefeated team, having already lost earlier in the day to Georgia in the Cotton Bowl, a tie probably would have locked up the national title (there was no overtime), but Osborne went for the two-point conversion and the win only to see Turner Gill's pass knocked down. "We wanted an undefeated season and a clear-cut championship," Osborne said after the 31–30 loss that led to Miami finishing No. 1, ahead of Nebraska. "I don't think we should go for the tie in that case. It never entered my head. I guess I'm not very smart."

Instead, after Byron Bennett's 45-yard field-goal attempt went wide-left in the final seconds of the Orange Bowl, an 18–16 loss to Florida State to decide the 1993 title, Osborne had to wait until 1994 to win his first consensus national championship—although it was anything from simple or easy despite Nebraska's 13–0 record.

Quarterback Tommie Frazier was sidelined after the fourth game by blood-clot problems in his right knee, and a partially collapsed lung slowed replacement Brook Berringer. He still managed to lead a 24–17 victory against Miami at the Orange Bowl, and voters rewarded the Cornhuskers despite Penn State also finishing unbeaten at 12–0.

With Frazier able to return, Berringer went back to the bench in 1995 when Nebraska was able to defend its title, and no opponent could come within 13 points of the Cornhuskers. Tragically, Berringer died the following spring in a plane crash. "The Brook I knew, there was nothing he could have done better," Osborne said. "The length [of his life] was not what you would have liked. But the quality couldn't have been better."

The split title came after a 42–17 victory against No. 3 Tennessee in the Orange Bowl, Osborne's final game, when the coaches' poll leapfrogged Nebraska over Michigan. Osborne called the squad "probably a little more talented than '94, certainly not near as controversial as '95. That was nice. So it was just kind of a nice way to go. Great leadership on the part of the players, and I didn't have to do much."

In the 1990s Nebraska lost just three home games. Although few programs have won 100 games in a decade, Nebraska is the only one in NCAA history to do it in consecutive decades.

Overall, Osborne had an incredible 255–49–3 record from 1973 to 1997, when the Cornhuskers recorded 15 10-win seasons. Their worst showing was

Nick Saban vs. Tom Osborne

Category	Saban	Osborne
Seasons	18	25
Consensus national titles	4	2 (Z)
Top five finishes	4	8
Top 25 finishes	11	25
Overall record (%)	165–57–1 (74.2%)	255–49–3 (83.6%)
Losing seasons	0	0
Bowl record (%)	8–7 (53.3%)	12–13 (48.0%)
Conference titles	5	13
Conference record	101–39–1	160–23–2
Consensus All-Americans	23	30
First-round draft picks (through 2013)	19	21
Record against ranked teams (%)	51–35 (59.30%)	62–37–1 (62.50%)
Record against top 10 teams (%)	27–17 (61.63%)	27–32 (45.76%)
Ratios/percentages		
National title seasons	One every 4.5 seasons	12.5
Consensus All-Americans	1.28 every season	1.2
First round draft picks (through 2013)	1.12 every season	.84
Average wins vs. ranked teams	2.83 each season	2.48
Wins over top 10 teams per year	1.50 every season	1.08

Z-Nebraska split the national championship with Michigan in 1997.

9–3–1 in 1976, with a trip to the Bluebonnet Bowl—a 27–24 victory against Texas Tech. Between Devaney and Osborne, who in 2000 won a seat in the U.S. House of Representatives and served for six years, Nebraska appeared in a record 35 consecutive bowl games (1969–2003), including 17 straight January bowl appearances (1981–97). Consequently, all 25 of Osborne's teams received a bowl invitation and finished ranked in the final Associated Press poll.

However, to give an idea of how times have changed in college football, over his whole career Osborne was involved in just three No. 1–vs.–No. 2 games, going 1–2. When Alabama defeated Notre Dame for the 2012 national title, it was Saban's fifth over the previous 49 months.

Ara Parseghian

Ara Parseghian is directly cut from the "If you can't beat them, join them" philoso-phy, only with college football coaches the word *join* needs to be replaced by *hire*. Although best known for his successful years at Notre Dame, he first was a player and coach at Miami of Ohio as a running back/defensive back in 1946–47 for Sid Gillman and spent a year as an assistant coach under the direction of Woody Hayes. After he took over in 1951, Miami went 39–6–1 over the next five seasons, with three of the losses coming the first year, and the 1955 team finished No. 15 in the final Associated Press poll.

Miami had already become a successful launching point for coaches (including Paul Brown, Weeb Ewbank, George Little, and Paul Dietzel), but to the surprise of some, the school to come calling for Parseghian was Northwestern. The Wildcats had made a Rose Bowl trip at the end of the 1948 season but were coming off a winless 1955 schedule. After taking the job, he too had a winless season in 1957, but five years later he had Northwestern ranked No. 1 during the 1962 season.

Led by quarterback Tom Myers and receiver Paul Flatley, the Wildcats got off to a 6–0 start and spent two weeks atop the Associated Press poll until the team was knocked off its pedestal by both No. 8 Wisconsin and Michigan State. However, Northwestern defeated Notre Dame four straight times, including 35–6 in 1962, which more than got the Fighting Irish's attention. Consequently, after five straight .500 or worse seasons, including records of 2–8 in 1960 and 2–7 in 1963, Notre Dame hired Parseghian in 1964 to turn the tables.

In addition to winning nine straight games against his former team, which went 17–41–1 during its first six seasons without him, Parseghian led Notre Dame to a 95–17–4 record over 11 seasons.

Under his direction (and with Heisman Trophy winner John Huarte), the Fighting Irish were poised to win the national championship during Parseghian's first season in South Bend in 1964, only to blow a 17–0 lead in the season finale at Southern California. Instead, Parseghian had to wait two more years, when Notre Dame went 9–0–1 and won an extremely controversial title over undefeated Alabama—the two-time reigning champion. The tie came against Michigan State in what was billed the "Game of the Century," only to result in a 10–10 finish when Parseghian decided to have his players not go for the win after getting the ball back at their own 30 with 1:24 to play. "We'd fought hard to come back and

Nick Saban vs. Ara Parseghian

Category	Saban	Parseghian
Seasons	18	24
Consensus national titles	4	2
Top five finishes	4	7
Top 25 finishes	11	12
Overall record (%)	165–57–1 (74.2%)	170–58–6 (73.9%)
Losing seasons	0	2
Bowl record (%)	8–7 (53.3%)	3–2 (60.0%)
Conference titles	5	2
Conference record	101–39–1	41–33–2
Consensus All-Americans	23	23
First-round draft picks (through 2013)	19	14
Record against ranked teams (%)	51–35 (59.30%)	21–30–4 (41.82%)
Record against top 10 teams (%)	27–17 (61.63%)	16–23–3 (41.67%)
Ratios/percentages		
National title seasons	One every 4.5 seasons	12
Consensus All-Americans	1.28 every season	.96
First-round draft picks (through 2013)	1.12 every season	.58
Average wins vs. ranked teams	2.83 each season	.88
Wins over top 10 teams per year	1.50 every season	.79

tie it up," he explained later. "After all that, I didn't want to risk giving it to them cheap. They get reckless, and it could cost them the game. I wasn't going to do a jackass thing like that at that point."

Alabama and Notre Dame were both undefeated when they met in a No. 1–vs.–No. 2 showdown in the Sugar Bowl at the end of the 1973 season, and the Fighting Irish pulled out a dramatic 24–23 victory. With the coaches' poll holding its final voting before the bowls, the last time it did so, Alabama could claim a split title, but Notre Dame was the clear consensus champion.

Although Parseghian resigned in 1974 for health reasons after 11 years at Notre Dame, he got involved in the fight against Niemann-Pick Type C, a genetic, pediatric, neurodegenerative disorder responsible for the buildup of cholesterol in cells that results in eventual damage to the nervous system. Three of Parseghian's grandchildren—Michael, Marcia, and Christa Parseghian—were diagnosed with NP-C in 1994, and all died by 2005. "Ara Parseghian probably was as classy a coach and as classy a human being, not only relative to what he did as a coach but all that he's done since he's not been coaching in terms of raising funds and money for research and fighting disease and different things that have affected his family," Nick Saban said. "I just think he's one of the all-time classy coaches who has ever had success. A lot of things that he did and the way he represented the program are things that we would like to be sort of remembered for as well."

Joe Paterno

It was a moment in which everyone knew that they were witnessing history but no one would completely appreciate until years later. Prior to kickoff at Bryant-Denny Stadium on September 11, 2010, Nick Saban stood at midfield with opposing coach Joe Paterno and special guest Bobby Bowden. The three laughed and smiled, enjoying the once-in-a-lifetime occasion, with the one fresh off a national championship graciously hosting the two winningest coaches in major college football history.

It certainly wasn't lost on Saban, though even he didn't realize that the photo op was really a sort of passing of the torch. "I think the thing you take from guys like Bobby Bowden and Joe Paterno is that they are good and have been good for a long time," Saban said that week. "They have also been great ambassadors for the game and they have done what they do in a classy way. They don't talk about other people. They don't run other programs down. They just do it in a first-class way. I think that is probably the biggest thing that I have tried to emulate [from] Joe Paterno, Bobby Bowden, and those types of guys…because of how they've done what they do, the kind of people that they are, and the kind of character they have. I think that is important for college football. I think that is an important part of the integrity of the game."

A lot changed during the years to follow, including the Penn State child-sex-abuse scandal involving an assistant coach and subsequent toppling of an icon. Saban went from telling Crimson Tide fans before the previously mentioned game that he would take it as a personal insult if anyone booed when the Nittany Lions took the field to handing Paterno his final loss a year later.

At the time there were few, if any, coaches that Saban respected more. "Coach Paterno is probably one of the greatest coaches of all time in college football, not in terms of how many games he's won, but how he's contributed to the game in so many positive ways," Saban said. "To give you an example, he was part of an academic committee. When I was at Michigan State, we had a player who sort of tried to get a waiver for a sixth year because he broke his leg twice. But he really couldn't get into graduate school. He had to get into a continuing-ed program. At that time, you had to get into graduate school to be able to do that. Joe was the

Joe Paterno and Nick Saban embrace after Saban's Tide defeated Paterno's Nittany Lions 24–3 in September of 2010. (AP Images)

Nick Saban vs. Joe Paterno

Category	Saban	Paterno
Seasons	18	46
Consensus national titles	4	2
Top five finishes	4	13
Top 25 finishes	11	32
Overall record (%)	165–57–1 (74.2%)	298–136–3 (68.54%)*
Losing seasons	0	5*
Bowl record (%)	8–7 (53.3%)	18–12–1 (59.68%)*
Conference titles	5	1 (B)
Conference record	101–39–1	31–54 (B)
Consensus All-Americans	23	33
First-round draft picks (through 2013)	19	33
Record against ranked teams (%)	51–35 (59.30%)	66–85–1 (43.75%)*
Record against top 10 teams (%)	27–17 (61.63%)	29–47 (38.16%)*

Ratios/percentages		
National title seasons	One every 4.5 seasons	23
Consensus All-Americans	1.28 every season	.72
First-round draft picks (through 2013)	1.12 every season	.72
Average wins vs. ranked teams	2.83 each season	1.43 (Z)
Wins over top 10 teams per year	1.50 every season	.63 (Z)

*All wins from 1998 through 2011 were vacated from his career 409–136–3 record. His original bowl record was 24–12–1. Without vacated wins, Paterno was 86–85–1 against ranked teams (50.29%), 35–47 versus top 10 opponents (42.7%).

Z-Without vacated wins his ratios would be 1.87 (ranked teams) and .76 (top 10).

B-Penn State was independent until it joined the Big Ten in 1993. Before vacated wins, his league record was 95–54.

head of that committee and he actually got it passed through and all that for us at Michigan State. What was amazing was, we were playing at Penn State. I forget the exact score of the game, but this guy that he got eligible ran for a touchdown with about a minute to go in the game [and] put us ahead. They went down and kicked a field goal and won the game. He did things for players and made decisions based on what was right, not what was politically correct for him or his school or anything else. I have a tremendous amount of respect for that because he's done it a hundred times for lots of players and lots of people involved in college football."

Paterno, an English major from Brown University who initially said that he never wanted to coach football, was hired as an assistant and subsequently named Penn State's head coach in 1966. Over 46 years he won 409 games, only to have 111 erased by an NCAA decision, and won two national championships, 1982 and 1986.

Under his direction, the school's string of consecutive non-losing seasons wasn't snapped until 1988 at 49. He notched wins at the Orange, Cotton, Fiesta, Liberty, Sugar, Aloha, Holiday, Citrus, Rose, Hall of Fame, Outback, Capital One, and Alamo Bowls, and over the years Beaver Stadium's capacity went from 46,284 to 107,282.

He had a Heisman winner with running back John Cappelletti in 1973 (1,522 rushing yards and 17 touchdowns), an amazing collection of linebackers ranging from LaVar Arrington to Jack Ham, and had some epic matchups against Alabama along the way. Among them was the Sugar Bowl to decide the 1978 national championship, which was highlighted by a goal-line stand, and the 1981 game to set up Paul W. "Bear" Bryant's record-setting 315th win the following week at Auburn.

Paterno and his wife, Sue, donated more than $4 million to Penn State for building projects and to endow faculty positions and scholarships and began a campaign to raise millions for the construction of a new library that bears his name. Yet despite all that, time will still be the deciding factor when it comes to his legacy.

Darrell Royal

If you ever want to stop a Texas fan dead in his or her tracks, just mention that the best coach in Longhorns program history was first an All-American quarterback for rival Oklahoma.

Yeah, well, he had a better career with the Longhorns.

After Darrell Royal was hired away from Washington at the age of 32, he and coordinator Emory Bellard changed the face of college football by unleashing the wishbone offense in 1968—which many imitated and coaches such as Paul W.

Nick Saban vs. Darrell Royal

Category	Saban	Royal
Seasons	18	23
Consensus national titles	4	2
Top five finishes	4	9
Top 25 finishes	11	14
Overall record (%)	165–57–1 (74.2%)	184–60–5 (74.9%)
Losing seasons	0	0
Bowl record (%)	8–7 (53.3%)	8–7–1 (53.1%)
Conference titles	5	11
Conference record	101–39–1	120–38–2
Consensus All-Americans	23	14
First-round draft picks (through 2013)	19	7
Record against ranked teams (%)	51–35 (59.30%)	30–31–3 (49.22%)
Record against top 10 teams (%)	27–17 (61.63%)	18–21–1 (46.25%)

Ratios/percentages		
National title seasons	One every 4.5 seasons	11.5
Consensus All-Americans	1.28 every season	.61
First round draft picks (through 2013)	1.12 every season	.30
Average wins vs. ranked teams	2.83 each season	1.30
Wins over top 10 teams per year	1.50 every season	.78

"Bear" Bryant visited to study and learn. The Longhorns quickly ascended to the top of the college football world, culminating in 1963 with an 11–0 record and 28–6 victory against Navy—and Heisman Trophy winner Roger Staubach—in the Cotton Bowl to win its first consensus national championship.

"Tune in your television to the Cotton Bowl, and you'll laugh yourself silly," Pittsburgh sports journalist Myron Cope made the mistake of saying beforehand. "Texas is the biggest fraud ever perpetrated on the football public."

For an encore, though, Texas just missed repeating with a 10–1 record in 1964 and in 1968 not only finished atop the Southwest Conference for the first of six straight years, but began an epic run of 30 straight wins, of which eight were against ranked opponents.

Not surprisingly, 1969 was probably Royal's best team, with the running attack led by three All-Americans (halfback Steve Worster and tackles Bob McKay and Bobby Wuensch). The result was a 10–0 regular season. Texas defeated Notre Dame 21–17 in the Cotton Bowl to secure another title.

Even though the Longhorns lost the rematch in 1970, 24–11, a few organizations still named Texas No. 1. It finished third in the Associated Press poll, and Nebraska was considered the consensus champion. Texas didn't claim another title until 2005, when Mack Brown and quarterback Vince Young shocked Southern California in the BCS National Championship Game.

Nevertheless, Texas has won two Heisman Trophies (Earl Campbell in 1977 and Ricky Williams in 1998) and used to all but dominate the SWC before it folded, the heart of its legacy stems from the man whose name now appears on the Longhorns' home, Darrell K Royal–Texas Memorial Stadium. During his 23 years as a head coach, including two at Mississippi State (1954–55), Royal accumulated a record of 184–60–5 for a 74.9 winning percentage and retired after the 1976 season at the age of 52.

Bo Schembechler

Even though he never won a national championship, Bo Schembechler deserves a mention among the all-time greats after being one of the sport's icons during his 27 years as a head coach, mostly at Michigan.

After six years at his alma mater, Miami of Ohio, where the Redhawks went 40–17–3, he was hired away by Michigan to deal with one of his former bosses, Woody Hayes at Ohio State. Their rivalry could only be described as "epic," and Schembechler had one of the best records in college football. Only Joe Paterno and Tom Osborne reached 200 wins in fewer games (Division I).

Although they weren't able to hold on, Schembechler had four teams reach No. 1 in the Associated Press poll and 16 finish in the top 10, including 10 straight (1969–78). The Wolverines also won 13 Big Ten titles, but the coach went 2–8 in the Rose Bowl against the Pac-10 champion. Overall, Schembechler went 194–48–5 with the Wolverines (1969–89) and 143–24–3 in conference play.

Nick Saban vs. Bo Schembechler

Category	Saban	Schembechler
Seasons	18	27
Consensus national titles	4	0
Top five finishes	4	6
Top 25 finishes	11	19
Overall record (%)	165–57–1 (74.2%)	234–65–8 (77.5%)
Losing seasons	0	0
Bowl record (%)	8–7 (53.3%)	5–12 (29.4%)
Conference titles	5	15
Conference record	101–39–1	170–32–4
Consensus All-Americans	23	25
First-round draft picks (through 2013)	19	14
Record against ranked teams (%)	51–35 (59.30%)	37–36–1 (50.67%)
Record against top 10 teams (%)	27–17 (61.63%)	16–22–1 (42.31%)

Ratios/percentages		
National title seasons	One every 4.5 seasons	None
Consensus All-Americans	1.28 every season	.93
First-round draft picks (through 2013)	1.12 every season	.52
Average wins vs. ranked teams	2.83 each season	1.37
Wins over top 10 teams per year	1.50 every season	.59

Amos Alonzo Stagg

Even though the University of Chicago dropped football in 1939 (it restarted the program for Division III in 1968), it won a national championship in 1905 and seven Big Ten titles from 1899 to 1924.

Jay Berwanger was the first winner of the Heisman Trophy in 1935 and subsequently the first selection in the first National Football League Draft. (He never played pro ball but is one of nine Chicago inductees into the College Football Hall of Fame.) The program also featured quarterback Walter Eckersall (1903–06) and guard Bob "Tiny" Maxwell (1902, 1904–5)—for whom both the Maxwell Club and Maxwell Trophy are named—but the person most associated with Chicago is legendary coach Amos Alonzo Stagg.

"The Grand Old Man of the Midway," who was at Chicago from 1892 to 1932, invented the end-around, hidden-ball trick, fake punt, quick-kick, man-in-motion, double reverse, huddle, backfield shift, Statue of Liberty play, padded goal posts, and having numbers on players' backs. Incidentally, he also invented the batting cage for baseball and the trough for overflow in swimming pools. "All football comes from Stagg," said Knute Rockne, whose football hero as a kid was Eckersall.

His championship team shut out every opponent except one, Indiana, which managed just five points. Chicago "rebounded" by winning 4–0 at Wisconsin and eventually beating Michigan 2–0. Over 11 games Chicago scored 271 points.

Nick Saban vs. Amos Alonzo Stagg

Category	Saban	Stagg
Seasons	18	56
Consensus national titles	4	1
Top five finishes	4	1 (I)
Top 25 finishes	11	1 (I)
Overall record (%)	165–57–1 (74.2%)	314–199–35 (60.4%)
Losing seasons	0	20
Bowl record (%)	8–7 (53.3%)	0–1(0.0%)
Conference titles	5	12
Conference record	101–39–1	NA (115–74–2 Big Ten)
Consensus All-Americans	23	10
First-round draft picks (through 2013)	19	1 (I)
Record against ranked teams (%)	51–35 (59.30%)	NA
Record against top 10 teams (%)	27–17 (61.63%)	NA
Ratios/percentages		
National title seasons	One every 4.5 seasons	56
Consensus All-Americans	1.28 every season	.17
First-round draft picks (through 2013)	1.06 every season	NA
Average wins vs. ranked teams	2.83 each season	NA
Wins over top 10 teams per year	1.50 every season	NA

I-The first Associated Press poll and NFL Draft were conducted in 1936.

During his 42-year coaching career at major schools, which began at Springfield, Stagg went 275–121–29 for a 68.1 winning percentage and 115–74–12 in the Big Ten. He had 10 consensus All-Americans. Stagg later coached at Pacific (1933–46), where he had five teams finish atop the Northern California Athletic Conference, giving him an overall record of 314–199–35.

Barry Switzer

When Chuck Fairbanks left Oklahoma for the New England Patriots after revitalizing the school's program (52–15–1 from 1967 to 1972), Oklahoma turned to the offensive coordinator who had used the wishbone to record the most prolific rushing season in college football history with 472 yards per game. The Sooners had also scored more than 500 points in 1971 and finished second in the final Associated Press poll for the second straight year.

At the time, Switzer was just 35.

Following his promotion from coordinator, Oklahoma won or shared the Big 8 conference title every season from 1973 to 1980, with back-to-back national championships in 1974 and 1975, and won another in 1985.

Switzer's teams featured some stellar players, including running back Billy Sims, who won the 1978 Heisman Trophy, and Lee Roy Selmon—considered by many to be the best player in Sooners history. With one of his brothers also on the team, "God bless Mr. and Mrs. Selmon" became a popular refrain among fans.

Switzer had a career record of 157–29–4, (for an .837 winning percentage). His Sooners never finished lower than second in the league, played in nine Orange Bowls, and only once finished a season unranked.

He is one of just two coaches to win both a collegiate national championship and the Super Bowl, the other being Jimmy Johnson. In 1996 Switzer led the Dallas Cowboys to a victory over the Pittsburgh Steelers in Super Bowl XXX, and he had a career NFL coaching record of 45–26.

However, his years at Oklahoma were filled with controversy as well, including the 1974 national championship. The Sooners were serving a two-year penalty for a recruiting scandal and were ineligible to play in a bowl game, but while the American Football Coaches Association had a rule that teams on probation were ineligible for rankings and national championship consideration, the Associated Press did not. The Sooners finished the season undefeated, averaging 508 yards of

Nick Saban vs. Barry Switzer

Category	Saban	Switzer
Seasons	18	16
Consensus national titles	4	3
Top five finishes	4	10
Top 25 finishes	11	15
Overall record (%)	165–57–1 (74.2%)	157–29–4 (83.7%)
Losing seasons	0	0
Bowl record (%)	8–7 (53.3%)	8–5 (61.5%)
Conference titles	5	12
Conference record	101–39–1	100–11–1
Consensus All-Americans	23	28
First-round draft picks (through 2013)	19	16
Record against ranked teams (%)	51–35 (59.30%)	43–21–4 (66.18%)
Record against top 10 teams (%)	27–17 (61.63%)	23–17–2 (57.14%)

Ratios/percentages		
National title seasons	One every 4.5 seasons	5.33
Consensus All-Americans	1.28 every season	1.75
First-round draft picks (through 2013)	1.12 every season	1.00
Average wins vs. ranked teams	2.83 each season	2.69
Wins over top 10 teams per year	1.50 every season	1.44

total offense while winning by an average score of 43–8. The AP had the team at No. 1, but the coaches' champion was Southern California (10–1–1).

Following numerous scandals, including prison time for shooting a teammate, cocaine sales to FBI officers, theft, and a gang rape, the NCAA found Oklahoma guilty of 20 violations and in December 1988 placed the program on three years' probation. Switzer resigned in June 1989.

Wallace Wade

Although everyone knows Alabama for Paul W. "Bear" Bryant and Nick Saban, the coach who landed the program's first three national championships was Wallace Wade. He wasn't just a tough disciplinarian but a cavalry captain during

Nick Saban vs. Wallace Wade

Category	Saban	Wade
Seasons	18	24
Consensus national titles	4	3
Top five finishes	4	2 (I)
Top 25 finishes	11	7 (I)
Overall record (%)	165–57–1 (74.2%)	171–49–10 (76.5%)
Losing seasons	0	1
Bowl record (%)	8–7 (53.3%)	2–2–1 (I) (.500%)
Conference titles	5	10
Conference record	101–39–1	113–28–5
Consensus All-Americans	23	3
First-round draft picks (through 2013)	19	2 (I)
Record against ranked teams (%)	51–35 (59.30%)	8–16 (I) (33.33%)
Record against top 10 teams (%)	27–17(61.63%)	4–11 (I) (26.67%)

Ratios/percentages		
National title seasons	One every 4.5 seasons	8.0
Consensus All-Americans	1.28 every season	.13
First-round draft picks (through 2013)	1.12 every season	NA
Average wins vs. ranked teams	2.83 each season	NA
Wins over top 10 teams per year	1.50 every season	NA

I–The first Associated Press poll and NFL Draft were conducted in 1936.

World War I. "The best you can do is not enough unless it gets the job done," Wade was known for saying.

Alabama went 7–2–1 during his initial season in 1923 and backed that up with an 8–1 finish that captured the program's first conference title. The team won the first three games by a combined score of 126–0 and didn't yield a point until its seventh game of the season, a 42–7 victory against visiting Kentucky.

Wade's team got off to an even better start in 1925, and after outscoring its nine regular-season opponents 277–7, an invitation was extended to play in the Rose Bowl (though Alabama was far from being the selection committee's first choice). The first southern school to make the trip to Pasadena was considered a heavy underdog to Washington, but it pulled out a 20–19 victory that had long-reaching effects and gave the region a dose of much-needed pride.

With its first national championship in tow, Alabama continued its winning ways in 1926, which included a third straight Southern Conference title and a return trip to the Rose Bowl. Although the Tide didn't win, the 7–7 tie against Stanford answered any questions about whether the previous year had been a fluke, and again Alabama could claim at least a share of the national title.

Wade had one more title run in 1930 when, even though he had turned in his resignation at the end of the previous season, he agreed to stay on for the final year of his contract before heading to Duke. It was arguably his best team yet, and the only points Alabama yielded that season were seven to Vanderbilt and six to Tennessee, while the offense cranked out 271.

A 13–0 victory against Georgia meant both a perfect regular season and fourth Southern Conference championship, resulting in another invitation to the Rose Bowl to play Washington State. That time the game wasn't close—a 24–0 Alabama victory, after which Wade's players carried him off the field. Clyde Bolton of *The Birmingham News* called it the "greatest swan song in the history of football."

Although Wade never won another national championship, he twice came extremely close. The 1938 team known as the "Iron Dukes" finished the regular season undefeated, untied, and unscored-upon, closing with a 7–0 victory in a snowstorm against No. 4. Pittsburgh. However, that still only earned a No. 3 ranking in the final Associated Press poll, and Duke subsequently lost in the Rose Bowl on a last-minute touchdown by Southern California. The Blue Devils were No. 2 at the end of the 1941 season, but instead of traveling back to Pasadena, they hosted the Rose Bowl due to West Coast safety concerns following the attack on Pearl Harbor. Although favored, Duke played flat and lost 20–16 to Oregon State. It remains the only time the Rose Bowl was not played in California.

Glenn "Pop" Warner

There are few, if any, names more synonymous with football than Glenn Scobey Warner, who when he played for Cornell from 1892 to 1894, was nicknamed "Pop" for being older than most of his teammates.

Warner's subsequent coaching career began at Georgia in 1895, when the entire student body was made up of 126 students. It included stops at Iowa State (1895–99, he coached teams from two schools simultaneously three times), Cornell (1897–98, 1904–06), the Carlisle Indian Industrial (1899–1903, 1907–14), Pittsburgh (1915–23), Stanford (1924–32), and Temple (1933–38).

Not including his 18–8 record at Iowa State, which was still a decade from joining its first conference, the Missouri Valley, Warner went 311–103–32 over 42 years for an outstanding winning percentage of .733. He had only three losing seasons and had four teams receive national championship consideration. His 1916 Pitt team was not only his best team but considered the overwhelming consensus national champion before the poll era began. (The other three were 1915 and 1918 teams at Pitt and the 1926 team at Stanford.)

Although Warner didn't lose a game with the Panthers until his fourth season, the 1915 team featured the unique war cry from center Bob Peck: "When Peck fights, the team fights!" The 1916 squad beat Navy, Syracuse, Penn, and Penn State while notching four of its six shutouts.

As for the 1926 title with Stanford, it was led by All-American end Ted Shipkey and sophomore fullback Clifford "Biff" Hoffman and finished 10–0–1. The tie came in the Rose Bowl against Alabama, despite outgaining the Crimson Tide 311 yards to 92, thanks mostly to a blocked punt. Stanford topped the power rankings computed by Frank Dickinson, a University of Illinois economics professor, but the majority of services preferred Alabama.

Warner also coached what's undoubtedly the best college football program most fans have never heard of, Carlisle, which was the first federally supported school of Native Americans to be established off a reservation. Over 25 years, before closing in 1918, it compiled a record of 167–88–13, thanks in part to eight future inductees into the College Football Hall of Fame.

At one time the entire Carlisle coaching staff consisted of Warner and an Oneida Native American named Wallace Denny, the trainer, who doubled as the school's night watchman. The team often played as many as 10 games in six weeks. In 1912 Warner's squad went 12–1–1 and scored 505 points. The following year it finished 10–1–1 with 289 points.

Warner's most notable player there was none other than Jim Thorpe, considered by some to be the greatest all-around athlete in United States history. As a

Nick Saban vs. Glenn "Pop" Warner

Category	Saban	Warner
Seasons	18	44
Consensus national titles	4	1
Top five finishes	4	NA (I)
Top 25 finishes	11	1 (I)
Overall record (%)	165–57–1 (74.2%)	319–106–32 (73.3%)
Losing seasons	0	4
Bowl record (%)	8–7 (53.3%)	1–2–1 (37.5%)
Conference titles	5	4
Conference record	101–39–1	36–13–5
Consensus All-Americans	23	23
First-round draft picks (through 2013)	19	NA (I)
Record against ranked teams (%)	51–35 (59.30%)	1–3–1 (I) (30.0%)
Record against Top 10 teams (%)	27–17 (61.63%)	0–0–1 (I) (50.0%)
Ratios/percentages		
National title seasons	One every 4.5 seasons	44
Consensus All-Americans	1.28 every season	.52
First-round draft picks (through 2013)	1.12 every season	NA
Average wins vs. ranked teams	2.83 each season	NA
Wins over top 10 teams per year	1.50 every season	NA

I-The first Associated Press poll and NFL Draft were conducted in 1936.

halfback in 1907–08 and again in 1911–12, he played 44 games with 53 touchdowns and 421 points. According to the College Football Hall of Fame, statistics for 29 of the games show he averaged 8.4 yards per carry. In 1912 he had 29 touchdowns and 224 points, which led the nation.

"Thorpe was the greatest athlete of his time, maybe of any time in any land," legendary sportswriter Red Smith once wrote, and with good reason. At the 1912 Olympics in Stockholm he won the pentathlon and decathlon. Thorpe went on to play Major League Baseball (1913–15, 1916–19), pro football (1915–28), and was said to excel in every sport he attempted, including golf, tennis, lacrosse, field hockey, riding, rowing, gymnastics, archery, bowling, darts, billiards, basketball, swimming, boxing, and wrestling.

Bud Wilkinson

He was a Minnesota guy and former aircraft-carrier deck officer on the USS *Enterprise* who quickly grew bored with the family mortgage-trading business. But Bud Wilkinson had a knack for football, which he used to turn Oklahoma into a perennial power, and started a wave of success that the Sooners continue to ride to this day.

Just a year after agreeing to join Jim Tatum's staff in 1946, he was the one to take over as both coach and athletic director when Tatum left for Maryland a year later. Wilkinson was just 31 when he unleashed his split-T formation on college football, which would never quite be the same again.

Nick Saban vs. Bud Wilkinson

Category	Saban	Wilkinson
Seasons	18	17
Consensus national titles	4	3
Top five finishes	4	10
Top 25 finishes	11	15
Overall record (%)	165–57–1 (74.2%)	145–29–4 (82.6%)
Losing seasons	0	1
Bowl record (%)	8–7 (53.3%)	6–2 (75.0%)
Conference titles	5	14
Conference record	101–39–1	93–9–3
Consensus All-Americans	23	15
First-round draft picks (through 2013)	19	9
Record against ranked teams (%)	51–35 (59.30%)	28–18–1 (60.64%)
Record against top 10 teams (%)	27–17 (61.63%)	12–15–1 (44.64%)
Ratios/percentages		
National title seasons	One every 4.5 seasons	5.7
Consensus All-Americans	1.28 every season	.88
First-round draft picks (through 2013)	1.12 every season	.53
Average wins vs. ranked teams	2.83 each season	1.65
Wins over top 10 teams per year	1.50 every season	.71

"His teams dispelled the Dust Bowl, Grapes of Wrath image of the Depression years," said former university president George Cross, who hired Wilkinson. "They made Oklahoma proud and called national attention to the state's potential."

The Sooners went 7–2–1 during his first season in 1947, winning the first of 13 straight conference titles when the league grew from the Big Six to the Big 8. He followed that initial season with records of 10–1, 11–0, and 10–1. Paul W. "Bear" Bryant's Kentucky Wildcats snapping a 31-game winning streak with a 13–7 victory at the 1951 Sugar Bowl. The 1949 team outscored opponents 364–88 and topped the season with a 35–0 victory against LSU in the Sugar Bowl.

In 17 seasons Wilkinson had an incredible record of 145–29–4, 93–9–3 in league play with just one losing season. Oklahoma won consensus national championships in 1950, 1955, and 1956 and finished off an 11-year run in which the Sooners always finished in the top five of the final Associated Press poll except once.

From 1953 to 1957, they racked up a major-college-record 47 consecutive victories (snapped by Notre Dame in a 7–0 victory in 1957) despite having stalwarts like Nebraska and Texas on the schedule. Center Jerry Tubbs was one of the players who after three varsity years finished his career without experiencing a single loss.

Additionally, the 1956 Sooners averaged 46.6 points per game, handed Texas its worst loss, 45–0, since 1908 and pounded Notre Dame 40–0 at South Bend. "Losing is easy," Wilkinson said. "It's not enjoyable—but easy."

Other Coaches

Frank Broyles: When he took over at Arkansas in 1957, Broyles inherited a program with just five winning seasons over the previous 19 years and went 144–58–5 over the next 19 years with 10 bowl games and seven Southwest Conference titles. (Note: He also went 5–4–1 one season at Missouri.) Although he never had a team finish atop the Associated Press or coaches' polls, Broyles came close numerous times including 1964 with a team that made a surprising 11–0 finish. The key win was a showdown with reigning national champion Texas, which had not lost a regular-season game in three years. It was decided by Ken Hatfield's dramatic 81-yard punt return for a touchdown for a 14–13 victory. Arkansas, which posted five shutouts that season, didn't allow another point until the Cotton Bowl, where Bobby Burnett's fourth-quarter three-yard touchdown plunge capped an 80-yard drive to finish a 10–7 comeback victory against Nebraska. Among those associated with the team were future football gurus Jimmy Johnson, Johnny Majors, Barry Switzer, and Jerry Jones.

Walter Camp: It would be impossible to do a book about college football coaches and not mention Camp, perhaps the game's greatest innovator. He played at Yale from 1877 to 1882 and was the program's first official football coach, compiling a 68–2 record from 1888 to 1892. Three of his undefeated teams (1888, 1891, and 1892) are essentially considered undisputed national champions. Among his many notable achievements was to standardize the game's rules, thus becoming known as the "Father of American Football." He created the line of scrimmage, the 11-man team, signal-calling, the quarterback position, and was the originator of the rule whereby a team had to give up the ball unless it had advanced a specified distance within a set number of downs. Camp also coached three seasons at Stanford, then an independent, where he had a 12–3–3 record.

Lloyd Carr: After being an assistant coach at Michigan from 1980 to 1994, Carr was finally promoted to head coach after Gary Moeller resigned. Over 13 seasons his Wolverines went 122–40, won five Big Ten titles and the 1997 national championship, though it was largely viewed as a split title with Nebraska. After quarterback Brian Griese completed 18-of-30 passes for 251 yards and three touchdowns to lead the 21–16 victory against Washington State in the Rose Bowl, Associated Press voters selected Michigan by a wide margin. However, the coaches' poll leapfrogged Nebraska over the No. 1 Wolverines by a mere two votes. All but one of his teams finished the season ranked, and he also coached 1997 Heisman Trophy winner Charles Woodson.

Larry Coker: With Butch Davis leaving for the Cleveland Browns, Coker inherited the 2001 Hurricanes, considered to be one of the best in college football history. They outscored opponents 512–117 for an average score of 42.7–9.8. He went 60–15 during six seasons at Miami with three top-five finishes. In 2011 he was named the first head coach of Texas at San Antonio (UTSA) and led the Roadrunners to an 8–4 first season.

Fritz Crisler: He's considered the father of two-platoon football and was also known for single-wing offense while compiling a record of 116–32–9 for a

.768 winning percentage at Minnesota (1930–31), Princeton (1932–37), and Michigan (1938–47). Crisler enjoyed two undefeated seasons at Princeton, but his final season saw the pinnacle of his coaching career, when Michigan ran the table in 1947 and defeated Southern California 49–0 in the Rose Bowl—his only bowl game. Although Notre Dame finished atop the Associated Press poll, many considered the Wolverines the real national champions. Crisler also coached a number of other sports and was Michigan's athletic director from 1941 to 1968.

Duffy Daugherty: During his 19 years as Michigan State's head coach (1954–66), Daugherty went 109–65–5 and coached 13 consensus All-Americans. Three times his teams finished second in the final Associated Press poll (seven in the top 10), with the 1966 title one of the most controversial in college football history after Michigan State tied No. 1 Notre Dame, and No. 3 Alabama didn't have such a blemish. Daugherty's teams won two Big Ten championships and split their two appearances in the Rose Bowl, both against UCLA.

Dan Devine: Over his 22-year career, he had three collegiate stops in addition to a brief stint heading the Green Bay Packers. Devine posted a 27–3–1 record at Arizona State (1955–57) and went 92–38–7 at Missouri (1958–70), where six of his 13 teams finished ranked in the final Associated Press poll. However, he's best known for his six years at Notre Dame (1975–80), where his teams went 53–16–1 and claimed the 1977 national championship by beating previously undefeated Texas in the Cotton Bowl. Devine went 172–57–9 (.742 winning percentage), 7–3 in bowl games, and had one other top-five finish, No. 5 with the 1960 Tigers. (Note: Kansas beat Missouri 23–7, but the Tigers were later awarded the win due to the Jayhawks using an ineligible player.)

Paul Dietzel: After creating a unique three-team platoon, including the second-string defensive unit called the "Chinese Bandits," Dietzel led LSU to an undefeated season and national championship in 1958. During his seven seasons the Tigers went 46–24–3 and finished in the top five of the Associated Press poll three times. After the 1961 season, Dietzel accepted the head coaching job at Army, making him the first non-Army graduate to hold the position. The former assistant coach under Paul W. "Bear" Bryant at Kentucky went 109–95–5 (.533 winning percentage) over 20 years and led South Carolina to its only league title in 1969 (Atlantic Coast Conference).

Vince Dooley: During his 25 seasons as Georgia's head coach, the Bulldogs went 201–77–10 (.715 winning percentage) and played in 20 bowl games. With running back Herschel Walker, Georgia dominated the Southeastern Conference from 1980 to 1982, winning three league crowns and a national championship. From 1979 to 1988, Dooley also served as athletic director. While his teams also had a strong academic record, they averaged more than eight wins a season, captured six league titles, and finished ranked in the final Associated Press poll 12 times, (eight in the top 10).

LaVell Edwards: During his 29 years at Brigham Young, the Cougars won 20 conference titles with 22 bowl appearances. They also captured the 1984 national championship at the end of a 13–0 season when BYU only had to defeat unranked Michigan in the Holiday Bowl 24–17 to claim the title. However, to help put the numbers into perspective, consider that prior to his arrival in 1972, the program had won just 173 games with 16 winning seasons out of 47 and been shut out 72 times. That happened only once under Edwards, whose pass-oriented offense averaged 32 points in 361 games. He went 257–101–3 (.716 winning percentage). Of his 12 teams to finish ranked, three were in the top 10, and the Cougars were 7–14–1 in bowl games.

Dennis Erickson: After four years at Idaho, one at Wyoming, and two at Washington State, where he only had an 18–16–1 record at the Division I level, Erickson was tapped to replace Jimmy Johnson after he left Miami to take over the Dallas Cowboys and won two national titles with the Hurricanes. In 1989 Miami didn't allow a touchdown for a 10-quarter stretch during the regular season, held six opponents without a touchdown, and allowed just 9.3 points per game. Miami bounced back from a loss to Florida State to defeat No. 1 Notre Dame 27–10 and beat No. 7 Alabama in the Sugar Bowl. Two years later, Miami benefited from "Wide Right I" to defeat No. 1 FSU and went on to crush Nebraska 22–0 in the Orange Bowl to cap a 12–0 season and split the national title with Washington, which finished No. 1 in the coaches' poll. However, after Erickson resigned to become the head coach of the Seattle Seahawks, the NCAA charged Miami with lack of institutional control and issued severe sanctions. After stints at Oregon State and Arizona State, Erickson was 147–81–1 at major schools (.644 winning percentage) over 19 seasons, 5–7 in bowl games, and nine of his teams finished ranked in the Associated Press poll.

Danny Ford: In 1981 Ford became the youngest coach ever to win the national title at age 33, but just days after the 1982 season ended, Clemson was found guilty of recruiting violations. Although most of them occurred under the previous coach, the NCAA found that they had continued under Ford, resulting in a two-year bowl and television ban. Ford rebounded by leading three straight 10–2 seasons before resigning in 1990 due to a falling out with school officials; he later coached Arkansas (1993–97). Over 17 seasons Ford compiled a 121–60–5 record (.664 winning percentage), went 6–3 in bowl games, and eight of his teams finished ranked in the Associated Press poll.

Phillip Fulmer: When Nick Saban and Alabama cruised to a 29–9 win at Tennessee in 2008 for its first back-to-back victories in the "Third Saturday in October" rivalry since 1991–92, the vultures were already circling. With UT's subsequent loss to South Carolina, the school announced the season would be Fulmer's last. From 1992 to 2008, Tennessee went 151–52–1 (.743 winning percentage), was 8–7 in bowl games, and was ranked in the final Associated Press poll 13 times. After finishing second to Florida in the SEC East four straight years (1993–96), the Volunteers finally broke through with Peyton Manning to win the SEC championship in 1997. After the quarterback left, the team won the first BCS title at the end of the 1998 season with a victory over Florida State in the Fiesta Bowl. Saban cost Fulmer another shot at a national title in 2001 when No. 21 LSU pulled off a 31–20 upset in the SEC Championship Game.

John Gagliardi: With a record of 489–138–11, the coach with the most wins in college football history, Gagliardi of St. John's University, never worked at the Division I level. When he took the job in 1953, the previous coach, Johnny "Blood" McNally (a legendary player in the NFL) warned him that no one could win at St. John's. Gagliardi captured four national championships, two at the NAIA level (1963 and 1965), and two in Division III (1976 and 2003). During his 60 seasons, St. John's won 30 conference titles and played in 58 postseason games (39–19) while "Winning with Nos." In addition to refusing to be called "Coach," Gagliardi did not use a whistle, blocking sleds, require the players to lift weights, allow tackling during drills, and limited all practices to 90 minutes. The 1993 team, though, averaged 61.5 points per game. Gagliardi coached other sports as well and served as athletic director (1976–94). He was the first active head coach to be inducted into the College Football Hall of Fame (2006) and retired in 2012.

Percy Haughton: A major reason why Harvard had only one losing season during its first 50 years of playing football was Haughton, whose teams compiled a 71–7–5 record from 1908 to 1916 and at one point enjoyed a 22-game winning streak. The Crimson also won three early national titles with teams that finished 8–0–1 (1910), 9–0 (1912), and 9–0 (1913)—the last two of which were led by back Charles Brickley, who still holds the school career record for points with 215 (23 touchdowns, 25 field goals, and two extra points). After briefly coaching at Columbia, Haughton's last words in 1924 were: "Tell the squad I'm proud of them." Also, in his book *Football and How to Watch It*, he wrote, "Football is a miniature war game played under somewhat more civilized rules of conduct, in which the team becomes the military force of the school or university it represents." His overall career record was 97–19–7 for a winning percentage of 81.7.

John Heisman: The man, for whom the Heisman Trophy was named, played every line position while at Brown (1887–89) and Penn (1890–91) and began his coaching career at Oberlin in 1892. He remained on the move, to Akron for a year, back to Oberlin in 1894, followed by Auburn (1895–99), Clemson (1900–03), Georgia Tech (1904–19), Penn (1920–22), Washington & Jefferson (1923), and finally Rice (1924–27). According to his College Football Hall of Fame bio, Heisman "originated the hidden-ball play, was the first to place his quarterback at safety on defense, invented the center snap, dreamed up the concept of the scoreboard, introduced the 'hike' vocal signal for initiating a play, led the fight to reduce the game from halves to quarters, and was in the forefront of the move to legalize the pass in 1906." A Shakespearean actor during the off-season, he once ran up a 222–0 score on Cumberland College. During his 26 years coaching major programs, Heisman went 148–60–14 (69.8 winning percentage) and had just one losing season. His overall record was 185–70–17, and he won five conference titles, one national championship, and coached five consensus All-Americans.

Don James: Arguably Saban's biggest football mentor and the man who got him into coaching was James, who over 22 years at Kent State and Washington had a 178–76–3 record, including 153–57–2 with the Huskies. Under his direction, Washington played in the Rose Bowl six times from 1977 to 1992, winning four. The 1984 team went 11–1 and with a 28–17 victory against Oklahoma in the Orange Bowl finished No. 2, but the 1991 squad was unequivocally his best. Led by defensive tackle Steve Emtman, who finished fourth in Heisman Trophy voting, and quarterback Billy Joe Hobert, the Huskies ran the table and then punctuated the season with a 34–14 victory against Michigan in Pasadena, where Heisman winner Desmond Howard only had one reception. The result was a split national title, with Associated Press voters selecting Miami but coaches opting for Washington. The 1984 Huskies also finished second in the AP poll.

Jimmy Johnson: Although Johnson was only a head coach for 10 years at the collegiate level, he's already in the College Football Hall of Fame. After posting a 29–25–3 record at Oklahoma State, he had an epic run at Miami that included a 52–9 record and five New Year's Day bowl appearances, culminating with the 1987 national championship following a 20–14 victory over Oklahoma in the Orange Bowl. He had three teams finish in the top five of the final Associated Press poll (reflected in his 3–4 bowl record), coached the program's first Heisman Trophy winner in Vinny Testaverde, and started the NCAA-record 58 home-game winning streak (1985–94).

Larry Kehres: During his 27 seasons at Mount Union, Kehres had a remarkable 332–24–3 record and won 11 national championships in Division III. His .929 winning percentage is the best ever at the college level, and his teams enjoyed 21 undefeated regular seasons.

Johnny Majors: After stints as an assistant coach at Tennessee, Mississippi State, and Arkansas, the former Tennessee standout halfback landed his first head coaching job at Iowa State, where he went 24–30–1 and was subsequently hired to rescue a Pittsburgh program that had lost 56 of 72 games. In his first year, Pitt went to the Fiesta Bowl, its first bowl in 17 years, and his strategy of overrecruiting the roster helped lead to NCAA legislation limiting scholarships. During the 1976 season his alma mater called, and Majors announced he was leaving at season's end; the Panthers went 12–0 and beat Georgia 27–3 in the Sugar Bowl to win the national championship. From 1977 to 1992, he went 116–62–8 with the Volunteers, who finished ranked six times, twice in the top five. Majors returned to Pitt (1993–96) to finish his 29-year career with a 185–137–10 record (57.2 percentage), 9–7 in bowl games.

Bill McCartney: In 1981 Colorado hired McCartney away from Michigan, where he had been Bo Schembechler's defensive coordinator. His first three seasons resulted in a 7–25–1 record, but switching the offense to the wishbone in 1985 was a turning point. Colorado finished the 1989 regular season 11–0, went into the Orange Bowl ranked No. 1, but came up short against Notre Dame 21–6. Fast-forward a year, Colorado opened with a tie against Tennessee, barely squeezed out a 21–17 victory against Stanford, and then lost 23–22 at Illinois. After close wins against Texas and Washington, the Buffaloes benefited from the epic "fifth down" controversy at Missouri, where officials mistakenly gave Colorado an extra down during the closing seconds, which it used to score the game-winning touchdown. But against the toughest schedule in the nation, the team didn't lose again, rising back to No. 1 for a rematch against No. 5 Notre Dame in the Orange Bowl, and this time it won. Overall, McCartney went 93–55–5 (62.4 percent), led the Buffs to nine bowls in 13 seasons, and captured three Big 8 titles.

Leo "Dutch" Meyer: Meyer, who many credit for introducing the spread offense to college football, brought Texas Christian to national prominence and won three conference titles in addition to a consensus national title in 1938. While running the table (11–0), the team defeated No. 6 Carnegie Tech 15–7 in the Sugar Bowl after trailing at halftime for the first time all season. Led by quarterback Davey O'Brien, TCU scored on its first possession of the second half to take the lead for good. The Horned Frogs outscored their opponents that season 269–60. Despite being 5'7", O'Brien was the first player to win the Heisman, Walter Camp, and Maxwell trophies for most outstanding player, all in the same year. Today the Davey O'Brien National Quarterback Award is annually given to the best college quarterback in the nation. "Sammy Baugh was a better all-around player than O'Brien and a better passer, but as a field general, Davey has never been equaled," Meyer said about his two great quarterbacks. "He was the finest play selector I've ever seen." Meyer, known as "the Saturday Fox," had a record of 109–79–13 over 19 years (.575 percentage) and went 3–4 in bowl games.

Clarence "Biggie" Munn: An All-American at Minnesota, Munn only coached one season at Syracuse and seven at Michigan State but gets a brief mention here for winning the 1952 national championship before becoming the Spartans' athletic director. From 1947 to 1953, Michigan State went 54–9–2 and finished ranked six straight years, including top-five showings the last three. His final game was his only bowl, the Rose Bowl at the end of the 1953 season, which Michigan

State won 28–20 against UCLA. His overall record at major schools was 58–14–2 (.797 winning percentage).

Homer Norton: He was the head coach at Centenary College of Louisiana from 1919 to 1921 and again from 1926 to 1933 and at Texas A&M from 1934 to 1947, compiling a record of 143–75–18. His career peaked during a three-year stretch with the Aggies, when they went 29–3 from 1939 to 1941 and won the 1939 national championship. A&M went 10–0 during the regular season and outscored opponents 198–18 before edging Tulane 14–13 in the Sugar Bowl. A&M shared the Southwest Conference title in 1940 and won it outright a year later, only to lose 29–21 to Alabama in the Cotton Bowl.

Eddie Robinson: Robinson went 408–165–15 (70.7 winning percentage) during his phenomenal career, which spanned 57 years at Grambling and saw more than 200 of his players go on to play professionally, including Hall of Famers like the Kansas City Chiefs' Buck Buchanan, the Oakland Raiders' Willie Brown, and the San Diego Chargers' Charlie Joiner. He also coached quarterback Doug Williams, Super Bowl XXII MVP with the Washington Redskins, who succeeded Robinson at Grambling. Robinson won at least a share of 17 Southwestern Athletic Conference championships, nine black college national titles, and from 1960 to 1986 he posted 27 consecutive winning seasons. The Football Writers Association of America named its annual Coach of the Year award after him, and Baton Rogue, home of Grambling's biggest rival, Southern, named a street in his honor. When he retired in 1997, the College Football Hall of Fame waived the requirement that a coach be out of the game for at least three years before being considered for enshrinement.

Bill Roper: In addition to serving as the head coach at the Virginia Military Institute (1903–04), Missouri (1909), and Swarthmore College (1915–16), Roper had three stints at his alma mater, Princeton (1906–08, 1910–11, and 1919–30). His 89 wins top the program, and he had an overall record of 112–38–18. Princeton claimed four titles during his time, and almost no one disputes 1911 and the 1922 "Team of Destiny." Despite having just three returning starters, Princeton was picked to finish behind Harvard and Yale but got a 21–18 comeback win at Chicago on a Howdy Gray 40-yard fumble recovery for a touchdown and a Harry Crum one-yard touchdown plunge on fourth down. Princeton returned to the East Coast to beat Harvard 10–3 and Yale 3–0 to finish 8–0 while outscoring opponents 127–34.

Howard Schnellenberger: One of Paul W. "Bear" Bryant's offensive coordinators who helped Alabama win national championships in 1961, 1964, and 1965, Schnellenberger made a name for himself by starting Miami's incredible run in the 1980s and won the 1983 national championship. During his 24-year career as a college head coach, Schnellenberger spent one year at Oklahoma, started the program at Florida Atlantic, and left Louisville after 10 seasons when it joined Conference USA. He went 141–133–3 (.514 winning percentage), was a perfect 6–0 in bowl games, and had five teams that finished ranked.

Ben Schwartzwalder: He was a 95-pound quarterback in high school and a 146-pound center at West Virginia who became a paratrooper during World War II and was awarded the Silver Star, Bronze Star, Purple Heart, four Battle Stars, and a Presidential Unit Citation. After returning home he began his coaching career at Muhlenberg College, where from 1946 to 1948 he went 25–5 before going 153–91–3 at Syracuse from 1949 to 1973. Schwartzwalder was primarily known for two things there: having Jim Brown, Ernie Davis, Floyd Little, Jim Nance, and Larry Csonka as running backs and the 1959 national championship. That team averaged 313.6 rushing yards, 451.5 total yards, and 39 points per game while yielding only 19.3 rushing yards and 96.2 total yards. He had seven teams finish ranked, plus four more that were in the final coaches' poll, and went 2–5 in bowl games.

Andy Smith: Although he had enjoyed successful short stints at both Pennsylvania and Purdue in the early years of college football, it was after compiling a record of 24–13–3 during his first four seasons at California that things clicked for Smith. "The Wonder Teams" with standout Babe Horrell at center went 44–0–4 between 1920 and 1924, with the Golden Bears considered the 1920 national champions (and tabbed No. 1 by various services in 1921, 1922, and 1923 as well). Cal went 9–0–0 that season—giving up just two touchdowns, one during a 79–7 victory against Nevada—while scoring 510 points and capped it off with a 28–0 drubbing of Ohio State in the Rose Bowl. His team went back to Pasadena the following season and tied Washington & Jefferson 0–0 for a 9–0–1 finish. The Golden Bears didn't experience another loss until a 15–0 decision against the Olympic Club in 1925. Overall, Smith had a career record of 116–32–13.

Gene Stallings: It took one of Paul W. "Bear" Bryant's former lieutenants and Junction Boys to return Alabama to the national championship picture. Stallings ended Miami's domination with a 34–13 win in the Sugar Bowl to cap a perfect 1992 season. Stallings enjoyed a 28-game winning streak and had three teams finish ranked in the top five. While Stallings also had an extensive coaching career in the NFL, he first was the head coach at Texas A&M for seven seasons, where his biggest win arguably came against Bryant and Alabama in the Cotton Bowl. Over 14 seasons his teams went 97–61–2, though his record was later adjusted to 87–70–1 by the NCAA due to playing an ineligible player in 1993. He was 6–1 in bowl games.

Jock Sutherland: After closing out a five-year stretch at Lafayette College, where his last three teams combined to go 22–3–2, Sutherland had a fantastic winning percentage of .818 over 15 years (1924–38) and guided Pittsburgh to four Rose Bowls, only to decline the invitation after the 9–0–1 season in 1937. The previous year the Panthers made the trip to Pasadena and defeated Washington 21–0, but the players preferred going on Christmas vacation instead. Nevertheless, Pitt was still considered the overwhelming national champion. Sutherland had a combined record of 144–28–14 and 1–3 in bowl games. Various services had his 1921 Lafayette team and the 1929, 1931, and 1936 Panthers at No. 1, but they were in the minority.

"Big" Jim Tatum: Tatum was an assistant at his alma mater, North Carolina, where he got a taste for head coaching when Raymond "Bear" Wolf entered the navy, and after a 5–2–2 season, Tatum enlisted as well. He was assigned to the Iowa Pre-Flight School where he was an assistant under Don Faurot and mastered his trademark split-T offense. Following the service he spent one year at Oklahoma (8–3–0 record in 1946) before accepting the head coaching job at Maryland. During his nine seasons, the Terrapins went 73–15–4, had six ranked teams, and at one point won 19 straight games. Although they beat top-ranked Tennessee 28–13 in the 1952 Sugar Bowl, the 1953 team is credited as being national champions despite losing to Oklahoma in the Sugar Bowl, 7–0 (when final polls were held before bowl games). Tatum's coaching career ended back at UNC (1956–58). He was 100–35–7 (.729) overall and 3–2–1 in bowl games.

Frank Thomas: When Wallace Wade turned in his resignation at the end of the 1929 season, he suggested that former Georgia assistant coach Frank Thomas replace him at Alabama. As a college quarterback, "Shrewd Tommy" had been George Gipp's roommate at Notre Dame, and sportswriter Naylor Stone in *Coach*

Tommy of the Crimson Tide credited Knute Rockne with telling his coaches: "It's amazing the amount of football sense that Thomas kid has. He can't miss becoming a great coach some day. I want him on our staff next fall." Instead, Thomas chose to attend law school. Thomas was 26–9–2 at Chattanooga and 115–24–7 at Alabama from 1931 to 1946 before stepping down due to health reasons. Under his direction the Crimson Tide won the first Southeastern Conference title in 1933, and the school claims national championships for 1934 and 1941 (though Minnesota was a much more popular choice both years). It was during the undefeated 1934 season, when Alabama outscored the opposition 316–45, that Tennessee coach Robert Neyland commented, "You never know what a football player is made of until he plays against Alabama."

John Vaught: During his career (1947–70, 1973), Vaught complied a 190–61–12 record for a .745 winning percentage and 18 bowl appearances. The coach of Archie Manning preached diligence and preparation, but despite having three teams reach No. 1, he didn't have any finish atop the Associated Press poll. The 1959 and 1960 Rebels were both second, the latter being somewhat controversial, as No. 1 Minnesota subsequently lost 17–7 to Washington in the Rose Bowl, while the Rebels beat Rice 14–6 in the Sugar Bowl.

Murray Warmath: After two years at Mississippi State, Warmath took over at Minnesota and from 1954 to 1971 went 87–78–7 (.526) with two Big Ten titles and Rose Bowl appearances. The Gophers haven't won a league title since. Despite losing to Purdue, the 1960 team was voted No. 1 in both the final Associated Press and coaches' poll before losing 17–7 to Washington in the Rose Bowl. However, Minnesota went back to Pasadena a year later and defeated UCLA 21–3. To put the turnaround into further perspective, his 1958–59 teams combined to go 3–15.

George Woodruff: When the former Yale guard was hired in 1892, Pennsylvania all but destroyed the competition, beginning with a 15–1 record the first year and the only loss to Woodruff's former school. From 1894 to 1898, Penn compiled a 67–2 record, including a 12–0 season in 1894 to receive national title consideration, and was the clear choice the following year after shutting out the first 10 opponents and finishing 14–0. Penn was even more dominating in 1897 when led by four All-Americans, including tackle/halfback John Outland, for whom the Outland Trophy for best lineman is named; the team finished 15–0 and outscored opponents 443–20 with 12 shutouts. During Woodruff's 10 seasons at Penn, the team went 124–15–2 and outscored opponents 1,777–88. He subsequently coached a year at Illinois and Carlisle before taking over at Georgia for five seasons in 1923. The Bulldogs went 9–1 his final year in 1927, giving him a career mark of 172–41–3 over 17 seasons.

Fielding Yost: During his first five years at Michigan from 1901–1905, he went 55–1–1, outscored opponents 2,821–42, and won the first Rose Bowl game 49–0 over Stanford. The school claims six national titles for Yost, but with at least two, that opinion was in the minority. In 1903 the National Championship Foundation had Michigan at No. 1, but every other service opted for Princeton. In 1904 the NCF again liked the Wolverines, while most others preferred Penn. The 1918 title was basically a split between Michigan and Pittsburgh, and in 1923 Illinois was a much more popular selection. Although there are some discrepancies about Yost's career numbers, the NCAA has him at 196–36–12. He had one losing season (1919) and went 42–10–2 in the Big Ten. The school also claims that 64 men who either played for Yost or coached under him as an assistant went on to become head coaches in college football.

Robert Zuppke: The lively coach was at Illinois from 1913 to 1941, went 131–81–12, and coached arguably the two biggest football names in that state's history, Red Grange and George Halas. Grange helped Illinois win the 1923 national championship, but it probably wasn't the best team in program history. That distinction goes to the 1914 squad, which went 7–0 and outscored opponents 224–22 (though Army was the majority choice for national champion). While the defense posted four shutouts, halfback Bart Macomber and guard Ralph Chapman led the offense. Although Zuppke also won a title in 1927, perhaps his biggest victory came against Minnesota in 1916. While Illinois was 2–2, Minnesota was a 40-point favorite with five All-American candidates. With Halas out due to an injury, Illinois used only 11 players, went up 14–0, and held on for the 14-9 win. The headline of the *Chicago Herald* said: HOLD ON TIGHT WHEN YOU READ THIS!

★ ★ ★

How They Stack Up, Part IV: Winning Big Games

One of the reasons why so many consider Michael Jordan to be the best basketball player in history is that he was a perfect 6–0 in the NBA Finals while recording two three-peats. Through 2013, Nick Saban was undefeated in national title games and 4–1 in SEC championships, which for the most part have featured much tougher matchups. Two, of course, were against Urban Meyer at Florida, and those two coaches were a major reason why the SEC won an unprecedented seven straight national championships (2006–12). In 2012 the league also captured its fourth Heisman Trophy in six years (in contrast it took 37 years to win its first four), six teams finished in the top 10 of the final Associated Press poll, and during the subsequent NFL Draft it had a record 61 players selected.

His closest national title game was the first, 21–14 against Oklahoma.

After topping Alabama and Saban in the Sugar Bowl at the end of the 2013 season for a little bit of payback, Bob Stoops improved to 18–13 against teams ranked in the top 10, while Saban was 27–17—which also meant that on average Stoops faced 2.07 teams ranked that high, while Saban's average, even with his years outside of the SEC, was 2.44.

Here's how those numbers rate:

Record Against Ranked Opponents, Active Coaches (%)
Bob Stoops 50–23 (68.49)
Urban Meyer 25–12 (67.57)
Jimbo Fisher 9–5 (64.29)
Nick Saban 51–35 (59.30)
Brian Kelly 15–11 (57.69)
Les Miles 40–31 (56.33)
Steve Spurrier 63–52–1 (54.74)
Mark Richt 34–31 (52.31)
Frank Beamer 43–50–1 (46.28)
Bill Snyder 21–42–1 (33.59)

Average Wins Against Ranked Teams, Active Coaches
Bob Stoops 3.33
Les Miles 3.08
Nick Saban 2.83
Mark Richt 2.62
Steve Spurrier 2.63
Urban Meyer 2.08
Frank Beamer 1.59
Brian Kelly 1.50
Bill Snyder 0.95

Record Against Top 10 Opponents, Active Coaches (%)
Urban Meyer 12–5 (70.59)
Nick Saban 25–16 (60.96)
Bob Stoops 18–13 (58.06)
Jimbo Fisher 4–3 (57.14)
Les Miles 16–17 (48.48)
Steve Spurrier 26–31–1 (45.69)
Mark Richt 11–16 (40.74)
Brian Kelly 2–6 (25.00)
Frank Beamer 7–32 (17.95)
Bill Snyder 4–29 (12.12)

A master of big-game victories, Nick Saban leads his Alabama team onto the field.

Average Wins Against Top 10 Teams, Active Coaches

Nick Saban 1.50

Les Miles 1.23

Bob Stoops 1.20

Steve Spurrier 1.08

Urban Meyer 1.00

Mark Richt .85

Frank Beamer .26

Brian Kelly .20

Bill Snyder .18

Pete Carroll was 29–9 against ranked teams (76.3 percent) and 12–4 against top 10 opponents for averages of 3.2 and 1.3, respectively. After NCAA penalties Jim Tressel was 31–15 (67.4) against ranked opponents and 9–8 versus (52.9) top 10 teams.

With just the Crimson Tide (2007–13), Saban was 28–12 against ranked opponents (70.0 percent) and 16–6 when facing top 10 teams (72.7). He's averaging 4.0 wins per season against ranked teams and 2.3 versus top 10 opponents.

Over the years the ability to win big games or inability to do so has probably defined coaches more than any other factor and correspondingly led to reputations that could take years, if not decades, to overcome, if at all.

Tom Osborne's a perfect example. From 1987 to 1993, the Cornhuskers lost in seven straight bowls after losing only eight regular-season games during that entire time span. Finally, though, he became the first coach in 40 years to have two consecutive undefeated seasons en route to winning national titles.

So who are college football's top big-game coaches? Many are considered the best the sport has ever enjoyed. Although coaches can obviously influence how tough their schedules are, here's the average number of wins each has recorded against ranked teams and top 10 opponents.

Average Wins Against Ranked Teams, All-Time Coaches (Minimum 15 Years)

Bob Stoops 3.33

Les Miles 3.08

Nick Saban 2.83

Barry Switzer 2.69
Steve Spurrier 2.63
Frank Leahy 2.46
Tom Osborne 2.48
John McKay 2.13
Bobby Bowden 1.98
Paul W. "Bear" Bryant 1.71
Bud Wilkinson 1.65
Frank Beamer 1.59
Mack Brown 1.58
Lou Holtz 1.55
Joe Paterno 1.43 (Z)
Woody Hayes 1.37
Bo Schembechler 1.37
Shug Jordan 1.32
Darrell Royal 1.30
Bill Snyder .95
Ara Parseghian .89
Bob Devaney .75

Z-Without NCAA penalties Paterno's average was 1.86.

Average Wins Against Top 10 Teams, All-Time Coaches

Frank Leahy 1.69
Nick Saban 1.50
Barry Switzer 1.44
John McKay 1.31
Les Miles 1.25
Bob Stoops 1.20
Tom Osborne 1.08
Steve Spurrier 1.08
Bobby Bowden .95
Paul W. "Bear" Bryant .87
Lou Holtz .79
Ara Parseghian .79

Darrell Royal .78
Woody Hayes .77
Mark Richt .75
Bud Wilkinson .71
Shug Jordan .64
Joe Paterno .63 (Z)
Bo Schembechler .59
Mack Brown .38
Bob Devaney .38
Frank Bearmer .26
Bill Snyder .18

Z-Without NCAA penalties Paterno's average was .76.

Overall, among those who have faced at least 20 opponents ranked in the top 10, only one coach in history has had a better career winning percentage than Saban.

Winning Percentage Against Top 10 Teams (Minimum 20 Games)

Frank Leahy 86.54
Nick Saban 61.01
Paul W. "Bear" Bryant 58.77
Bob Stoops 58.06
John McKay 57.69
Barry Switzer 57.14
Woody Hayes 52.08
Les Miles 48.48
Darrell Royal 46.25
Bobby Bowden 46.39
Tom Osborne 45.76
Bud Wilkinson 44.64
Steve Spurrier 45.69
Bo Schembechler 42.31
Ara Parseghian 41.67
Mark Richt 40.74

Lou Holtz 38.57
Joe Paterno 38.16 (Z)
Shug Jordan 36.36
Mack Brown 25.58
Frank Beamer 17.95
Bill Snyder 12.12

Z-Without NCAA penalties Paterno's percentage was 42.7.

Finally, the tougher the opponent, the better Saban's winning percentage—for the most part. As previously shown through 2013 he won 59.3 percent of his games against ranked opponents and 61.6 percent against teams in the top 10. Against teams in the top five, he's 56.5 percent (13–10) and he is 66.7 percent against opponents ranked No. 1 (4–2).

Now check out his numbers at Alabama (2007–13), which have been even more impressive:

Top 25: 28–12
Top 10: 16–6
Top 5: 7–5
No. 1: 3–1

The four wins against teams ranked No. 1 are tied for the most by any coach since the Associated Press poll was created in 1936.

Wins Against No. 1 Teams in Associated Press

Joe Paterno 4
Lou Holtz 4
Jimmy Johnson 4
Nick Saban 4
Jack Mollenkopf 4
Paul W. "Bear" Bryant 3
Dennis Erickson 3
Bo Schembechler 3
Barry Switzer 3

Jack Mollenkopf was at Purdue from 1956 to 1969 and went 84–39–9. All but two of his teams were ranked at some point of the season, with the 1968 Boilermakers No. 1 in the preseason poll. However, his best finish was No. 7 in 1966, when Purdue went 8–2 and defeated Southern California in the Rose Bowl.

Of those coaches with three-plus wins, only one has a better record and percentage than Saban against top-ranked opponents:

Jimmy Johnson	4–1	80.0
Lou Holtz	4–2	66.7
Jack Mollenkopf	4–2	66.7
Nick Saban	4–2	66.7
Barry Switzer	3–2–2	57.1
Paul W. "Bear" Bryant	3–3	50.0
Dennis Erickson	3–3	50.0
Bo Schembechler	3–5–1	38.9
Joe Paterno	4–8	33.3

Bud Wilkinson is one of the few with a winning record against No. 1 teams, at 2–1, but his Sooners were 5–9 against opponents ranked in the top five. Meanwhile, USC's John Robinson was 2–0 against No. 1 teams. Some others of note include: Urban Meyer, 2–2; Bob Stoops, 2–2; Woody Hayes, 2–3; John McKay, 2–3; Mack Brown, 2–4; Steve Spurrier, 2–4; Ara Parseghian, 2–5; Frank Broyles, 2–6; Bobby Bowden, 1–5; Tom Osborne, 1–5; Les Miles, 1–5; Frank Beamer, 0–6; Jim Tressel, 1–1; and Frank Leahy, 0–1–1, while Pete Carroll never faced a No. 1 team.

Granted, you can't face the team atop the poll when it's your team, but on the flip side, Alabama's record when ranked No. 1 (BCS standings, otherwise Associated Press) under Saban was 28–4 (87.5 winning percentage) through 2013. All other No. 1 teams from 2007 to 2013 combined were 51–15 (77.3).

★ ★ ★

The Mount Rushmore of College Football: Nick Saban

★ ★ ★ ★ ★ ★ ★

"He was a hard-nosed coach and demanded a lot from us. If you can do it and you can do it well, why not do it perfect? That was his whole philosophy."

—Former Alabama defensive lineman Marcell Dareus (2008–10)

Like with so many other successful coaches, Nick Saban has numerous ways to get a point across, and anecdotes that get retold every few years to new and younger audiences.

"Saint," or now "Grandpa" Nick telling a story goes something like this: "I'll never forget fishing as an 11-year-old in West Virginia, and I'm fishing down by this lake where the hot water runs off from the coal mine because that hot water is where the catfish like to hang out. This guy is just sitting there pulling in huge catfish but throwing them back and then he'll catch smaller ones and keep them. I'm not catching anything at all, but I'm like, 'Hey, man, why do you keep those little ones and throw back those huge ones?' His answer was, 'Because I've only got a nine-inch skillet.' See? You have to know who you are."

So who is coach Nick Saban? Just the one everybody in college football is chasing and the man who might be piecing together the greatest dynasty the game has ever seen. His career numbers have been nothing short of spectacular, and the ones at Alabama can only be described as unparalleled and unprecedented.

In terms of national championships, he's set a mind-numbing pace. He arguably recruits better than anyone in college football history and Saban is set to reach two amazing accomplishments by 2017: having coached the most consensus All-Americans and the most first-round selections in the NFL Draft. Through 2012 he had a perfect record when a crystal football was on the line, and only two cohorts had a better winning percentage against top 10 opponents. He's the only coach in the modern era to win titles with two different programs and he's done so while competing in a conference that's similarly at its own unique level.

Moreover, his players graduate at a very high level and win academic awards. Not only is Saban the only coach to have a Heisman Trophy winner at Alabama, he, Steve Spurrier, and Phillip Fulmer are the only coaches to have two winners of the Campbell Trophy, the academic Heisman.

Saban hasn't just become the coach to beat and/or emulate; he's set a new standard while simultaneously taking his place in college football lore—alongside Notre Dame's Four Horsemen, Woody vs. Bo, and Doug Flutie's Hail Mary. Fans in Tuscaloosa especially have been experiencing and enjoying names, games, and seasons that soon will be described as "hallowed" and discussed more over time instead of less while helping redefine the sport and its place in our culture.

If you doubt the correlation, try substituting the world *football* for *life* with any famous quote from a player or coach. "Football is like life," Vince Lombardi once said. "It requires perseverance, self-denial, hard work, sacrifice, dedication, and respect for authority."

Saban may understand that as well as anyone. While so many other coaches and players have embraced the flashier "instant gratification" parts of the game, he has remained true to its core by promoting a power offense, an even tougher defense, and a relentless pursuit of excellence.

He plays to his team's strengths but looks to wear down opponents and take away their will to compete (which sometimes happens before halftime), no matter the setting. When preparing for the BCS National Championship Game at the end of the 2012 season, Notre Dame defensive coordinator Bob Diaco had someone put together a collection of Alabama defensive snaps on third-and-7 or longer and said after watching it, "We called it a day after that because we were all demoralized."

Imagine how he felt after the 42–14 thrashing.

Defense still wins championships, while turnovers and explosive plays decide the majority of games. But it's hard work and paying attention to the details that have led Alabama to its latest dynasty and becoming the NFL's primary resource of talent.

"He has everything in place at Alabama: recruiting, facilities, and support from the administration," an anonymous assistant coach at a rival SEC school told ESPN in 2013. "People ridicule him for always talking about the 'Process,' but there isn't a better blueprint for winning anywhere out there. It's been a perfect plan so far. I don't see Alabama slowing down unless he retires."

Unlike his previous stops, where Saban kept moving on after five years, this time he stuck around to enjoy the ride, in part because there were no more steps to take in college football. Finally reaching the pinnacle and landing at the perfect school at the right time, the championships started to flow. More than anything else, that will be his eventual legacy of pure greatness.

★ ★ ★

Acknowledgments

I would love to say that I came up with the idea for this book, but that wouldn't be accurate.

On January 3, 2013, I was already in the Miami/Fort Lauderdale area preparing for the upcoming BCS National Championship Game, where Alabama went on to repeat and win its third crystal football in four years, when I got an email from Tom Bast about possibly doing something on Nick Saban.

At the time I wasn't looking to write another book. It had been a really long season, with essentially no downtime, and my wife and I got married during the bye weekend. Our priority list was topped by ways to get away from work and deciding where to go on our delayed honeymoon (which we finally took in June).

Triumph Books had just published *Tom Brady vs. the NFL: The Case for Football's Greatest Quarterback,* by Sean Glennon, so the initial idea was to do something similar. My response was that I couldn't quite make the case yet that Saban was college football's greatest coach, but I could that he would be on its version of Mount Rushmore.

Tom liked the idea, and we hammered out the details over the next few weeks. Meanwhile, I came up with a format, reread Saban's books for background, and figured out all the necessary parameters, including the rigorous writing schedule that wouldn't overlap the 2013 season.

On March 1, after the project was officially green-lighted, I immediately started working on a section about the 2012 season, describing it as Saban's best coaching job yet, while it was still fresh in my mind. That part of the book, the first draft of which ended up being 75,327 words, wound up getting cut along with an appendix about quarterback AJ McCarron's place in history. Those sections just didn't fit with the rest of the project.

That and a 200,000-word manuscript was simply ridiculous. We're talking longer than the New Testament (181,253 words), and that would cause a lot of jokes about *War and Peace* (560,000 words). But that was the thing about this book, I didn't just want to do just anything about Saban. I wanted to write *the* non-autobiographical book about him while exploring and breaking down his coaching career nearly every way imaginable. The more I got into it and continued to dig, the more the numbers bore out that he's already one of the game's elite coaches and worthy of being labeled as such.

The entire first draft was completed by July 1, 2013, and a revamped version much closer to the finished product was finished by fall (training) camp. Fittingly, the manuscript was due on Saban's birthday, Halloween, and tweaked at the end of the 2013 season.

Of all the people I have to thank, first is my lovely wife, Megan, who also served as an editor once I got through a couple of rewrites. It wasn't quite the first year of marriage that she expected…well, yeah, it probably was, but she showed a lot of patience and was extremely understanding throughout the whole thing. It didn't hurt that she's a huge Crimson Tide fan.

Second is Tom and everyone at Triumph Books who worked on the book, especially editor Jeff Fedotin. I greatly appreciate you all making me look good.

Third is everyone at BamaOnLine and 247Sports. Hopefully this ends up being good enough for you all to show it off.

Also, special thanks to David Honeycutt for looking over an early draft for me, to the rest of my family for their support, and to the fans. You're the ones who really make this all possible.

★ ★ ★

Sources

A lot of the book comes from doing my regular job, which from 2004 to 2013 was covering Alabama football for BamaOnLine and *The Tuscaloosa News*. So any time Nick Saban or just about anyone else is quoted, it's from a press conference or an interview I've been a part of over the years.

For some of the stand-alone quotes, I also referred back to transcripts compiled over the years by asapsports.com, especially those from SEC Media Days. The quotes from the president are from transcripts of Alabama's visits to the White House. A couple of quotes from former LSU players are from a story I did while working for *The Tuscaloosa News*: "Former Saban players mainstays in Kansas City lineup," from August 2, 2008.

Anything else is sourced in the book. All of the charts I researched myself.

BOL readers got a sneak peak at the "How They Stack Up" sections with a 15-part series in June 2013 and a condensed version on July 4, 2013. An early version of the dynasty story also got a test-drive in Lindy's preseason preview: *Crimson Tide in the Huddle 2013*.

Information came from a variety of sources, including:
2013 NCAA Division I (FBS and FCS) Football Records Book
NFL.com
Team websites and media guides
The College Football Hall of Fame

Saban, Nick with Sam King. *Tiger Turnaround: LSU's Return to Football Glory.* Chicago: Triumph Books, 2004.

Saban, Nick with Brian Curtis. *How Good Do You Want to Be?* New York: Ballentine Books, 2005.

rolltide.com

My own online database: ultimatefd.com

sports-reference.com

My previous books, including *Who's #1? 100-Plus Years of Controversial National Champions in College Football*; *100 Things Crimson Tide Fans Should Know & Do Before They Die*; *Where Football Is King: A History of the SEC*; and the *Huddle Up* series, for which I authored editions for Alabama, Tennessee, and Texas.